MIND AND SOUL OF INDIA

MIND AND SOUL OF INDIA

Edited by

A.K. SINHA

ANAMIKA PUBLISHERS & DISTRIBUTORS (P) LTD.
4697/3, 21A, Ansari Road, Daryaganj, New Delhi 110 002
Phones: 23281655, 23270239
e-mail: anamikapublishers@yahoo.co.in

First Published 2013

ISBN 978-81-7975-557-0

PRINTED IN INDIA

Published by Anamika Publishers & Distributors (P) Ltd., 4697/3, 21A, Ansari Road, Daryaganj, New Delhi 110 002. Typeset by Aadil Printographics, Delhi 110 092 and Printed at Chauhan Offset, Shahdara, Delhi 110 032.

Contents

Editor's Note

On the eve of the 25th year of its existence Department of Ancient History and Culture, Mahatma Jyotiba Phule Rohilkhand University, Bareilly planned to organise a number of academic programmes to felicitates its silver jubilee celebrations in a graceful manner. One of the series of these programmes was the national seminar on the theme the 'Mind and Soul of India' which was organised on 27-28 April 2010. A good number of scholars, senior as well as young from various universities and other institutions across the country participated with great enthusiasm in the seminar. The seminar was inaugurated by the eminent historian Prof. K.K. Thaplyal, former Head of the Department of Ancient Indian History, and Archaeology, Lucknow University and the Key-Note Address was delivered by Prof. Om Prakash, the former Vice-Chancellor of M.J.P. Rohilkhand University and the former Head of the Department of Ancient History, Culture and Archaeology, University of Allahabad, Allahabad. The then Vice-Chancellor of M.J.P. Rohilkhand University Prof. S.P. Gautam presided over the inaugural session. Some other distinguished participants were Prof. U.P. Arora (JNU, Delhi), Prof. R.C. Thakran (Delhi), Prof. Vibha Upadhyay (Jaipur), Prof. O.P. Srivastava

(Allahabad), Prof. S.N.R. Rizvi (Gorakhpur), Prof. C.M. Agrawal (Almora), Prof. H.N. Dube (Allahabad), Dr. Aparna Mathur (Shillong), Prof. Prashant Srivastava (Lucknow), Prof. R.P. Tripathi (Allahabad,) Prof. Renu Shukla (Dehradun) and so on. We are extremely thankful to all for making the seminar a great success. The present volume is a collection of some selected papers presented in the seminar that reflect one or the other dimension of the theme of the latter. We thank to all the contributors for permitting us to include their articles in this volume. The seminar was generously financed by U.G.C. and I.C.H.R., New Delhi for which we are greatly thankful to the authorities of the both agencies, especially to Dr. Ishrat Alam, Prof. S.P. Gautam was kind enough in extending his wholehearted support and co-operation in organising this seminar very successfully. He also presided over the inaugural and the valedictory sessions of the seminar despite his very busy schedule. We are highly obliged to him. We are grateful to our colleagues Dr. Abhay Kumar Singh, Dr. S.B. Lal, Dr. V.B.S. Yadava, Dr. A.R. Mishra, Dr. Pankaj Sharma, and Shri Sunil Kumar who assisted us in a number of ways in organising the seminar and preparing the press copy of this volume. Thanks are also due to Shri Pankaj Sharma of Anamika Publishers and Distributors (P) Ltd., New Delhi for bringing this fruit of our hard labour into light. Once again we thank one and all who have been, in any way of help in this academic venture.

25.1.2013 **A.K. Sinha**

Contributors

Prof. K.K. Thaplyal, Former Head, Department of Ancient Indian History, Archaeology and Culture, Lucknow University, Lucknow.

Prof. Om Prakash, Former Vice-Chancellor, M.J.P. Rohilkhand University, Bareilly and Former Head, Department of Ancient History, Culture and Archaeology, University of Allahabad, Allahabad.

Prof. A.K. Sinha, Dean, Faculty of Humanities and Social Sciences and Former Head, Department of Ancient History and Culture, M.J.P Rohilkhand University, Bareilly.

Dr. Abhay Kumar Singh, Head, Department of Ancient History and Culture, M.J.P. Rohilkhand University Bareilly.

Prof. R.P. Tripathi, Former Head, Department of Ancient History, Culture and Archaeology, University of Allahabad, Allahabad.

Dr. Rajjan Kumar, Head, Department of Applied Philosophy, M.J.P. Rohilkhand University, Bareilly.

Dr. Dinesh Kumar Ojha, Reader, Department of Ancient Indian History, Culture and Archaeology, B.H.U., Varanasi.

Prof. C.M. Agrawal, Head, Department of History, Kumaon University, Almora, Uttarakhand.

Prof. Prashant Srivastava, Professor, Department of Ancient Indian History, Archaeology and Culture, Lucknow University, Lucknow.

Dr. Anil Kumar, Department of Ancient Indian History, Archaeology and Culture, Lucknow University, Lucknow.

Prof. R.C. Thakran, Head, Department of History, Delhi University, Delhi.

Prof. Vibha Upadhyay, Head, Department of History, University of Rajasthan, Jaipur.

Dr. Aparna Mathur, Reader, Department of History, North-Eastern Hill University, Shillong.

Prof. Hari Narayan Dube, Professor, Department of Ancient History, Culture and Archaeology, University of Allahabad, Allahabad.

Prof. Renu Shukla, Head, Department of Ancient History, Gurukul Kangri University, Women Campus, Dehradun, Uttarakhand.

Dr. Durgesh Kumar Tripathi, Department of Ancient Indian History, Archaeology and Culture, Lucknow University, Lucknow.

Dr. S.K. Jaiswal, Department of Ancient Indian History, Archaeology and Culture, Lucknow University Lucknow.

Dr. Sushma Srivastava, Reader, Department of Ancient History, Jagat Taran Girls College, Allahabad.

Sunil Kumar, Department of Ancient History and Culture, M.J.P. Rohilkhand University, Bareilly.

1. INAUGURAL ADDRESS
Mind and Soul of India

Kiran Kumar Thaplyal

In the following pages a brief survey of the contribution of Indian mind and soul in the fields of social, economic, political and religious institutions and in the fields of philosophy, literature, science and art is given.

The concept of land from the Himalayas to the sea, forming as one unit had been present in the mind of the ancient people of this land, despite the differences in geographical features, languages, religions, social customs and economic conditions. The land has been eulogized as more worthy than heaven, and as one where even gods love to be born. There was a concept of auspicious seven cities, seven mountains and seven rivers, most situated in the north and a few in the south, as especially sacred. Shankaracharya founded four sacred *dhamas* in the four corners of India—Badrinath in the North, Shringeri in the south, Puri in the east and Dvaraka in the west.

The Brahmi script, of which the antiquity may go to the sixth century BC (though the earliest extant inscriptions belong to the Maurya period), is the mother of all the north Indian scripts and has influenced some of the south Indian scripts as well. In course of time, its use spread in the neighbouring countries. Sanskrit as the *lingua franca* of India, provided a great cultural unity to the land, and was also in use in some other Asian countries. Sanskrit literature has rich heritage—vedas, which are the earliest literary works in the world, brahmana literature, the aranyakas and upanishads, the two epics the Ramayana and the Mahabharata, the largest epic in the world of which the Gita forms a part, the Puranas and the *Dharmasastra* literature. The works of Bhasa, Asvaghosha, Kalidasa, Bharavi, Magha, Bana etc. are of great literary merit. The *Ashtadhyayi* of Panini is the great and most perfect work on grammar, and the *Arthasastra* of Kautilya is the most significant ancient work on polity in the whole world.

There is a great emphasis on the learning. Besides the *gurukulas,* where the student resided and studied in the home of the teacher, great educational institutions also arose. Of these, the most important one was the Nalanda with 1,000 teachers and 10,000 students coming from various parts of India, as also from China and other neighbouring countries. Though a great Buddhist centre, it also taught religion, philosophy of other sects, as well as subjects other than religion and philosophy.

Indian society comprised of four *varnas—brahmana, kshatriya, vaishya* and *shudra*. First one, the *brahmana,* with learning and teaching, offering and accepting charity, performing sacrifices for themselves and for others. The *kshatriyas* were to study, offer charity, and perform sacrifices and provide protection to the people. The vaishyas were to engage themselves in agriculture, cattle-rearing, trade and commerce, and usury. The *shudras* were expected to serve the people of other *varnas*. In time of distress, the following of the vocation of other *varna* was allowed. There are a number of references to people following the vocation prescribed for other *varnas*.

The ancient Indians formulated a scheme of four *ashrama—brahmacharya, grihastha, vanaprashta* and *sannyasa,* as also the four *purusharthas*—dharma, artha, kama and moksha. In the *ashrama* scheme, for the first 25 years, a man was expected to lead the life of a *brahmacharin* and devote himself to learning, from 25 to 50 years, one as householder (*grihasthin*), was to earn livelihood and also physical pleasures (*kama*), from 50 to 75, he as *vanaprashtin* was to be partly detached from society, and after the age of 75 years he was to be completely detached from society and put all the efforts for the attainment of *moksha.* Not all people, however, following the ideal of *ashramas* and *purusharthas.*

In the sixth century BC, great intellectual and religious activities were witnessed in India, as in some countries. Buddha, Mahavira, Makkhaliputta Gosala and others lived in that age, whose contribution in the field of religion and philosophy is immense. Some of them challenged the authority of the vedas and denied the existence of God.

There developed six philosophical systems—nyaya, vaisheshika, sankhya, purva-mimamsa, uttara-mimamsa (the same as vedanta), and lokayata. Of these philosophical systems—vedanta, which is mainly propounded in the upanishads, became the most popular. According to this, in every individual, one-self is imminent, and as such, one should perform such acts as making gifts (*dana*), kindness (*daya*) and non-injury (*ahimsa*), and there is unity in *atman* and *brahman,* as seen in the expression *tat tvam asi* (thou art that) and *aham brahmasmi* (I am the *brahman*). That the supreme *brahman,* though not seen, is present in all beings, is well-illustrated by Uddalaka Aruni to his son, Shvetaketu. 'He then told his son to put some salt in water, which got dissolved. He then told him that as the salt is not seen, but its presence is felt from the water being salty, so *brahman* is not seen yet is present'. The upanishads show great subtlety and sublimity of human mind and guide men from *asat* to *sat*, and from *tamas* (darkness) to *jyoti* (light). The significance of upanishadic teachings may be realised from the statement of the German scholars, Schaupenhouer: 'In the whole world there is no study so beautiful and elevating as that of the upanishads. It has been the solace of my life, it will be the solace of my death.'

One of the most characteristic features of the Indian culture has been its cosmopolitan outlook. In the *Rigveda*, it is stated that Indra, Mitra, etc. are one and the same deity, though the learned call them by different names. Ashoka's inscriptions provide us with the finest examples of religious tolerance. He shows his respect for all the religious sects, and requests the followers of different sects not to unnecessarily eulogise one's own sect and condemn others' sects. He emphasises on the control of speech. He tells that he who condemns others' sect, harms his own sect. He exhorts people to listen to the teachings of others' sects, which will make them realise that the basic principles in all of them are the same, although there is difference of rituals followed by them. Listening to the tenets of others' religion will lead to the growth of *samavaya* and also to concord between different sects. He also expresses his wish that the followers of different sects should reside in all places within his kingdom. The depiction of deities related to various pantheons—Indian, Central Asian, Iranian, Greek and Mesopotamian—on his coins by Kanishka I shows eclecticism. King Harsha Pushyabhuti is known to have worshipped the Buddha, Surya and Siva while his father, Prabhakaravardhana, was a worshipper of the sun, and his brother,

Rajyavardhana, was a Buddhist. In several ancient texts, belonging to different sects, such words as *esha dharmah sanatanah* (this is eternal precept) occur quite frequently, showing great respect for ancient traditions. Ashoka, too, states that the noble thought should be followed as it formed a part of ancient tradition.

There was great activity in the economic field. The artisans (*kulikas*), the merchant-cum-bankers (*shreshthins*) formed their own guilds, and there is the evidence of the Vaishali sealings for the existence of the joint corporations of the *shreshthins, sarthavahas* (caravan merchants) and *kulikas*. Caravan merchants, in large groups, with 500 or more bullock carts, loaded with goods, used to travel to distant lands for the sale of their goods. There are several references to rich merchants, like Anathapindaka, who is said to have bought the Jetavana by spreading coins on its whole surface as its price. The kings were keen to be friendly with the merchants. There was trade with the Roman empire by land and sea, as is testified by literature and by the find of large number of Roman coins, mostly from coastal areas of India, and also with some southeast Asian countries by sea. The balance of trade was greatly in favour of the Indians.

In the field of art may be mentioned the smooth and tapering monolithic pillars of Ashoka, huge in size and heavy in weight. The pillars were crowned with capitals, topped with animal figures. The famous Sarnath Lion capital, showing four lions back to back on the top, and a bull, an elephant, a lion and a horse on its abacus, is classed among the best pieces of the world art. The art that flourished in the Gandhara from about the first century BC to about third century AD, shows the figures of the Buddha, bodhisattvas, etc. based on Indian iconography and Greek features. The Gupta sculpture, of which the best pieces—the seated Buddha image at Sarnath and the standing red sandstone image from Mathura—is known for its high aesthetic quality. Of the rock-cut architecture, the best example is Kailasa at Ellora. The Ajanta rock paintings are extremely artistic. The iron pillar at Mehrauli, belonging to King Chanda (Chandragupta II Vikramaditya), has been standing in the open for about 1,500 years without any significant sign of rusting, is a proof of highly advanced metallurgy.

Aryabhatta, the great mathematician and astronomer, for the first time discovered the decimal system and also the fact that the earth rotates on its axis and moves around the sun. He almost correctly determined the value of *pi* (π). Brahmagupta and Varahamihira were also astronomers. It is also interesting that the Indians had not only the knowledge of Greek astronomy, but have also incorporated their views in their own works, which they refer as the *Paulish Siddhanta* and *Romaka-Siddhanta.* A Syrian monk, in AD 662 said, that the discoveries of the Indians were more indigenous than those of the Greeks and the Babylonians.

The ideals prescribed in the ancient texts for the kings to follow are laudable. According to the *dharmashastra* literature, the king was entitled to spend one-sixth of the produce by way of pay for providing protection by the subjects to him, and performing activities for their welfare. Still nobler is the idea that the king is unto his subjects as father is unto his children, and should do his best for the good of the subjects as he would do for his children. Ashoka also states that all his subjects were his children (*save munisapajamama*). Kautilya states that in the happiness and welfare of the subjects lies the welfare and happiness of the king (*praja sukhe sukham rajnaya, prajanama ca hita hitam*). The king was to enact laws after taking into consideration the traditions of caste, region, guilds and family.

There was decentralization of power, and the village was the smallest administrative unit, with the headman and *grama-sabha*. The latter comprised of senior members of the village, who helped and guided the headman in administration and in imparting justice, and also in performing works for the welfare of the village. The *grama-sabha* also provided a check against the headman turning a tyrant.

In ancient texts, three types of conquests have been mentioned. Of these, the *asura-vijaya* is the conquest in which the enemy loses his life and kingdom. In *lobha-vijaya,* the wealth of the enemy was taken, and in the *dharma-vijaya,* the accepting of the suzerainity of the conqueror was enough. In the *Raghuvamsa,* Raghu is mentioned as a *dharma-vijayin,* since he captured and later released the lord of Mahendra, and thus took away his glory but not his land. Samudragupta's south Indian conquests, in which he first captured the kings and then liberated and reinstated them, was also a *dharma-vijaya.* In Ashoka's concept of *dharma-vijaya,* there was no war, but conquering of the heart of the people by working for their material and moral welfare. Significantly, Indians did not aim at conquering land outside India by force, but spread Indian culture by peaceful methods to Sri Lanka, Myanmar, Siam, Malaya peninsula, Annam, Sumatra, Java, Bali and Borneo in southeast Asia, as also in central Asia, China, Korea and Japan.

A number of people of foreign origin, such as the Iranians, Greek, Shakas, Pahlavas, Kushanas, Hunas, etc. who came to India and settled here, were absorbed in the Indian population. The foreign conquerors did not fit in the *varna* scheme, but since they were mostly warriors, and some rulers, they were placed in the *kshatriya varna,* but to differentiate them from the traditional Indian *kshatriyas,* they were called *vratya* (fallen) *kshatriyas.* There must have been give and take and the Indian society, too, was influenced by the foreigners.

2. MIND AND SOUL OF INDIA
Keynote Address

Om Prakash

Mind and soul pre-suppose a body in which they, according to common understanding, dwell. Mind and soul of India metaphorically specify that body as India, not so much as geographical entity but as a people authored a superior civilization as an expression of themselves. Platform to the quest of mind and soul of India was provided by the need of national identity to counteract the dubbing of her people as niggers of India, ignorant, barbaric and despicable. "No people, how .rude and ignorant soever," remarks the first British historian of India, James Mill, "have ever drawn a more gross and disgusting picture of the universe." (Mill, James, [1820] 1975). The missionary discourse was far more attacking than this Colonial/Imperial discourse inspired by utilitarianism. It openly disparaged Indian art by saying that the artistic images of Indian deities have to be subjected to amputation of their surplus limbs and heads before presenting them for appreciation (Archer cited in Coomarswamy).

At the dawn of modern history writing Europe too was struggling with the questions of identity and origin. The adventitious Biblical origin myths raised serious issues of historicity and chronology. Yet, in the absence of any better alternative people of Europe had to adhere to these and even after they got a viable alternative they retained the Old Testament stage settings of the story. The breakthrough came in 1786 when Sir William Jones' following quote laid the foundations of historical or comparative linguistics, shifting the question of origin from religious to historical myth-making:

"The Sanskrit language, whatever may be its antiquity, is a wonderful structure, more perfect than the Greek, more copious than the Latin, and more exquisitely refined than either, yet bearing to both of them a stronger affinity, both in its roots of verbs and in the forms of grammar that could possibly have been produced by accident; so strong, indeed, that no philologer could examine them all three without believing them to have sprung from some common source which, perhaps, no longer exists: there is a similar reason, though not quite so forcible, for supporting that both the Goethick and the Celtick, though blended with a very different idiom, had the same origin with the Sanskrit; and the Old Persian might be added to the same family" (Jones, W., 1788, 415-31).

The Old Testament myth provided a kinship and genetic origin to Europeans from the Hebrew Noah and his sons after his Ark, following the Great Flood, rested at Mount Ararat in Armenia where they constructed the tower of Babel and as a result of divine intervention ceased to understand each others' tongue which providentially turned into mono-languages and dispersed with that of their kin drifting to areas between the Oxus and the Euphrates rivers, including the Mount Caucus and frontiers of India within Iran (Parsons, J., 1767). This religious myth provided the following assumptions, which continued to be basic in the construction of people with a mind and soul to create a superior civilization:

1. Blood relationship or kinship is the biological bond that creates a race or people.
2. By divine intervention, the language of the kin-groups, originating from different sons of Noah, became different. That is to say, the racial identity is coeval with linguistic identity pushing kinship to background by the will of God.
3. The locale of the resting of Noah's Ark and linguistic-cum-racial dispersal of the kin-groups, initiated by his sons having a common language, is well identifiable.

In the later part of the eighteenth century, perhaps for reasons of their experience with the Jews intruding upon European society as traders, particularly in Germany and France, people frowned upon the Biblical myth of the origin of Europeans. Derivations, based on religious myth, also looked obnoxious to the mind and soul of the Europeans of the Enlightenment era which worshipped the light of Reason and hated the darkness of religion based on faith without reason. The following quote of Voltaire hinted at the source of the superiority of European civilization as per his dispassionate, reasonable investigation: "What is Europe really but a sterile trunk which owes everything to oriental graft." (Poliakov, L., 1971: 11). Herder in 1803 remarked, "the pains that have been taken to make all the people of the earth..., descendants of the Hebrews, and half-brothers of the Jews, are contrary not only to chronology and universal history but to the true point of the narrative itself." To him, "the central point of the largest quarter of the globe, the primitive mountain of Asia, prepared the first abode of human race." (Herder, J.G., 1803: 517-18). According to

Bryant, Herder introduced the passion for India into Germanic lands and fired the imagination of the Romantics to look to mother India rather than to the father figure of the Jews for origin and excellence.

Sir William Jones' Aryan hypothesis more or less satisfied all these consternations and expectations in one stroke while retaining the above-mentioned basics of the Biblical myth of origin and dispersal. It took language as a given structure without going into its structural elements, power of signification and communication and the distinctions and complementarity of *langue* and *parole.* It joined linguistic units with the racial units of past and present speaking them, taking race too as given biological unit. It worked out family affiliations among languages and their speakers more or less on the lines of kinship and on one to one basis. The entire procedure of comparative or historical linguistics was only apparently and outwardly historical but it was essentially a historical and mythical, to say the least. That is why it was open to political manipulation by British colonial and Nazi national socialist interest. The hypothesis put forward by Jones already contained room for such manipulations. By removing religious overtones in the Biblical myth it reduced the question of the quest of the origin of Europeans to racial-cum-linguistic proposition. How could Germans and their economic oppressors, in their real and imagined perceptions, be of the same race and brotherhood particularly when their respective languages had no filial affiliation? The hypothesis also left the antiquity of Sanskrit language as a vague and open question with a clear hint of the likelihood of a hypothetical non-existent language prior to Sanskrit which might have mothered the Sanskrit, Greek and Latin languages despite vast gulf of time separating them from Sanskrit and that protolanguage was taken for granted to have been already Indo- European. Needless to say, such a ghost language was, since its inception, only a matter of opinion. Yet ambitious projects were afloat to reconstruct it by an enormous feat of research through abstract-back derivations from relatively more evolved phonetic and semantic form of common words and grammatical structures, creating the lost language with words which one does not know how to pronounce and what was their meaning. Such a ghost language was supposed to be the common source of Greek and Latin, including the Sanskrit. The myth of this language extinct beyond reconstruction led Bopp and others to deny all attempts to ascribe the origin of the ruling race of colonial India from that of the despised and despicable niggers. Interchangeability of race and language was a convenient tool provided by the above hypothesis of Jones to put to any use, as was done by the Britishers in India to construct a social, cultural and historical base for turning their power into some kind of an authority and by Nazis in Germany to extract sentimental approval for the genocide of Jews. The British historians both rejected and accepted the hypothesis. They rejected it for not to ascribe the status of motherhood to India, the bearer of the oldest and still surviving Indo-European language, Sanskrit with the *Rigveda* as its oldest record, as did the Germans and the French in the second half of the eighteenth century and a little later. They accepted it to propagate the historical myth that the *dvijas* from among the speakers of Indo-European languages in India, were Aryan in race while the entire south India speaking non-Indo-European, i.e. Dravidian languages, belonged to a different race, including the non-*dvijas* of northern India even though they speak the Indo-European languages. The hypothesis became a handy tool in the hands of colonial masters to divide and rule the people of India on the basis of a historically propagated myth which the *dvijas* also enthusiastically shared and those of south Indians too who could claim the *dvija* status by virtue of their immigration to south India or on any other religious, historical, customary or *dharmasastric* pretext. Sociological theories of dominant caste and Sanskritization merged with the concept and practice of westernization to consolidate hierarchy of ruling classes of Indians despite their racial, ritual, religious and cultural differences and contradictions.

If Utilitarian and Missionary reason put a full stop to the Romantic inclination of French and German people produced by the new historico-linguistic discourse to take hold of the Britishers, the revolt of 1857 in India prevented the colonial rulers to go whole hog the Utilitarian or the Missionary way. They had to have a source material for a history of India different from and more authentic than a history derived from linguistic observations and the data furnished by them for deriving useful conclusions while sparing some select platitudes of the linguistic reconstructions of history from rejection, which they thought, were necessary to please and divide Indians against themselves. Military and administrative reforms militating against caste and religious pride and prejudice had to be pushed aside and anti-Muslim stance had to give way to a policy of patronage and feer to Muslims as a tool to control the Hindu drive to nationalism and freedom from the colonial rule, now under the Crown.

The new phase of British rule was determined to give India her true history (despite Indians lacking historical sense and consequent absence of chronicles and other authentic records and other source material for writing history) with a view to capturing the mind and soul of India immanent in her monuments and informing the religion, society, customs and costumes, pursuits of pleasure, asceticism and salvation together with ethnographic traits of Indian people depicted therein. The source of this history had been adjudged to be the architectural and archaeological remains of India, besides buildings surviving intact. According to Fergusson, "Compared to literature, architecture was seen as far more reliable index of the past" (cited by Tillotson, G.H.R., 30). He further looks upon Indian architecture as "a great stone book in which each tribe and race has written its annals and recorded its faith." (*Ibid.*, 18). Architecture never shifts its locale and it does not change with time. Cunningham looks upon architecture as only one of the four categories of archaeological remains, the other three being sculpture, coins and inscriptions and further sub-divides these as Buddhist, Indo-Scythian, Jain, early Brahmanical, later Brahmanical and early and late Muhammadan. The Archaeological Survey of India was founded in 1861 to locate monuments intact as well as in ruins and subjects the same to cleaning, retrieval, reassembling to nearest approximation of the original preserving and documenting. The study, though painstaking, was basically a museumizing process, reduced to systematic and chronological order the variegated relics, and monuments formed the rock-book of India, which, as per British historians, told a tale of decline from an ancient era of greatness. It proceeded from the Buddhist period, known for its simplicity, creativity and originality, to a corrupt and degenerate idolatory of medieval Hinduism. To Curzon, India's great artistic achievements were all "exotics imported into this country in the train of conquerors, who had learnt their architectural lessons in Persia, in central Asia, in Arabia, in Afghanistan" (*Ibid.*, 18). Significantly, the Indian stone-book repeated what the Brahmanical, Buddhist and Jain theories of time conceptualized by placing the golden age in the past to be followed by continuous decline till the cyclic order of cosmic time brought back the golden age again. The colonial view projected colonizers to have landed in a declining and degenerating India, as did earlier invaders bringing in their train all sorts of exotics. But the British alone were shown to have the distinction to bring striking progress in an exotic and unprecedented manner which is likely to stop the inherent decline and degeneration in India's mind and soul while making Indians to receive inspiration from their authentically revived and museumized great past as gift from their enlightened colonial rulers. The colonial historiographers of Indian art and aesthetics firmly fixed India's past as a fully compartmentalized section of historical time that can never seep down to the present and remained permanently locked out there as a well-ordered museumized entity to be proud of. But Indian artists always saw the past as flexible, fluid and running into the present.

The point call be illustrated by bringing forth the conception behind the arrangements of the investiture ceremony of Queen Victoria on January 1, 1877 for which Lord Lytton and Benjamin Disraeli were responsible and those of Lord Curzon's Delhi Darbar in 1903. For Her majesty's proclamation as Kaesar-e-Hind in the first ceremony the Queen was seated on the throne of Great Mughals whom she replaced but the decorations and rituals were not Mughal. They were feudal, not in any Indian form, real or imaginary but in the form they prevailed in the pre-modern Europe. In place of feudal lords, however, Indian princes, bound by subsidiary alliance, were there. Curzon's Darbar was marked by exquisite decorations in Mughal and Indo-Saracenic style but the exchange of presents or *nazrana* was not allowed. Both these events suggest the kind of mind and soul the colonial rulers were ascribing to India. It was the mind and soul of a feudal set-up, supposedly presided over by the throne of once glorious and powerful Mughals whose power decayed to a final extinction giving way to the most modern and powerful Crown of the world which does not look back upon it as a continuing legacy but retains it as a magnificent ornamental crest of jewel to be publicly worn on ceremonial occasion. Mughal and Indo-Sarascenic to Lord Curzon represented but one category, the signature of an exotic Islamic architecture indistinguishable for the colonial power, irrespective of their distant location in India, Arabia and Egypt. The Imperial/Colonial masters have power to further decorate the beauty of Taj Mahal by an Indo-Saracenic lamp to be hung there. As pointed out by Tillotson, the colonial aesthetic is an aesthetic of difference, of distance, of subordination, of control holding the past firmly into the past after ordering it with scrupulous attention to details and methodology. A Shah Jahan could never have comprehended it, (*Ibid.*, 24). In the name of giving *India* her history from the stone-book the colonial rulers were only ascribing the mind and soul of deactivated ingenious slave to her. Anachronistically, the puppet princes of India were made to enact the investiture ceremony of Queen Victoria as Kaesar-e-Hind in a feudal paradigm that had never existed in India and in Europe too which was already a thing of the past, as the Mughal power in India was kept alive for a long time after its mind and soul had already departed. What is more wonderful, however, is that the motif thus presented making things topsy-turvy as a show off of what power can do was so powerful, even in independent India, that her many British trained historians worked hard to show that there was a thing like. Indian feudalism as an early medieval socio-economic formation brought about by history. Needless to say, the colonial hold over the mind and soul of India persists with profound vigour despite independence.

As against the colonial wont of holding the past firmly into the past by a process of museumization Indian artists, to judge from the pages of the great stone-book of Indian itself, used it as something fluid and flexible and bridging the gulf between the past and the present making them continuous rather than divided by such drastic breaks that imprison the past in an airtight compartment beyond which it can never move. Thus elements of Indus civilization managed to jump over the so-called Vedic retardation and inform the second urbanization characterizing the Buddhist-Kusana period. Buddhist architecture likewise complemented the Muslim architecture of Fatehpur Sikri. The Diwan-e-Khas interior column was Hindu in outline and details, yet it bore Muslim decorative carvings. Jahangir brought the Asokan pillar, already inscribed with his and his Queen's edicts and the inscription of Samudra to Allahabad Fort and recorded on the same his own regnal titles and genealogy reaching back to Timur. Outside India, for example, in the Selengor Secretariate building in Kuala Lumpur, Malaya (1897), even the British designer C.E. Spooner mingled Islamic Arabesque with Hindu details and in Victoria Memorial Hall, Madras (1906) H.C. Irwin attempted a Fatehpur Sikri style building in red sandstone. Preference for Muslim elements of architecture in some of the colonial buildings in outside India mismatches with the ignorance of Muslim cities of Delhi housing a number of medieval monuments and the capital of colonial India. Giving extraordinary attention to the documenta-tion of the deserted Mughal city of Fatehpur Sikri and Mandu of outside Delhi is striking. It surely reveals a shrewed play with India's selectively museumized past highlighting the one part of it while putting under shadow the other.

Shifting the use of Jones Aryan hypothesis from tracing the ancestry of European people, including the British, to a non-Semitic source, i.e. Sanskrit speaking Vedic Aryans of India who represented the oldest Indo-European people of the world to establishing brotherhood with colonial rulers as Big Brothers selectively with the *dvija* category of people of north and south India, irrespective of their mother-tongue marked a far reaching change which not only divided Indians into racially, culturally and politically superior and inferior blocks but also engaged brother Indians in the search of their glorious pre-Muslim history into unwritten sources pointed out by the Big Brothers. This change is amply reflected in the directive of Lord Canning (post-1857 Viceroy of India) given to the Royal Asiatic Society, London, which launched in 1860 a project to survey and document the ancient monuments of Orissa. The directive stressed the need to describe and investigate the history and tradition associated with the ancient monuments of India with a view to capturing the light these monuments can throw on the religious and cultural history of the period to which they belonged. (*Ibid.*, 57). The trained Indian investigator, Rajendralal Mitra, of this project demonstrated by his work how the national art tradition monumentalized in Orissan architecture was able to leave behind the purest and the most pristine relics of itself due to the insulation in time and space of the region. Escape from Muslim vandalism, in particular, argued Mitra, left the tradition of Indian art and architecture to its own in Orissa. In a continuous development from earlier times excessive decoration and ornamentation in Orissan monuments do not constitute a sure sign of decline and degeneration of Indian architectural development as propagated by Fergusson and others but its culmination and grandeur. This break from the colonial mode of reading the stone-book of India took the purist line that tended to attribute all degeneration and decadence to Muslim intervention devastating as well as peaceful. Mind and soul of India thus started receiving a new edition which gradually drifted to a kind of Indian nationalism with the otherness affixed largely on Muslims, as colonial intervention was already thought to be brotherly in view of the linguistic past of India as shown above. R.D. Banerji's *Pasaner Katha* in Bengali makes a stone fragment in the Bharhut Stupa to narrate a story that situates the Indian reader into a national perspective. It is a veritable microcosm of nation's history (Tapati Guha-Thakurta, 27). The call for Indians to write their country's history themselves, as no foreign historian can do justice with it, came from Bankim Chandra Chatterji. The stone-book to which were added texts of inscription, legends and depictions on coins and accounts of the foreign travellers now constituted the basic source material. Focusing on architecture now gave way to discovering new dynasties of Indian rulers and emperors, extent of their empires and public policies contrastingly different from the colonial ones, besides discovering a Napoleon in Samudra Gupta and a uniquely enlightened and philanthropic ruler in Asoka. All this emerged mainly from inscriptions, coins, Puranic text on *vamsanucharita* and genealogies, great and small, together the exploits, wars and diplomacy of their kings extracted from the epigraphic sources and corroborated by literary texts too. The new approach not only managed to fill a large number of gaps and dark ages of India's political history in an undeniable manner but also worked to delineate expansion of Indian culture beyond the boundaries of the country to Southeast Asia which in the first flush of national enthusiasm was called colonization of Southeast Asia, Central Asia and China. Nationalism which thus epitomized the mind and soul of India, was seeking expression in the form of India's history by its own historians employed and trained by colonial rulers in the techniques of photography, surveying, measuring, drawing and mapping of ancient monuments, exploring documenting and digging archeological sites and deciphering inscriptions and coins with a view to giving India her history. But the history they gave refused to be totally museumized and imprisoned into the compartmentalized past of colonial conception. Blasting the colonial mould it not only restored India to her ancient glory but also made her to proclaim to the world that the fallen shall rise. Bankim in his *Anand Math* gave India the image of a Mother, not of Europeans but of all Indian past and present and most perceptively made the *vande mataram* sung to her by a band of ascetics out to lay down their lives to liberate her from the shackles of the foreign rule. India's glorious past was thus made to ultimately inspire and inform her none too happy a present firing her children's mind and soul to find their lost freedom and glory.

This drive to rediscover and acquire the lost mind and soul of India in the form of Nation personified as Mother India, however, begged the question: which India? The India of image worshippers who look upon her as the Mother, the goddess or the India of iconoclasts or atheists who look upon her as the Mother, the giver of birth and the sustainer, or else the India of those marginalized and disempowered down-trodden Dalits, backwards and the women who look upon the kind Mother for justice, social, educational, political and economic? Can Mother India embody the mind and soul of all these India's and grant their expectations as the reward of their offerings of blood and worship or should they enter into a scramble for claiming the portions of the body of the Mother as a matter of right for the satisfaction of their mind and soul? Failure to evolve politically and spiritually along lines of much adumbrated fundamental unity of India and/or to integrate all these India-s into a nation having a common denominator like the historically observable principle of fundamental unity of India or having an understanding to concede the just claims of all the India-s without 'pandering a false sense of national pride' (Thapar, 1996: 12) by proving that the largest minority constituting the first of the above three India-s 'came to India in historical times as foreigners' (Sharma, 1998: 91) finally led to the partition of the country. Successful integration of the Dalits to the nation on the principle of reservation arrived at in the negotiations of the Poona Pact saved a tripartite partition of India. Politics of violent direct action as against the non-violent direct action of Gandhi to secure partition for the largest minority on the principle of two nation theory reached to the extent of shameful partition riots which left behind a trail of the charges and counter-charges of chauvinism and fanaticism against each other by the contending parties. Such riots keep on rocking even independent India sporadically even after paying the price of partition. The die-hard legacy of social, educational and economic discrimination with all kinds of disabilities operating from historical times and still persisting despite being illegal and immoral promoted Dalit consciousness, Dalit discourse and Dalit politics as also Backward consciousness, Backward discourse and Backward politics. Women are also catching up fast. The common source of these politics is the policy of reservation and affirmative action and the issues of their proper implementation which is usually problematic because of the failure of the legal and administrative provisions to generate commensurate sense of duty and commitment for the social and national cause. Hidebound prejudices and attitudes to the contrary generally come in the way. The mind and soul of the nation are not at peace, as nation building and politics of vote bank after independence have been running a good deal against each other grain. The resultant disappointment produced by this inherent disharmony between nation building and the politics of vote bank is responsible for the conflict between mind and soul of the nation, which has been pathetically voiced by Hindi poets like Sarveshwar Dayal Saxena and Dhumil as follows:

> राष्ट्रगान में अरे कौन वह भारतभाग्य विधाता है।
> फटा सुथन्ना पहन के जिसका गुण हरिचरना गाता है।।
>
> — *सक्सेना*

> आजादी क्या तीन थके हुए रंगों का नाम है
> जिन्हें एक पहिया ढोता है।
> इसका क्या कुछ खास मतलब होता है?
>
> — *धूमिल*

The colonial and nationalist approaches to India's past respectively to keep her under the exploitative foreign rule and to free it from the same lost their relevance after India became a Sovereign Democratic Republic after paying the price of partition. The question now was that of nation building on Gandhian line which placed mind and soul of the people above unscrupulous mechanization and industrialization in imitation of the West or nation building on Nehruvian line of heavy industrialization and mechanization under the planned supervision of a centralized welfare state by combining features of both the capitalist and communist economy. The Gandhian way somehow became a synonym of backward looking nationalism, reconstruction of the lost ethos of the self reliant rural life, institutions and economy, cottage industry with moderate use of machines and energy with a view to giving to the downtrodden, the backward and the socially and educationally retarded unto the last man the necessary means and knowledge/training input to enable them to earn their bread and live with dignity and honour. Their empowerment and contribution to the nation and the world under this Gandhian scheme was to follow as the poor, the helpless and the discriminated cruised their way to them relying on their own effort, skill and labour. For Gandhi, the question was not to provide them crutches of welfare doles but to boost their confidence with necessary means and skill input just enough to pull themselves out of the historically imposed disabilities, attain equality and contribute to the nation and the world. The Nehruvian way, on the other hand, was a programme of maximizing production and need as per market hype to create wealth and comfort to make India a powerful nation at par with other powerful nations of the world and also help the poor, the down trodden and the victims of social injustice and discrimination through reservation, especial welfare schemes and public distribution system. Representation through reservation of seats in the Parliament and assemblies, and also in municipal, block and village Panchayat councils constituted for Nehru the tools of empowerment of the weaker sections of Indian society, including women. The fruits of planned development accomplished and to be accomplished on a mass scale by increasing application of science and technology were also to reach the people of these sections by a process of percolation of benefits from top to bottom. But the caste ridden and compartmentalized society of India responded these Nehruvian initiatives of nation-building by generating a politics of vote banks and a malpractice of corruption on an unprecedented scale which flopped much of the intended and produced the contrary result of enormously increasing the gap between rich and poor, cities and villages, the educated and the uneducated, the ideal and the real, not to speak of unemployment and price rise which increased in leaps and bounds. The whole trend of actual economic growth under the Nehruvian model shifted the attention of the nation from the mind and soul-oriented development of India, not totally ruling out necessary material concerns, to maximizing the material development of the individual and the nation thereby diluting the Gandhian concern for mind and soul as an evaporating ideal. It also paved the way for the rise of Marxist historiography in India which outlined the socioeconomic formations of the past around slavery and feudalism of a different kind, called Indian, finally giving way to capitalism qualified by colonialism and nationalist aspirations in pre-independence days and socialist, Marxist and welfare leanings of post-independence days. Reordering of Indian history as a socio-economic process unfolding through class conflict rather than as ruler-centered political and cultural history concentrated on struggles for material gains and losses and empowerment and dis-empowerment of tribes, communities and castes through power and religious discourses. It also highlighted the rural, urban and rich and poor divides and economic integration of trade and commerce of the world of their time by Romans and Arabs. While Roman integration which was more of the nature of a trade network developed, not so much for monetary or wealth gain which the Roman Empire already had in plenty but for the supply to Rome of exotic products of the East brought about the climax of urbanization in India, the Arab integration was for turning the balance of trade in their favour and for monopoly of Eastern trade to Europe had supposedly plunged India into a phase of de-urbanization, demonetization and feudalism. Predominance of Marxist historiography in India practically made all talks of mind and soul of India a taboo among historians.

The Nehruvian model of development on the lines of mixed or welfare economy with a predominant public sector over a practically subordinate private sector with lots of precessual and bureaucratic bottlenecks and national as well as private banks received a fresh state socialist input during and after internal emergency proclaimed by Indira Gandhi in 1975 in the form of bank nationalization, abolition of privy-purses and integration of territory notionally ruled over by native rulers who agreed to remain with Indian Union and twenty-point programme of the Prime Minister. The two wars with Pakistan and terrorism taking its toll in Kashmir and Punjab leading to operation Blue Star and its sad aftermath, the Sikh riots and assassination of Rajiv Gandhi had a destabilizing effect on Indian economy of the prevailing order and created the balance of payment crisis which Narsimha Rao successfully tided over under the ministration of economic reforms formulated by the then Finance Minister, Manmohan Singh. The reforms devalued the rupee and inducted privatization, liberalization and globalization of Indian economy which led to the boom of service sector and foreign investment in particular. Preceding Narsimha Roa as Prime Minister, Rajiv Gandhi had already prompted the ship of Indian state policy to the direction of this sea change in India's economy hitherto following Nehruvian model with state socialist tinkering here and there by bringing in the New Education Policy, emphasis on TV culture and computer technology which led to the opening of a number of private engineering colleges and decentralization at the rural and urban local bodies through Seventy-Third and Seventy-Fourth Constitutional amendments. The agenda of social justice through OBC reservation, initiated by Indira Gandhi was implemented by Prime Minister V.P. Singh, which made the development along new lines to look inclusive, though rightly or wrongly it is also accused of generating vote bank and caste politics and sometimes viewed as causing the Babari Masjid and Ram Mandir counterblast that brought BJP to power. The world also saw a sea change in the end of Cold War with the fall of the USSR in 1991 following a grave economic crisis in Soviet Union. The capitalist economies of the western world saw in this event the vindication of their free market economic system enshrining liberalism and private enterprise as its corner stones over that of the Marxist Socialist system represented by the second pole of the bipolar world of the cold war days. Collapse of the second pole ushered in globalization and apparently added itself to capitalism as its third principle. But apparent is not always accepted as real. That is perhaps why globalization is looked upon not as an expansion of capitalism but as something making it to outgrow itself as post-modernism. Modernity, in fact, dates back to Enlightenment of which

Capitalism and Marxism are the two faces. Regarded as an expansion of capitalism alone, globalization would be leaving out Marxism despite collapse of the USSR but considered as bringing in post-modernism both capitalism as well as Marxism stand outgrown together with all the Enlightenment values, including Reason.

Modernity and post-modernity represent an attitude to power as a means to conquer and control through contrivances based on reason, strategy and technology, which is a product of science. Modernity developed from Enlightenment with capitalism and socialism/communism as its twin representing the socio-economic binary and constitutional and totalitarian governments as also colonial/imperial and nationalist governments as its political binary. Another political binary was that of revolutionary nationalism in conflict with the entrenched order of ancient regime, as in the France, or open war of independence against the colonial regime, as in the America. Modernity represented a clean break from the past or progress to future and opposed the grip of religion on society and state by applying the concepts of secularism and rule of law. It preached freedom for the individual which nationalist and communist socialisms opposed on the principle of equality being sacrificed at the altar of liberty to exploit the common man. In the name of preventing individuals from lapsing into license, socialist states of Nationalist and Communist kind degenerated into totalitarian regimes. The conflict between open and closed/structured propaganda societies led to world wars that entailed enormous suffering, including the Great Depression.

If modernity rejected the past as full of faith and superstition, a dead weight antithetical to reason and progress to a vision of the future, an attitude generated by Enlightenment, post-modernity rejected modernity along with its source, Enlightenment had tended to imbibe the anti-Enlightenment rhetoric of religious opposition to scientific rationalism, nationalism, universalism or humanism, Romantic anti-capitalism or socialism as well as liberal democracy. Philosophically it is traceable to the mood represented by later writings of Nietzsce, Spengler and Hieidegar. Globalization is also the rhetoric of post-modernism which it brings about. Its economic interface is free market, financial and corporate capitalism dominated by multinational corporations integrated by the hegemony of the power dominating the unipolar world. The world-wide web of invisible economic coercion swallowed, like a bait, by helpless nations of developing and the under-developed world and punctuated by strategic wars with a show of hightech sophisticated weapons of mass and limited destruction is openly arm-twisting, which dominates the so called sovereign nations of the much adumbrated open and free society. It is turning all the values into economic value, all relations into business relations and all men either into skillful tools of increasingly mechanical production or lots of consumers ranging from those given to wasteful profligacy of the developed world to those on the bare survival or poverty levels of developing and the under-developed world. The rhetoric of development which has so far integrated the three worlds in terms of international pacts for trade, arms deals, infrastructural and other kinds of development, aids and loans has already entered a blind alley, as development on wasteful American model has been pronounced as unviable on India and China scale, not to speak on that of prosperous but fanatic Arab world. Protectionism as against the free market principle going with globalization, has come back against Chinese goods in U.S. and other countries. Unless eternally replenishable green energy sources are in place and more free space for unlimited expansion of man is made available by enormous feats of science and technology by colonizing other planets of the solar system as the entire resources of the world fall too short of the total need of the three worlds at the present rate of consumption and development. To prevent this eventuality India, China and the prosperous Arab countries will have to switch off their growth of machine and fanatic vandalism let loose by way of terrorism or otherwise has to be effectively checked by force, if the limits of peaceful solutions is reached. This is what justifies of unchecked accumulation of power and resources by the developed world and rules out sharing of available resources with continence. It is more imperative for the developed world to keep their average per capita consumption rate which is 32, as against India at less than 1, and China at less than 3 than to let it scale down a little for a better and meaningful sharing of available resources with the rest of the world. Limitations of the already overexploited nature disallow limitless growth and development and needs of leadership and hegemony prevent reasonable, if not equitable, sharing of available resources for the greater good is the great question that the post-modern world is facing, and facing to the finish of a final collapse characteristic of all large scale and far-flung conquests. The spirit of the post-modern world perhaps lies in going strong at the cost of those who, for any reason, cannot do or are not allowed to do the same while keeping them always below its level of power and resources. Mind of the post-modern world is unfurling the flag of knowledge as power, that of power as the tool of aggression and that of aggression as a signal for final collapse of the world order while yet assuring the disheartened underprivileged world that nothing is impossible for this genie (knowledge) of Alladin's lamp. It is giving a call for inclusive development while keeping their own development as exclusive as ever and also for alleviating poverty while adding further to it by increasingly monopolizing resources and enhancing the purchasing power of the developing and under-developed world to create markets for their finished goods through aids and loans to alleviate poverty, to promote education, to ensure gender and social justice as far as possible to control population, and to develop infrastructure for facilitating world trade and expansion of free market. The present world is thus having both mind and soul with all its high sounding scientific pretensions to the contrary. One only needs eyes to see the pathology inside its outer rhetoric. To talk of mind and soul of India is, therefore, not untenable, though there is a possibility of a pathology inside Indian rhetoric too. But then it is a question of discovering and remedying the same.

Let us have a look on Indian mind and spirit with reference to attitude to knowledge as it is obtained from tradition. There is no such division of knowledge between science and arts although the term *vijnana,* by which science is generally translated, is there but in traditional usage it stands for intuitive cognition of the self or *atman,* as in the Upanishadic example of *yena vijnatena sarvamidam vijnatam bhavati* (by knowing which all this is automatically known). Knowledge as such is called *vidya,* i.e. cognitive knowledge and is divided into four categories: *anvikshiki* (knowledge of reasoning), *trayi* (knowledge of the three corpuses of revelation, viz. *rik, yajush* and *saman*), *varta* (knowledge of agriculture, animal husbandry and trade) and *dandaniti* (knowledge of statecraft). *Anvikshiki* has been lauded as the illuminating lamp of all knowledge (*pradipah sarvavidyanam*), the approach of all actions (*upayah sarvakarmanam*) and refuge of all *dharmas,* i.e. duties—religious, social, economic, political and moral (*asryah sarvadharmanam*). It is important to see that duties of various kinds have not been dichotomized as religious and secular. They are viewed in continuity and interrelatedness rather than in terms of binary breaks. The content of *anvikshiki* has been spelled out as *sankhya,* i.e. metaphysics, *yoga,* i.e. union or relation honoured in appropriate spirit or spirituality and *lokayata,* i.e. interaction with the world of material richness. The English word religion derives from the Latin word *religere* meaning relation. *Anvikshiki* is, therefore, a triumvirate of theories going beyond grossly perceptible physics (metaphysics), spirituality (of non-material ties or relations) and attitude to material world. Unlike Western Reason it not only enlightens but also shows the right approach to all human actions and provides refuge or shelter to all kinds of duties and indebtments. Unlike Hegelian Reason, it does not march on earth in the form of state to ensure freedom, nor does it operate as historical materialism to produce the ultimate goal of classless society out of class conflicts against the three pre-modern class formations of human society, viz., slavery, feudalism and capitalism. The attitude of the Barhaspatya school of thought to the three Vedas incorporating revelation as pious fraud has been controverted to show that they provide the path to heaven and infinite bliss and the basis of *varnasrama,* i.e. organization of Indian social order into *varnas* and *asramas.* Admiring the role of *trayi* in the material world it has been said that protected by it the *loka,* i.e. the material world prospers and does not decline. Derived from *vritti, varta* denotes livelihood, while *artha* and its opposite *anartha* the subject matter of statecraft or *dandaniti* also denotes livelihood. The distinction between the two is that while *vritti* stands for individual livelihood *artha* means livelihood of the people (*manusyanam vrittih*) to be managed by the state. Livelihood in this collective aspect has been redefined as populated territory (*manushyavati bhimi*). The approach/technique (*upaya*) concentrating on the acquisition and protection/ sustenance of it constitutes the *sastra* of *artha,* i.e. state economy. *Dandaniti* or statecraft is a wider term as it includes *artha* as well as the opposite of it *anartha. Artha* in *dandaniti* has been defined as acquiring of that (territory) which has not been acquired (*alabdhalabhartha*), protecting and sustaining that which has been acquired (*labdhaparirakishini*) enhancing the value of that which has been protected/sustained (*rakshitvivardhini*), and investing the enhanced value to further the activities of the departments of the state (*vriddhasya tirtheshu pratipadini*). A state approach contrary to it constitutes *anartha* or absence of value addition. *Artha* thus depends on the state and includes conquests for acquisition of new territories, populated or otherwise, and defence and development of the same to enhance its value by what has been prescribed as *janapadasannivesa,* i.e. steps to convert an unpopulated territory into habitat and source of livelihood of the people by encouraging them by remission in taxes and other concessions to settle there and bring the fallow land under cultivation and also develop commercial, mining and industrial activities, with or, without state help, as per the scope available. State might also subject strategically important territories to *durganivesa,* i.e., garrisoning the same by converting it into a fort town. Mind of pre-modern India as revealed by this scheme of knowledge has reason, that is *anvikshiki* as a threading tool that stitches religious, social, economic and political relations of the individual with the territorial, kinship and functional groups of the people and those of state activity on all these levels with that the harmonious participative whole. This relational web does not rule out aggression and scope for power play aimed at consolidating material gains by violence and value-addition by peaceful activities under individual, group and state supervision without reducing things into ideological binaries justifying genocides, revolutionary or progressive, or violence for realizing theoretically conceived future visions, radical or moderate, that turn the other end of the binary essentially retrograde, superstitious and barbarous as a logical necessity. Unlike Reason of Enlightenment and modernity *anvikshiki* is not reductionist and condemnatory of what has been or is beyond it. It does not attribute everything bright and brilliant to itself excluding the rest as dark, shabby and abominable. It unites, stitches together also the opposite perceptions that inspire harmonious or conflicting resolving actions. Man has been defined not as a political, tool-making or economic being or animal but as a one who stitches the fabrics of his action to fit configurations of his attitude, faith or perception to whatever he relates with (*manushyah kasmat? matva karmani sivyanti*), be it Nature, God or gods, State, animals or his fellow beings. Unlike modernity it does not reduce law to rational or irrational command of the sovereign or the contract or covenants entered into by sovereign, autonomous or individual parties with or without an agreed mode of enforcement, nor to legislated or traditionally obtaining customary or Prophetic codes of commands. It gives supremacy to relational justice (*dharmanyaya*) which has power to override the authority of *sastra* codifying and interpreting rules of law.

This broad generalization based on some salient sources about the mind of pre-modern and pre-medieval India was perhaps most compatible to her soul and sounded nearer to the ideal than real in subsequent times, though the real did not emerge without its seed in the ideal. It is also doubtful if the gap between ideal and real was ever totally absent. After all, ideal is always the presentation of the best, people are capable of rising upto or falling down from. It is also a fact that no one time ideal is an ideal for all times to come and considerable changes take place even in the ideal with the passage of time and the challenges of real life braved and negotiated. It is a datum of conduct contextualized in the attitudinal and perceived web of relationships acted upon and honoured in the expects, unexpected or condemnable spirit of crisscrossing ties of that web. Actions on ritual, material, social or moral plane tend to lose their spirit and become a merry-go-round of travelling for the sake of travelling on the rails of given ties even if they cease to be compatible with the attitudes and perceptions underlying them. The scope of aggression and power game left in what has been said above was confined to state and restricted to the given purpose of expansion of and value addition to the old and newly acquired territories for the larger good of enriching, if not providing means of livelihood to the people. But as new invaders from across the borders poured in giving rise to violence, wars and non-native regional states and, as agriculture, trade and commerce expanded with innovations or trade contacts they brought with them. Bringing in new people from among the jungle tribes and foreign diaspora, and men of arms on Indian soil within the ambit of the *varna* order gave rise to gaps between ideal and real. Out-dated and obscure ideals were obviously followed more in breach than in observance. Was it progress or regress? Was it enrichment of Indian people and the traditionally obtaining mould of their life by way of introduction of multicultural elements such as new beliefs and practices and new peoples, gods and customs, dress, ornaments, languages, scripts, skills and art or was it a phenomenon of impoverishment and decline, vandalism and destruction? Perhaps both, as they strand differently perceived. The crisis needed new ideals to be formulated and adhered to and shunning of some of the old ones. Although emergence of new religious movements in the form of Buddhism and Jainism, rise of Magadh followed by Nanda and Maurya political unification and of second urbanization succeeding with a clear break with the first one brought about by the rise of Harappan cities in proto-historic times and culminating in Kusana urbanism distinguished by religious, commercial and cultural expansion overeas and overland reaching Southeast Asia, Central Asia and China has to be looked upon as progress beyond and over and above the circumscribed ideals of the past and pushing the prevailing social, religious, economic and cultural order to a compulsory change. Yet, socially and educationally circumscribed mind of the guardians of the *sastric* view preferred to conceive all this as fall from the golden ideals and worked out necessary adjustments by way of *apaddharma, kalivarjya,* notion of mixed caste (*varnasankara*), social, gender and all sorts of disability rules and provisions. It responded to change by bringing in rigidity from the front door and flexibility from the back door. This distorted, on the empirical level of understanding, the spatial and temporal sequence of events and developments. It is also responsible for dispensing with the need to modify the *sastric* view on the basis and a faithful recording and generalization of the phenomena of change, though only a few isolated and regional exceptions to this can be pointed out. Such an attitude to change inducted the cyclical theory of *yugas* and *manvantaras* in the *sastric* view of things that placed the golden age of pristine purity and all time ideal in the past leading to the assumption that decline compulsorily sets in and moves in leaps and bound as one progresses within a particular cycle of time consisting of four *yugas* till the golden age of the first *yuga* of the next *kalpa* is reached and new cycle of inevitable decline starts. Change and developments on the empirical plane are only a meaningless trash in this overall inevitable scheme of successive decline and getting back to golden age which unleashes a new cycle of decline and degeneration. It created a religious predilection for going back to Vedas and Vedic rituals while harbouring an empirical ambition to push forward in the material world for power, riches and glory.

This faulted mind of India characterizes and controls to a large extent the practice of life, culture and thought in Gupta, post-Gupta and early medieval times of Indian history though strong tendencies to this effect started earlier. Sale/donation of land for construction of monasteries and cash investments in the form of *akshayanivi* to earn religious merit by perpetually feeding monks or arranging for a lamp to be daily burnt at the specified shrine, and the like from the interest proceeds of the amount of money deposited with the *srenis* was an old practice to support and patronize Buddhism and Jainism. Land grant deeds in the form of inscriptions started from the time of Satavahana rulers. The Gupta and Vakataka kings used this device to support education of Vedic learning and rituals and to propagate the practice of the latter by setting up examples by performing *asvamedha* and other Vedic sacrifices themselves. Earlier still a couple of *asvamedha* sacrifices were performed by Pushyamitra Sunga perhaps to mark a break from Asoka's pacifist policy of *dharmavijaya* which declared the cessation of all wars and violence. This tendency to revert to Vedic rites and rituals coincided with the effort to fight back foreign invasions and uproot states ruled over by foreign rulers and also native chiefs of tribal origin in different regions. Rescuing the submerged earth from the primordial ocean by Vishnu in his *varaha* incarnation became a religious and artistic motif of rescuing territories lost to invading foreigners and emerging tribal chiefs establishing themselves as rulers of independent states in different regions. But as early as the time of Samudragupta it became impractical to uproot and keep in control distant kingdoms even though they were ruled over by newly emerging tribal chiefs and foreigners. This led to the formulation of a new concept of *dharmavijaya* and, contrasting the same from *asura* or *lobhavijaya*. The new concept visualized a conquest that led to acknowledgement of the supremacy of the conqueror while agreeing to pay him a stipulated tribute at regular intervals. Samudragupta claims in his Allahabad Pillar inscription to have uprooted nine kingdoms of Aryavarta region annexing them to his empire while the twelve kingdoms of Dakshinapatha region were set free after the conquest on condition of paying tribute. A third category of foreign and bordering kingdoms, also of those situated in the islands, is noted as those which submitted without being conquered and started paying tribute and receiving orders from the imperial power as subordinate allies. Conquests by subsequent rulers of the Gupta, post-Gupta and early medieval dynasties treaded more or less on these policy lines. This model of political and military expansion also saw a parallel process of overseas and overland commercial and cultural expansion which accompanied expansion of agriculture over to forest-covered and uncultivated land. Chola conquerors Rajaraj and Rajendra added naval campaign overseas perhaps to achieve some sort of commercial hegemony for Indian traders. It can be clearly seen that the revival of Vedic orthodoxy as an ideological and/or ritual instrument for fighting back foreign invasions and suppressing the rise of tribal chiefs as political and military powers did not switch off the growth machine, economically and culturally speaking. But the principle of Vedic orthodoxy as a source of power to push back foreign invasions and the rise to political and economic power of tribal chiefs probably fell too short to crop down the drive for inclusiveness and restrict the same to its exclusive confines. It not only brought to the forefront the Puranic and Tantrika gods and goddesses' rites, rituals and philosophies initially frowned upon but later adjusted with orthodox Vedic exclusivism through various symbols and motifs but also socio-economic formations known as castes which were theorized in a complicated manner as products of inter-*varna* marriages of *anuloma* and *pratiloma* types. Factually, however, castes appeal to have been scatterings of the forceful currents and cross-currents of stock-oriented nation forming forces around the economic and military might of new monarchies that foundered at the breakwaters of imperial drives supported by the social, ritual and economic discrimination and disabilities imposed in the name of Vedic orthodoxy as mediated by the ingenuity of its *dvija* ambassadors acting in drastic collusion of discourse and the power of imperially backed arms and agro-commercial and handicraft economies propagating progressively caste ridden *varnasrama* hierarchies as the mainstream of socio-economic order religiously and ritually sanctioned on pan-Indian basis. This gave rise to a tremendous crop of *dharmasastra* literature arranged topically without reference to time, space or authorship (which is wholly legendary) and giving subtly but systematically the mass of prevailing customs an imperceptible push towards *dvija* discourses operating both at the top and grass root levels, sometimes accommodating and sometimes contradicting customs, as and when necessary and/or manageable, in order to give them a turn to fit in the schematic patterns of broad-based but multi-grooved Vedic orthodoxy indirectly and on a long term basis. At the same time, like wheels within wheels, it replicated hierarchies by primary exclusion and also among the excluded by secondary, tertiary and so on, exclusions based on ritual distinctions and disabilities to be realized or kept as deactivated, as the case may be, by the ability of a caste community unit under overall orthodox direction mostly of a discursive kind to muster effective domination or power in terms of number, wealth or arms or opportunity of equation/collaboration, no matter temporary, with powers that had been. A fusion of political, social, religious, economic, ritual, and cultural colours, like those of the spectrum, power in India had thus become discursive and divisive: divisive along the lines of Vedic, *Dharmasastric,* Pauranic and Tantrik discourses. These discourses submerged within themselves the heretical dissent of Buddhism, Jainism and other prominent religious challenges by transforming their character from within rather than subduing them by an intolerant opposition and bloody wars or inquisitions. They provided for the high, middle and low or subaltern needs of ritual, piety, spirituality and philosophy separately and tried to make them all converge in their concept of a common essence of supreme consciousness or spirituality to be reached ultimately by travelling along diverse routes of beliefs, and practices. They inspired innumerable power centers in society, polity and economy and their essentially hierarchical organizations to litter the entire subcontinent with lots and lots of monuments, temples, forts, *mathas, mathikas, chaityas, tirthas* and shrines with an equally large number of motifs and symbols, sculptural, architectural, musical, dance and drama traditions. They also inspired poets, dramatists, *siddhas, sadhakas* and scholars to contribute to literature and folklore of India with rich crops of their creative writings, speeches, songs and liturgies, *sastras, kathas* and *mahatymas*. Power in India was never exclusively and narrowly political. It consisted of a whole spectrum. It was broadly divided into two polarities and hierarchies: political including its social and economic levels and spiritual including its religious and cultural levels. It thus bypassed the assumption of and inherent contradiction between the particular and the universal, between the aggressive contest of the stocks of people emerging as nations organized under European style 'new monarchies' aggressively contesting the sacred universalism of the Church as sole and supreme masters of the profane and the conservative orthodoxy of the Vedas. There was no such polarization that suited the needs of a binary opposition between the national and the colonial/imperial, including an aggressive war of independence, no matter non-violent, but paying the price of partition before a determined programme of direct action of a violent kind. The Indian notion of particular and universal consists of an inherent drive to attain the universal and to be one with the same. It is a process of rising above what is particular in order to attain the universal rather than fighting its way to conquer the universal. Politically and/or diplomatically motivated aggressions of one kingdom against the other or 'others represent' a deviation on the level of negotiating hard realities of material life and individual, political and military ambition of the king and kingdom managing political power. This train of factual development in India in the period noted above does not neatly conform to any given map of historical development which is considered as a universally applicable model for any country's history writing. It also did not neatly fit in the requirements of Indian mind and soul indicated above. If the non-conformatory one makes Indian historical development unique to a large, the other led to the emergence of a number of pathologies of power to be debated by the participants of this Seminar.

I wish the Seminar on this rather inconvenient theme a grand success.

3. MIND OF INDIAN CULTURE

A.K. Sinha

"One attribute that sharply distinguishes man from the rest of nature is his highly developed capacity of thought, feeling and deliberate action. Here and there in other animals rudiments approximations, and limited elements of this capacity may occasionally be found; but the full-blown development that is called a mind is unmatched elsewhere in nature."[1] Mind, thence, transforms man from a mere biological being into a value-conscious being who develops a culture as the systematic totality of values[2] in a sequential succession of the priorities and the primacies in his objectives of life making his journey of life as a march from good to better and from better to the best.[3] This is how a culture develops and keeping an eye over the stages of its development, the mind of that culture can be grasped, which, in the present context, is being attempted to know Indian Culture in a characterized manner.

All values are human values as they originate from the 'urge', 'need' or 'desire' of a human person and are aimed at the fulfillment or satisfaction of this urge, need and desire of him.[4] To be a human person, therefore, is a value. And man, the human person who is a 'desirer of desires', seeks a conscious satisfaction of his desires, and all values arise from the conscious satisfaction of this man, who is a 'desirer of desires'.[5] Man and Culture are thus inseparably interrelated on an axiological plane and all cultural developments are meant for and aimed at the highest stage of man's betterment through the development of a society as the best expression of the inherent social instincts rooted intrinsically in human nature that defines and determines the dual nature and character of the same.[6] The mind of a culture can therefore, only be known by knowing the notion and concept of man in that culture.[7] That is why if in ancient Greek Culture that essential dualism of the original nature of man brought the Greeks to consider him, in a rational way, as a social or political animal seeking his ultimate end in the development of society and state, in Indian Culture he was considered as a spiritual being for whom the ultimate end of life was attaining *moksa* and all social and political developments were those mid-way achievements that form the *trivarga* of Indian value-system, making him conscious and aspirant also for the attainment of the *chaturth varga* viz., the *moksa* for realising the sense of perfection.[8] Indian Culture is thus, without any doubt, a spiritual or transcendental culture[9] though empirical part of life is also taken as an unavoidable reality in its philosophy of life. The *preya-sreya* dichotomy is the essential part of it which develops a specific character of Indian way of life that undoubtedly establishes the superiority of *sreya* over *preya* but *preya* also is accepted respectfully as the values of life.[10]

(II)

The Mind of Indian Culture is best represented in the *Pancakosa* theory of *Taittiriya Upanisad*[11] and the theory of the four *Purusarthas* which speak of man and his values in a very systematic manner and lay the foundation for the development of Indian Culture. The *Pancakosa* theory takes man as a developing being from the lowest to the highest level of consciousness. While at the lowest level of *Annamayakosa* he is, in no way different from any other biological animal for whom all values rest in mere satisfaction of his biological needs. Next to this is *Pranamayakosa* at which survival becomes the highest concern that initiates a process of systematization and management of physical conditions and material resources ensuring protection of life not only in present but in future also at all level. *Manomayakosa* is the next higher level of consciousness which is expressed in the feelings, sentiments and sensitivity etc., being the essential factor for all artistic, creative and aesthetic development leading to the state of enjoyment and pleasure. Then comes the *Jnanamayakosa,* the intellectual level of consciousness exhibited into the thoughtful activities and finally the *Anandmayakosa,* the highest level of blissful consciousness of realizing the perfection as the highest and ultimate end of life conceptualized in *moksa.*[12] There is a sense of gradation in these five levels of consciousness[13] and the desired values at every level, yet what is important to mention here is the tangential connection between all these levels of consciousness presenting man as an integrated body of the same that prepared the ground for the development of a systematic value-system which could make a combination of all these values that separately were concerned with two different worlds of objectives—the empirical and the spiritual or transcendental respectively.[14] *Purusarth-Catustaya* is that complex whole of values in which all human urge, need, want, dreams and aspirations etc., are merged into one combining earthly and heavenly pursuits together and also transcending the both.[15] If *artha* and *kama* represent the highest totality of all worldly values, *moksa* is conceptualized into the highest form of spiritual or transcendental values and *dharma* makes a bridge between the two.[16] *Moksa* in this system comes to be the highest value that gives a spiritual or transcendental colour to Indian Culture and if Indian Culture is called a spiritual culture[17] it is only on account of taking *moksa* as the ultimate value of human life.

(III)

The philosophy of *Purusartha* begins with a firm belief in the *Pancakosa* theory and it makes very clear that all the four values are not for every one. The desire for attaining a specific value presupposes the realization of a definite level of consciousness. It is the *sadhna* and *abhyasa* that prepares one realize from lower to the higher level of consciousness and aspire, consequently, for the higher end of life.[18] The *asrama* system is a theoretical practicality in this process that provides the ground for the physical training and the mental preparation of this realization.[19] By developing the notion of *svadharma* ensuring everyone to realize perfection in his own way, *asrama* system prepared the ground for the development of the *varna* system in an accommodative manner and they, jointly, brought a sense of dynamism in the philosophy of *purusarthas* resulting into a sort of variation in the notion of ultimate value at different levels and also in the way of realization of the same.[20] Thus, for a king ultimate value of his life rests in the performance of his kingly duties of *Prajaraksana* and promoting the *Yogaksema* of his subject with full dedication, while for a trader it lay in the performance of his job with honesty and sincerely. This is very clearly indicated in the various stories in the *Mahabharata,* especially those related with King *Jajali* and a trader Tuladhara, a *Vyadha* and a *Ganika* and so on. It is in this spirit that we find each of *artha, kama* and *dharma* having been declared as the ultimate end of life in different sources with different visions without a sense of ideological clash with the traditional system of values.[21] This dynamism presents a new dimension to Indian value-system by redefining the end-means interrelation in new way declaring that means are not always the means and so are the ends also.

(IV)

Keeping an eye over the development of *Purusartha-Catustaya* vis-à-vis *asrama* and *varna* systems giving rise to the notion of '*svadharma*'[22] as indicated earlier; enables one to underline the path to the formation of Indian Culture as the reflection of Indian value-system in its totality. What forms the 'mind' of Indian Culture is a deep sense of inseparable interrelation between all these essential 'elements' of the latter that manifests itself in the well-known and highly advocated characteristics viz., broadmindedness, tolerance, acceptability, adjustment and accommodation etc., that mark a sense of identity and individuality of Indian Culture and also the form and feature of the same. *Dharma* signifies all these virtues in totality and hence reflects the 'mind' of Indian Culture. In its various forms and types, viz., *Varnadharma, Asramadharma, Kuldharma Jatidharma, Desadharma, Yugadharma* etc., it develops a multidimensional notions of *svadharma* that enables everyone to follow the path of what is just and right, i.e., *Dharma* in all and every situation, condition and station of life with a feeling of devotion and dedication developing a perfect sense of dutifulness in him.[23] *Sva* meaning personal in a narrow sense which, when attached with *dharma*, gets itself broadened gradually to *'para'* meaning 'others' and then *'param'* meaning the highest or ultimate including everything or value beginning from the mere biological satisfaction to the ultimate good of life embracing other social, aesthetic, and political values in its domain. *Dharma* throughout in this process appears as a link or bond of attachment between apparently opposites, viz., ideal and real, individual and society, impirical and spiritual, religiousity and morality and so on and hence sometimes it might seem to be a controversial notion but its inherent essentiality of being 'right and just' in all circumstances leaves no room for any such confusion and *dharma* remains always 'right and just' running between its two poles of 'greater good' and 'lesser evil' providing itself a dynamic nature within specific references to the time and space for establishing its validity.[24] *Dharma* thus is the key-concept to understand the nature and character of Indian Culture that presents in real sense the 'mind' of the latter in its working of combining and uniting the opposites and the extremes and developing the path of oneness that leads to state of perfection and that is all.

REFERENCES AND NOTES

1. *The Encyclopaedia Britannica*, Vol. 24, 15th edn., New York, 1997, p. 152. This may be compared with *'dharma'* or *'jnana'* in Indian tradition that distinguishes a human being from the world of animals.

   आहार निद्रा भय मैथुनं च सामान्यमेतद् पशुर्भिनराणां।
   धर्मों हि तेषामधिको विशेषो धर्मेणहीनाः पशुर्भिसमानाः।।

   Mahabharata, 12.264.49 At some places *dharma* has been

replaced by *jnana.*
See, Hiriyanna, M., *Indian Conception of Values,* Mysore, 1975, p. 6.
2. Pande, G.C., *Consciousness Value Culture,* Allahabad, 2006, pp. 12-13.
3. This makes Culture defined as a constant process of Value-Seeking. Pande, G.C., *The Meaning and Process of Culture,* Agra, 1972, p. 121.
4. Pandey, R.B., *Bhartiya Niti ka Vikas,* Patna, 1965, p. 4; Pande, G.C., *Mulya-Mimamsa,* Jaipur, 1973, p. 33; Sinha, A.K., 'Mulya Ki Avadharna evam Svarup' in the *Journal of G.N. Jha Kendriya Sanskrit Vidyapeeth,* Allahabad, Vol. 39.
5. Nikam, N.A., *Some Concepts of Indian Culture,* Shimla, 1973, p. 47.
6. Sinha, A.K., *Some Aspects of Ancient Indian Society and Polity,* Delhi, 2005, pp. 14-15.
7. The volume entitled *Concept of Man* edited by P.T. Raju and S. Radhakrishan presents very emphatically this fact with a reference to the important cultures of the world.
8. Sinha, A.K., 'On the Problem of Cultural Identity (with special reference to Ancient Indian and Greek Cultures)' in U.P. Arora (ed.), *Graco-Indika — Demetrius Galanos Memorial Volume,* Delhi, 1991, pp. 281-82, also, Sinha, A.K., *Time, Materialism and Historiography — Some Indo-Hellenic Parallels,* Delhi, 2004.
9. "... A spiritual aspiration was the governing force of this (Indian) Culture, its core of thought, its ruling passion. Not only did it make spirituality the highest aim of life, but it even tried, as far as that could be done in the past conditions of human race to turn the whole of life towards spirituality..." Aurobindo, *The Foundations of Indian Culture,* Pondichery, 1980, p. 121. (Bracket is mine).
10. *Kathopanisad,* 1.1.23-25; Recognising *trivarga* as conceptualized in the symbolical totality of all worldly and other worldly pursuits and pleasures and considering it a pre-condition for seeking *moksa* is a very important tradition of Indian Culture and philosophy of life simply makes this view established.
11. *Taittiriya Upanisad,* 1-2-8.
12. Sinha, A.K., 'Subha ki Avadharna evam Manava-Svabhava ke Sath Uske Antarsambandhon ki Vivechana' in *Paramarsha,* Year 5, No. l, Jaipur, 1983; Sinha, A.K., 'Value and Social Structure in Ancient India' in *Journal of Oriental Institute,*

Vol. 40, Pt. 1-2, Baroda, 1990; Pande, R.B., *op. cit.*, pp. 63-64.
13. *Kathopanisad,* 1.3.10-11, 2.3.7-8; Rajbali Pandey, however believes in three level of consciousness corresponding to the theory of the three *gunas,* viz, *tama, rajas* and the *sattva* respectively. See, Pandey, R.B., *op. cit.,* pp. 63-64.
14. The notion of dharma as *'Yato abhyudaya nihsreyasasiddhi so dharmah'* develops in the same spirit. *Vaisesika Sutra,* 1-1-3, Mukerjee, Radha Kamal, *Indian Scheme of life,* Bombay, 1951. p. 20.
15. Sinha. A.K., *Some Aspects of Ancient Indian Society and Polity,* p. 16.
16. Sinha. A.K., *Pracina Bhartiya Vaiyaktika evam Samajik Mulyabodh* (2[n] ed.) Delhi, 2009, Ch. 5, entitled, 'Vaiyaktika, evam Samajik Jivana Ka Samanjasya-Sutra——Dharama'.
17. Aurobindo, *op. cit.,* p. 121.
18. See, Pande, G.C., *Bhartiya Parampara Ke Mula Svara,* Delhi, 1981, p. 11.
19. Ibid. pp. 69-71; Sinha, A.K., *Santiparva mein Vislesîta Naitika Vicar a,* Allahabad, 1985, p. 67.
20. Sinha, A.K., *Pracina Bhartiya Vaiyaktika evam Samajika Mulyabodh* (2nd ed.) Delhi, 2009, pp. 48, 56 fn. 95.
21. Development of the traditions of *Dharmasastra, Arthasastra* and *Kamasastra* through the *Dharmasutra* and *Smriti* texts, the *Arthasastra* of *Kautilya* and the *Kamasutra* that declare *Dharma, Artha* and *Kama* as the supreme value respectively with a reference to one another clearly establish this way of thinking but they all accept *moksa* as the highest value of life.
22. This 'Svadharma' has clearly been described in the *Bhagvadgita* and the *Santiparva* of the *Mahabharata* which very strongly establish the path of action over the way of ascetism and renunciation.
23. For a detailed information regarding this aspect of dharma See, Creel, A.B., *Dharma in Hindu Ethics,* Callcutta, 1977, Ch.l. and Singh, R. Dharma Ki *Hindu Avadharna,* Allahabad, 1977. Ch-I, also, Pande, G.C., *Bhartiya Parampara Ke Mula Svara,* pp. 66-67.
24. *Mahabharata,* 12.110.10; Dasgupta, S., *Development of Moral Philosophy in India,* Bombay, 1961, pp. 15, 91.

4. INDIAN CULTURE AND GLOBALISATION
Threat and Response

Abhay Kumar Singh

"O Veritable Asia, origin and home of mankind;
Search well the treasure lying in her ruins.
May sap from thy (very) thirst awaiting deliverance,
In her bottomless well stagnates the water divine."
(Henry Frank, *The Dance before the Arch*)

Globalization[1] is very different from the bygone days concepts of "humanism" or "internationalism"; "universalism" or the "one-world order". Despite its tall claims of doing universal good, the advent of globalization has become a threat to the cultural spirit of the Asian countries which were the cradles of civilisations and culture. That is so, because we are value-based cultures, God-fearing societies and humanity-loving nations, to whom the vicious ideals and vile goals of the western-capitalistic world do not appeal. In the Orient, materialism has limited fascination, while non-materialistic ideals and spiritual ends are venerated. To fulfil the economic goals of the multi/trans-national companies and their favouring political powers, the plot of imposing a western culture of consumerism in Asia amounting to de-culturing the Orient has been designed today as supportive of 'globalization'.[2]

Asian cultures are being meddled with under subtle marketing strategies, suggesting out of context or construed relationships between cultural symbols and beliefs with consumer goods; emotional appeals with technological progress ascribed to the West. New tastes and wants are being created, whereas basic needs are awaiting solutions in the poorer parts of our world. India is treated a market rather than a society. Are we consumers first and not humans? The paper is an anxious evaluation of the like, and similar past and present situations and objects to the culture umpiring by the powerful and elite, which used as a lever to promote globalization. We should beware of taking pride in being West (-t-) oxicated modernised people and think about the reinforcing and rejuvenation of our finer traits of culture.

Present Crisis

In 1929, when contemporary industrialisation and scientific growth were causing a state of unsettlement Dr. S. Radhakrishnan had written: "Civilization today seems to be passing through one of its periodic crises. The world is casting off its old garments. Standards, aims, and institutions which were generally accepted even a generation ago are now challenged and changing. Old motives are weakening and new forces are springing up."[3] He also mentioned, "Man, the combative animal, is still untamed. Economic success is our highest ideal, and almost all our wars are due to economic causes. Economics is our religion. Empire is big business. We wage wars to increase our trade, extend our territories and acquire colonies. Modern civilization is in the stage of economic barbarism. It is concerned more with the world and its power than with the soul and its perfection."[4]

Whatever he had observed at that time seems true even today.[5]

The same scene is repeated since the end of the twentieth century, and the only difference being the addition of new factors like information technology and economic liberalisation. Recently, an eminent educationist has commented, that "globalization has brought about a certain kind of economic fundamentalism as an ideological fact across the world,.....economics has become a kind of theology, which is pretending to be a science."[6] Another eminent journalist opines that "the whole process of globalization has not only produced an elitist bias in our public discourse but it has also moved the standards of our own moral and ethical values and judgements away from our anchorage to those which we feel are in conformity with the West."[7] "What we now have is both a frightening process of dominance by economically powerful groups shifting the way we think about ourselves away from the egalitarian concerns towards a selfish and consumeristic social order, and a process of democratic movements to connect both within and across States against whosoever the oppressor may be."[8]

In fact, the economic phenomenon of globalization is not only transforming the world-economy, rather at the same time more seriously affecting the social and cultural fabric of the East, not only marginally or substantially, but grossly and blatantly. At an ultimate of capitalism, man is becoming, first and foremost, a consuming being. He is urged to bargain for material benefits and pecuniary gains in every aspect of life. He is enthused to possess the solitary aim to consume more and grossly enjoy everything to the point of optimal satisfaction. He is praised for his gluttony and absolved for his wastefulness. Peoples and nations, world resources and environment are exploited and devastated by the greed of the capitalist man. In the course of his consumerism, such a man loses his sensitivity, sensibility, sympathy and sentimentality, which are the true and vital virtues of humanity. To such a class of men, every object has become a mere commodity, may it be art or culture. In the apt words of Oscar Wilde, "Too many people today know the price of everything and the value of nothing."

Apprehensions

There are questions like "What is globalization bringing in?" Erosion of our culture. "What would happen, then?" The prevalence of western ways, whatever they may be.[9] There is fair amount of truth but also certain errors in comprehending the situation. Globalization is interfering in our cultural evolution.

The fears about the future in countries like ours relate to the fate of the factors of strength that have sustained us till now. They are our ideals, approaches and ways of life. Our resistance is reposed in our culture, which we feel are weakening and threatened. Apprehensions are heightened by the rapid incumbent changes in the nature of their society, the transformation of the culture and traditions, the vanishing of the identity, the weakening of the national state, the economic disparity, the change in education[10] and resultant servitude of the people and brain-drain.

Presently, "the incompatibility of modern civilization with our tradition-bound civilization is one of the most important causes of the crisis in our society."[11] The sense of insecurity not only connects to the dreaded 'erosion of culture' or its 'supplanting by Western traditions'[12] but also to the professed 'inevitability of globalization'[13] and 'western as the only model for our transformation'.

It is imperative to reflect upon the views of some intellectuals who have discussed these apprehensions from the academic point of view. The stances of the exclusiveness of each culture and the problem or risks arising from interaction with other cultures are at the core of our fears. But culture is not as delicate or tender as feared. It is a misconception that culture is exclusive and segregated. In past global links were war and religion, but cultural inter-connectedness was subject to limitations imposed by geography, ecology and technology. States in the past were not absolutely sovereign as there were number of institutions competing with the state. Thus, there have been many factors and forces, other than economic policy, that has brought about cultural interaction and has left impressions on different cultures and societies. There is need to rectify our misunderstanding and misapprehensions. If a culture is active and alive then it is neither closed nor secluded from the outside world. It always remains under engagement with other cultures.

Under the globalization there is intense interconnectedness between societies and nations, we need to recognise certain facts (as enumerated by Prof. Bhargava) that (a) "cultures are not bounded, they are open-ended and they overlap" (b) the cultures are "connecting with each other, shaping each other. Interconnection is something which is internal to every culture." Cultures are not like billiard balls[14] sometimes colliding otherwise separate. Cultures are "always intermeshed with each other." (c) Cultures are not homogenous, internal differentiation is really at the heart of every culture. Cultures are being constantly negotiated, constantly imagined, and re-imagined.[15]

Opposition to Onslaught

The conditions under the globalization are no different from what were observed long ago by Dr. Radhakrishnan. "The tyranny of a high power civilization hardly leaves us any time for the saner pursuits of the mind. It is inimical to that repose, detachment, and concentration of spirit without which genuine reflection cannot go on. Greater knowledge has not resulted in greater wisdom." Further, "Education is valued for its utility in cutting a man for success in the competitive economic struggle, science is respected for its useful knowledge, the comforts and conveniences which it makes possible, its power of organization and its capacity to devise machinery for increased production. The outer acquisition does not, however, bring about inner retirement.....This stage of society is one of economic or intellectual barbarism, since it confuses civilization with comfort, morality with convention, religion with routine, and politics with trade, exploitation and opening of markets."

As a principle, "no single historical culture or civilization can lay claim to an absolute universality."[16] "If there is a single goal for all civilization, it does not mean that all shall speak a common tongue or profess a common creed, or that all shall live under a single government or all shall follow an unchanging pattern in customs and manners. The unity of civilization is not to be sought in uniformity but in harmony......The faith of the future is in co-operation and not identification, in accommodation to fellowmen and not imitation of them, in toleration and not absolutism."[17]

Recently, Dr. Seyed Mohammad Khatami, former President of Iran, has commented on the situations in the present world. It can be best to put in his own words: "All human beings are entitled to participate in the activities that will shape the world in the third millennium. No nation should be left on the sidelines because of some philosophical, political or economic arguments.........The world should be shaped by the massive cooperation of all human beings. Though this notion upto the early twentieth century sounded like a humanist motto, today it is a necessity for the continuation of human life."[18] "We have been relegated to being passive consumers of the West's modern civilization. But if we use our rationality and wisdom, we will have the opportunity to break out of our current second-rate status, and we will be able to affect the course of human destiny."[19]

Western Culture: A Mediator of Globalization

The capitalistic civilisation and its Western culture has been discredited for its inherent shortcomings by prominent Indian thinkers. "A community which is almost entirely preoccupied with life and body, physical and economic existence, scientific and technical efficiency to the exclusion of the higher humanistic ideals of mind and spirit is not truly civilized. Body, mind and spirit form distinguishable aspects of an inseparable unity. Human nature is all of a piece and unification of the three is the true aim of civilization."

However, the West is still a dominant reality and through its cultural tentacles is reaching out to poison the sap of Asian strength.[20] Through these tentacles does economic globalization tends to take roots in Asia.

"Western civilization is the powerful reality of our age," wrote Dr. Dhatami, "The West has indeed brought great achievements to humanity, but it has also created great difficulties."[21] In his writings he has taken a considerate view and declared that "the whole of the West is a civilization that has its own culture, and this civilization is based on a specific worldview and value system. Without understanding these values, our grasp of the West will be superficial and misleading. At the point of appraisal, we must shun the extremities of hating the West or being completely enchanted by it, so that on one hand we can guard against the dangers posed by the West and on the other hand utilize its human achievements."[22] However, he objected to the western model and said that ".....development in its western sense is merely one form of transformation, not the only form."[23]

What Do We Fear to Lose in Our Asian Cultures

The goals and ideals in Asian cultures have been historically and philosophically, different from the West. By culture we are referring to the cultural spirit, and not strictly to the outwardly manifestations of that in rituals, codes, style of living etc. The outward manifestations may change with time, but the essence of culture which reflects in values, attitude, beliefs and goals, needs to be protected. However, former being the body of that spirit also has no mean importance.

During the course of history since the dawn of the capitalism and industrial age, it has been the Orient that has seen more erosion and suppression. "Before the advent of industrial revolution, we had other standards of social valuation..........The days when poverty could be clean, healthy, and self-respecting are over. Money-making has become one of the most popular industries of the world."[24] We subscribe to solutions in resorting to cultural solace. "The end of life is not pleasure (*preyas*) but the realization of the good (*sreyas*). A life of joy and the joy of life are not the same."[25] It is in these values that we are rooted.

The threat to the Westoxytocin or homogenising of the Asian cultures by the globalization, however, superfluous it may be reckoned, is still real. It may not be the worry of the imposing factor, but it should certainly be the concern of the suffering part to caution in what shape it shall emerge and how.[26] It may be questioned as to what is so special about our cultures. Are we an ideal and egalitarian society or a fair and honest society? No, surely not. We concede that we are imperfect, but like all others! We are not the only imperfect souls on the planet. There are more and worse than us in the more wealthy and civilised quarters of the world. And they have no merit to act as ideals to be emulated or civilisational role-model to be followed.[27]

Past Reactions and Wisdom

In every age people have (i) felt apprehensive to change, and also (ii) recognised the efficacy of culture. There have similar upheavals during the transitory phases of history and each time there were some serious discussions and thinking about the future of the changing society.

In England, the Victorian Age was a time of doubts and change, when Matthew Arnold lived and wrote (since 1849). He witnessed the "difficulties" after the Reform Bill of 1867 which brought the second democratization of England. The issues of the Non-conformists, the views and actions of the three classes of the British society (Barbarians, Philistines and Populace), induced Arnold to write essays which subsequently were published as *Culture and Anarchy.* Arnold believed that democracies tend inevitably to anarchy unless they are permeated by intelligence and tolerance, which he termed as "sweetness and light". By anarchy he meant "doing as one likes" and for anarchy not to prevail it was imperative for everyone to cultivate the spirit of sanity and cooperation with the State, which culture[28] fosters. His contact with modern social[29] and political movements led to his belief in the healing power of culture for times troubled by restless agitations. What democracy needed was intelligence and patience, both of which were fruits of culture. Arnold concluded that "Through culture seem to lie our way, not only to perfection, but even to safety." Later on H.G. Wells lamented and wrote, "Had we listened to Matthew Arnold, we might have avoided the Great War."

After the First World War, there was a great thrust to the Industrial Revolution. The great philosopher-teacher Dr. S. Radhakrishnan wrote (1929) *Kalki* or *The Future of Civilization* and discussed the world situation. He wrote, "An industrial age believes in the creation of new wants. The consumer's appetite grows by what it feeds on. To want more, and to get more, is the way of material progress. By means of this exciting competition we are concealing from ourselves the barrenness of life." He added, "A community which gives greater importance to mind than to life and body is higher in scale. But unless the 'mind' is taken in a larger sense so as to include aesthetic development and ethical perfection, i.e. unless the mind is interpreted as one with spirit, we have not reached the ideal of civilization."

Safeguarding Preferences: Building Immunity; Introspection and Reforms

The defence against the Western cultural intrusion and globalization may range from reactionary stances, fundamentalism, and intense nationalism (which are desperate and damaging) to adopting suitable and preferable modernisation (which is sensible statesmanship). Among the latter may be counted the stances of immunization or empowering the society with moral consciousness to reject the unworthy, unaffectedly; as also the social introspection or critique of traditions and to accordingly bring in reforms giving new lease of life to culture and flow with the tide of modernity.

In modern times, Mahatma Gandhi was observant of the crisis caused by the foreign rule, western capitalistic thought and its impact on countries like India. The social and economic models for the development of the country proposed by Gandhi differed from the western models.[30] But he was tolerant to new ideas. He sided with the idea of generating moral force within the being and advocated steadfastness. His views were not to disconnect with the rest of the world or to revert to the hiding in our shells, but in seeking strength in character to oppose what defies our ideals by firm refusal to be influenced. In his peculiar style, we shall not close our doors and windows to the world and shall let in fresh air from all corners, but we shall refuse to be blown off our feet by that gust of wind. We shall be masters of our own houses.

Dr. S.M. Khatami has also favoured the dialogues between civilizations to continue and slogan the strategy of development of internal immunity in our people to resist any unwanted habits.[31] "An active, evolving society must be in contact and communication with different, sometimes opposing, views to be able to equip itself with a more powerful, attractive and effective thought than of the opponent........we have no other choice but to offer society sophisticated and adaptive thinking." "As a progressive religion, Islam shuns building fences around people's consciousness. Instead, our strategy must focus on making our people immune, raising and educating them to resist the cultural onslaught of the west on their own. Only a strategy of immunization represents a viable solution for today and tomorrow. This requires us to allow disparate views to engage one other in our society."[32] "To make our society stable and strong, we must teach the young a more worthy path than hedonism, such that they gain pleasure out of abstinence."

"We must reach a level of historical evolution and social maturity to be able to judge accurately the thoughts and efforts of others so that we know our place in the world and can put our own house in order,"[33] adds Dr. Khatami. He refers to the option of reform by way of critique of tradition, the dismantling of obsolete traditions to revitalize the culture,[34] can also bring modernity and development. However, "we can only critique tradition if we have a firm sense in our own identity."[35] Dr. Khatami finds it a "simplistic conclusion that to reach development, it is necessary to embark on modernization, and modernization can only come about through dismantling tradition."[36] He argues that "even in the effort to dismantle tradition, there is no escaping tradition."[37] "If a people are to evolve, they must understand their past to see where they are in their process of historical evolution. Thus, dismantling aspect of tradition must be based on indigenous models, not imported and artificial." "The people who once created one of the most glorious civilization in history still enjoy the potential to create another, provided, of course, that they lend themselves to reason and reflection."[39]

From Umbrella to Shield

A cursory glance over the histories of Asian countries like Iran, China and India can give us the information that they could retain their goodness across the span of thousands of years, despite odds. It was not by way of forceful unification or regimentation, but by methods which permitted diversity to flourish. The Achaemenid emperor Cyrus (the Great), despite his immense powers, chose the policy of assimilation, religious tolerance and cultural autonomy for his vast heterogeneous empire. Emperor Ashoka saw the futility of repressive war and took up peaceful means to harness his vast empire. Consolidation by *'sambhao'*; reforms through persuasion on *'dhamma'*; and control with an anxious paternal outlook, were the preferred means adopted to achieve the objectives. The spread of Buddhism from India to China and Japan united the region without disturbing the diversity. The South-Central Asian nations traversed by the Silk Route flourished and the economic chain binding the entire region again was more on sharing than domination or suppression. Asian nations also had their own traditional responses in the struggle against British imperialism, e.g., the emphasis on the soul-force, *satyagraha, swaraj, swadeshi,* were also novel appeals for reconstruction.

It may be noticed that in the social, cultural and religious spheres, the syncretic, assimilative attitude of the Indian could avert collapse and disorder rather shape the future more beautifully towards enrichment. The transformation from Vedic Brahmanism to Puranic Hinduism was one such process in the ancient India that legitimised (not Indianised) the variety within assimilation. The Bhakti Movements of medieval days also brought reforms avoiding social conflicts and disturbances. On one side, some might annoy to the passivity and lack of disturbance, but that (anarchy) is what does not find favour in evolution. On the other side, (there were and still are) many view that change as towards a decline.[40]

The weakening of the 'Nation State'[41] does adversely affect reforms, but that does not close the fate. More than the state, it is the society that has been considered as the source of energy that can bring change. Reform movements in our communities originated from the common class in the society and the leadership seldom with political class. Buddha and Mahavira, belonged to the elite ruling class, but while in leadership they were not as political masters. The Bhakti Movement was dominated by saints from the common class. The Indian National Movement was nurtured and furthered by those who were without political power. The Revolution in Iran was also a social movement.

Present times demand greater cooperation, mutual respect and closer interaction. Time is inappropriate for eulogising own past glories and criticising others imperfections; but still enough for weaving interdependence and knitting a mutual connectedness, as a safeguarding effort. We need stronger bonds than boundaries. Social integration is essential even across the boundaries in Asia. For creation of understanding we need to promote the learning of the each others languages and arts. The features that are common to us must be highlighted. Respect for each others identity is good but it shall better if we give greater recognition to the commonness in our different identities. And the best will be our understanding of the fact that each identity is an evolutionary entity which has borrowed from others in its development and shall continue to borrow if it has to develop further and survive.

Asian Shield

We have noted that the options open to us are mainly building immunity with the vitality provided by our own cultures;[42] moving forward with self-introspection and reforms, dismantling traditions on own models and providing adaptive thinking and higher goals to the society; or building concerted defence through closer cooperation[43] in Asia. We will prefer to greater interaction in our society for building social bonds and create economic ties and inter-dependence. Not discussing the possibilities of the economic cooperation in Asia, we shall limit to the cultural issue only.[44]

The trajectory of hybridization of culture or projection of each identity[45] cannot deliver the goods. If an Asian Shield is contemplated, it can be a composite one only, where each identity is important and visible, complementing the others, while the hybridization shall not be a deliberate or conscious policy, but an unhampered natural process. The Asian cooperation would rest upon this Asian identity. Surmounting the national identity we must concern about the nascent Asian identity and for building this outlook we shall rely on writing a composite history for Asia. It shall neither advocate nor propagate any ideology nor should it glorify particular episodes and cultures. History for peace should reject exclusiveness and accept the mutual borrowings. Achievements should be considered heritage of all and failures as defeat of humanity. Recognition to such a history should not be withheld nor denied nor objected. Identities are not drowned in a composite culture; they swim like fishes in the stream. The stream, the water, the fishes and the vegetation, all shall be part of one scene. Wherever we differ, we must admit it as diversity. Diversity is natural to the world and does not negate equality. Wherever we can blend, or wherever we can harmoniously tolerate our differences, we can produce a composite culture.

Firstly, we must learn to offer our own answers to our peculiar and general problems. Committed to this approach we can further our assimilation or cooperation in a better way. Secondly, we must surprise the Western globalization with our answers which should be different from the anticipated ones. Our watchwords should be Avoid, Refuse, Innovate, Compete.

And we must optimistically look forward believing the dictum from an allegory told by Attar of Nishapur: "This, too, will pass."

REFERENCES

1. Prof. Rajeev Bhargava, basing upon David Held and Anthony Giddens defines Globalization: "It refers immediately to two things. It refers to the scope of activity. Something that may have had a very particular location now has allegedly spread worldwide. There has been an intensification of inter-connectedness of various social-economic and cultural activities. And this inter-connectedness has become chronic," Bhargava, Rajeev "Globalization and Culture" in Prof. Achin Vanaik (ed.), *Globalization and South Asia, Multi-dimensional Perspectives*, (ATWS & Manohar, N.D., 2004), p. 302. Further, "Globalization in a rather vague term refer to the enormous commercial revolution.........Globalization in its more meaningful sense refers to a specific phase of capitalist development, which started around 1970-3...........flexible accumulation meaning that investments.......... become more mobile .... units of production........gets more and more decentralized.........decline in .....stereotypical image of advanced capitalism..........power of organized labour has suffered a major decline.........enormous human retrogression throughout the world.......total glorification of the free market." *Ibid.*, p. 319.
2. The prevailing world view is of "a colour-blind religion-blind and culture-blind globalization which many have rightfully criticized as a disguise form of Westernization of the world." Mr. Rajiv Malhotra 'Comment on Nico Stehr's Special Feature Article, "Nothing has been decided: The Chances and the Risks of Feasible Globalization'" in *Journal of Inter-disciplinary Crossroads* on Internet.
3. Radhakrishnan, Dr. S., "*Kalki* or *The Future of Civilization*,

(Kegan Paul, Trench, Treubner & Co., London, 1934, first edition 1929), "Anyone who has an insight into the mind of the age is vividly conscious of its restlessness and uncertainty, its dissatisfaction with the existing economic and social conditions and its yearning for the new order which is not yet realized."

4. Radhakrishnan, Dr. S. *op.cit.*, p. 46. "In the first triumphs of scientific progress it tended to cast aside philosophy, despise thought, and almost succeeded in slaying religion. Though we are more learned and scientific than our ancestors, we cannot say that we are less brutal and more humane."
5. Compare the similarity in the present situation when an educational expert opines: "We're talking about the question of regulating capitalism...... We should also perhaps be talking about regulating science and technology....Nanology...have made... association between science and curiosity, or between technology and curiosity, quite obsolete.........there is a very important need for us to fearlessly look at the issue of science as a progress value once again, without the fear of being labelled as being neo-Gandhians.........we have to open up the Chapter of the scientific temper because science is no more what Jawaharlal Nehru has learned in his childhood..." Prof. Krishna Kumar, "Globalization and Education" in Prof. Achin Vanaik (ed.), *op.cit.*, p. 251.
6. *Ibid.*, p. 241.
7. Harish Khare, "Globalization and the Media" in Vanaik, Achin (ed.) *Ibid.*, p. 270. Harish Khare adds "Suddenly the country has decided that it has had enough of the past. It must now look to the twenty-first century", "...what we seek is the approval of not the people of this country, but of what the outsider will do and of what the outsider thinks." *ibid.*, p. 270. "So now you don't want to judge yourself by your own past, or be nourished by the aesthetic, cultural, spiritual enrichment which is there in the whole glorious saga of the freedom struggle that lasted more than 50-60 years." *ibid.*, p. 270. "As we move away from the legacy of that struggle against a Colonial power, we are seeking legitimacy from those Colonial powers." *ibid.*, p. 273.
8. *Ibid.*, p. 272.
9. Mr. Harish Khare writes : "The most vocal constituency of the liberalization process and of globalization is the new middle class, which doesn't care for seeking approval; it

doesn't want to be the part of the poor India; it wants to be a part of the rich United States." *ibid.*, p. 271 "...there is a new elitism of the elites wherein they no longer show the kind of the earlier concern for the underprivileged and the larger masses." *ibid.*, p. 275. Also, "...the newly empowered Indian is not interested in the Third World. He will not be interested in famine in Ethiopia or in floods in Bangladesh.....A new jugalbandhi is taking place between the consumer of the new media, the provider of the new media, and the financier of the new media. The 100 million middle class may consume in India but thinks about Nottingham or Pennsylvania. This process is inherently anti-democratic because it does not seek legitimacy from the aspirations, dreams and values of the society at large but rather it seeks approval from the pages of The *Wall Street Journal* or *the Times*, London." *ibid.*, p. 271.

10. On convergence of curricula across the world and favouring people for diplomas encashable in specific economies : "All this takes away the intellectual, the theoretical function, almost entirely out of higher education, rendering the products of higher education highly susceptible and highly vulnerable to these shifts and changes in the economy." Krishna Kumar, *op.cit.*, p. 246.
11. Dr. Seyed Mohammad Khatami's lectures and writings are published as *Islam, Dialogue and Civil Society*, (JNU, New Delhi, 2003), p. 79. It has been so diagnosed by the eminent statesman and former President of Iran, Dr. S. M. Khatami, and very well explained in his own words: "When a new civilization is created and the culture appropriate for it is entrenched, people who still carry around vestiges of the previous culture experience a contradiction when encountering a new civilization....."
12. "Globalization is not the same as cultural homogenization.... there is a lot of cultural heterogeneity. As ideas and models moved from one place to other communities they were transformed and in some ways indigenized......... some forms of hybridity...Furthermore we must not think of globalization as Americanization, or even Westernization......Bhargava, Rajeev *op.cit.*, p. 305.
13. Prof. Krishna Kumar writes "Regarding the slogan of globalization, and the attendant slogans of liberalization and privatization, when they began there was an air of

inevitability about them......How can we make the future discussible in unless deterministic terms, in more reversible terms, in terms that permit us to assert our right to be human beings and for us to say that human beings have always written their own destiny and the twenty-first century will be no different......" Krishan Kumar, *op.cit.*, p. 251. "Critics like Chomsky argues that human beings have created the roles of the WTO, they can reverse them too. Then there is the model of correctibility where people like Anthony Giddens and others say that there are various positions that can be taken or Roberto Unger telling us that there is a second alternative or a third way..." *Ibid.*, p. 258.

The observation of Dr. Radhakrishnan, seventy-five years ago, compares so well with the present state of affairs: "The world is becoming outwardly uniform. Europe and America as well as Asia and Africa are moving in the same direction, only the former faster than the latter India and China are being sucked into the maelstrom. The unrest in the East is due to the new consciousness that, if the Oriental nations are not to decay and die they must strive to stand as equals alongside of other nations whose spirit of enterprise and power of organization, have spread their sway to the uttermost parts of the earth."

14. James Tully had proposed a 'billiard ball concept of culture' which has not convinced many intellectuals. Prof. Bhargava explains, "This newly identified concept of culture is more like an ecosystem where there is a cluster of variegated elements with diverse origins, not an internally homogeneous system very clearly bounded from, and clearly demarcated from (and hence the billiard ball concept) other cultures. It is as if each of us belongs to one culture, which is to be demarcated from and which is excluded from every other culture. These cultures may interact, may collide, may come to conflict with each other, and so on." Bhargava, Rajeev *op. cit.*, p. 314. "This conception of culture as separate bounded, clearly demarcated, internally homogeneous... give rise to what we call the politics of multi-culturalism." Multicultural conceptions is grounded on the billiard-ball conception of culture. Identity is a matter of orienting towards this cultural space. Notions of cultural identity depend upon this separate bounded internally homogenous culture. Even the politics of majority and minority, of cultural identity, depend on this

billiard ball conception. *Ibid.*, p. 309.

15. *Ibid.*, pp. 309-10.
16. Radhakrishnan, Dr. S. *op. cit.*, p. 11. Dante proclaimed: 'There is not one goal for this civilization and one for that, but for the civilization of all mankind there is a single goal.'
17. *Ibid.*, p. 13.
18. Dr. Khatami, *op. cit.*, p. 32.
19. *Ibid.*, p. 70.
20. Rajiv Malhotra, *op. cit.*, asks "Disregarding the merits and demerits of Western living, if the economic planners cannot guarantee the practical achievability of the "good Western lifestyle" to all, is it not fraud to promote it as the sought-after legitimate lifestyle across the globe today? Why have intellectuals made it fashionable to denigrate the Indic traditions which offer a comprehensive lifestyle alternative, complete with culture and spirituality that has passed the test of time for eco-friendliness and non-dependence on capital?"

    Is it that consumerism *ad infinitum* is a pre-requisite for the growth of incomes on the world financial markets without which stock prices (based on future income growth projections) would crash and jeopardize the Western lifestyles today? The third worlders are being dislocated from viable native cultural alternatives that they have lived for several millennia, under the false promise of an alternative "progressive" lifestyle which no economist has proven to be achievable in practical terms."
21. Dr. Khatami, *op. cit.*, p. 44.
22. *Ibid.*, 51.
23. *Ibid.*, p. 86.
24. Radhakrishnan, Dr. S. *op. cit.*, p. 26.
25. *Ibid.*, p. 61.
26. See note 20, para I,
27. *Ibid.*, Rajiv Malhotra says, "American culture has only two life-stages, juvenile and senile. Everyone is expected to be "young," fueling a juvenile culture of dying hair, breast implants, Viagra, etc., just to be seen as youthful for as long as possible. Eventually, upon failing to keep up this artificial youthfulness, i.e., upon accepting the inevitability of one's aging, one faces rejection by society and lives in an old people's home waiting to die. This is why so many older Americans turn senile, unlike in

traditional India.

28. Matthew Arnold believed that 'Culture' was an effort towards perfection "through all the voices of human experience which has been heard upon it, of art, science, poetry, philosophy, as well as of religion". Culture works both for inward expansion in the individual and for general expansion in society.

    Elsewhere, he wrote, "Culture being a pursuit of our total perfection by means of getting to know, on all matters which most concern us, the best which has been thought and said in the world; and through this knowledge, turning a stream of fresh and free thought upon our stock notions and habits, which we now follow staunchly but mechanically vainly imagining that there is a virtue in following them staunchly which makes up for the mischief of following them mechanically." "But culture, which is the study of perfection, leads us, to conceive of true human perfection as a harmonious perfection, developing all sides of our humanity; and as a general perfection, developing all parts of our society." Arnold, Matthew, *Culture and Anarchy* (W.S. Knickerbocker, ed.), Macmillan & Co., New York, 1925 reprint, 1928.

29. Matthew Arnold: "... for us the framework of society, that theatre on which this august drama has to unroll itself, is sacred...... without order there can be no society, and without society there can be no human perfection."

30. Rajiv Malhotra, *op. cit.*, "Once economists can publicly admit that they are unable to present a convincing model of 'development' that would bring the world to average Western standards in the foreseeable future, they would have to consider radical alternatives. As an example of such a radical alternative, to what extent would the burden on India's infrastructure, capital and natural resources be eased if a significant percentage of Indians (say around 25%) were to voluntarily opt for what I call 'dignified poverty', a lifestyle of non-consumerism exemplified by Gandhi and lived today by lakhs of sadhu? Is the sadhu, when seen in this manner, not a subaltern who has used spirituality to achieve contentment without dependence on material consumerism?"

31. "We must be active on three fronts : (i) we must understand the peculiarities of our era and treat the Western civilization

as our era's ultimate manifestation and symbol, (ii) we must try to come to grips with our own historical identity which has brought many valuable gifts to humanity, (iii) pay attention to the problems that threaten our society from outside—the hegemonic nature of Western politics, economics, and culture." Dr. Khatami, *op. cit.*, p. 72.

32. *Ibid.*, p. 62.
33. *Ibid.*, p. 72.
34. "Culture, the way I conceive it, is the collection of rooted beliefs, as well as habits of thought and emotion in society........Civilization is the basis and foundation of a culture, on the basis of its schism with culture, civilization loses its innovative and creative power actually becoming an impediment in the way of development, for it is not deeply-rooted and gradually comes apart." *Ibid.*, p. 44.
35. *Ibid.*, p. 85.
36. *Ibid.*, p. 75.
37. *Ibid.*, p. 85.
38. *Ibid.*, p. 84.
39. *Ibid.*, p. 16.
40. The *dharma* texts mention the Kaliyuga, and the state of *yuga-ksheya* and *varna-sankara* (admixture of social classes) when the social order had gone topsy-turvy, mainly due to usurpation of economic duties of other classes; non-observance of prescribed *dharma* duties and rituals; inter-marriage and indiscriminate social interaction. The solution prescribed was holding on to the cultural roots. However, we learn that it was the broadening of the social stratification, increasing the caste fold and adopting the approach of acculturation and syncretism that saved the situation.
41. Harish Khare: In the pre-globalization stage all the three relationships (i.e. between the individual and the State; individual and market and individual and global; civil society) were to be negotiated by the State. That process was suddenly questioned...the nation-state has become weaker....within a nation-state, the elites, particularly the economic elites have become stronger... and they have come to acquire a far greater say in the media. Harish Khare, *op.cit.*, p. 269.
42. Rajiv Malhotra, *op. cit.*, suggests, "If world-wide consumption of industrial production at Western levels is simply unachievable, then what alternative lifestyles have been

encouraged as parallel options? Before jumping to the conclusion that people today do not want any non-Western lifestyle, let me say this: The *ashrama* system of Indic culture divides a person's life into four quarters and provides four different lifestyles, one for each. It advocates consumerism only for 25% of one's life, namely as the householder in stage 2. Stage 1 is as a student living a simple life. Stage 3 is as a retired person offering voluntary community service to others. Stage 4 is as a renunciant not necessarily abandoning the home today, but living a simple introverted life. Under such a lifestyle, only 25% of Indians at any given time (i.e. those in stage 2 as householders) would be consumerists."

43. Recently, Mr. Mani Shankar Aiyar urged, "It is time Asian countries woke up to the imperatives of Asian cooperation" (*Times of India,* 10 February 2005).
44. Rajiv Malhotra, *op. cit.,* "Globalization should be modeled as a game among competing cultures." He adds, "Dr. Stehr points out several legitimate risks facing the current dominant paradigm, and his thesis calls for serious consideration to be given to other alternatives. Forecasting globalization is not about what is good or worthy, but about likely trends, including concerning those that would be unworthy or worse." Writes President Khatami, "Why not focus on the coming civilization, and adjust all transformations to fit that ideal. Such an ambitious plan requires that we critique both modernity and tradition." Dr. Khatami *op. cit.,* p. 86.
45. "We have the paradoxical but still very important phenomenon: that globalization which supposedly unites people is coincident with the development of numerous kinds of often mutually conflicting identity politics all over the world." Sumit Sarkar in Achin Vanaik (ed.), *op.cit.,* p. 321.

5. SPIRITUALITY, DIVINITY AND CULTURAL IDENTITY IN EARLY INDIA

R.P. Tripathi

In this paper, an attempt has been made to deliberate upon the complex issue of understanding mind and soul of India. It invites a through probe into Indian thoughts, attitudes, beliefs, norms, customs, ideas, traditions and practices which were evolved during a long span of time.

Spirituality

Our country has a long history of human endeavour for developing a system for making this world fit for the emancipation of the soul from the eternal bondage of death and rebirth. The highest goal of life has been the attainment of salvation or *moksha*. Though it is very difficult to pursue the path of attaining *Moksha* or heaven, it has been attracting the people since later Vedic Age.[1] In one of the inscriptions of Ashoka it has been mentioned that the main aim of the propagation of *Dhamma* was to enable the people to enjoy happiness in this world as well as the other world.[2] Thus *dharma* was considered as the main source of happiness. The Indian philosophy laid emphasis on the role of *dharma* in ensuring people's happiness in this material world and also in the next world. It would be incorrect to suggest that the people of

India were more concerned with the heavenly pleasure than the happiness in this world. Neglecting worldly duties was never intended in India.[3]

Spirituality helped in realizing self or the soul. It purifies the mind and helps in self-introspection. Spiritual power restrains the mind from going astray. Control of the senses is possible only through spiritual power. This invokes the power of true judgement. Anger, temptation, jealousy and ill-will disappear as a result of the enhancement of spiritual power. Liberality, humanity, mercy and benevolence emanate from spirituality. According to the Upanishads it is the knowledge (*jnana*) and knowledge alone which leads to *moksha*. *Brahman* is the ultimate reality and the self of man emanates from *brahman*. The unity of self with *brahman* results in *moksha*.[4] The philosophy of the Upanishads is unique in the sense that the knowledge of self is not possible without the help of a *guru* (teacher) and meditation, the last stage of attaining *moksha*. The other schools of thought lay emphasis on *karma* (Action) and *bhakti* (devotion to God) for attaining salvation. This is elaborated in the *Bhagawadgita*. The light of spirituality spread far and wide with the efforts of our great saints and sages and the whole world owes considerably to them.

Divinity

The role of divine power in the evolution and growth of Indian culture has been emphasized from time immemorial. Most of the institutions—social, political and educational owe their origin to divinity. The four-fold social division known as *varna* is said to have been emanated from different limbs of the *Viratpurush* or the Almighty. *Brahma*, the Creator of this universe has also been credited with the emergence of the *varnas*. Similarly, the State in India is said to have been evolved with the grace of God. It is stated in the *Mahabharata* that Prithu was appointed king by the gods[5] as he pledged to protect the *vedas* and the *brahmanas*, to maintain social and ethical norms and also prevent the inter-mixture of the castes. Manu also holds that the king was created by God. In fact God himself created *danda* and *dharma* to help the king in administering this earth. Though the theory of divine origin of the state and the kingship has been refuted by several scholars, the element of divine power in the evolution of political institutions cannot be denied altogether. Unlike his western counterparts the king in India was made responsible to the people and the gods. He could hardly wield dictatorial powers. If he failed to protect his people from internal and external dangers he could be removed from his office and even put to death.[6] The literary evidences would reveal that *Brahma*, (the Creator) himself produced the art of writing for educating the people. In the absence of the art of writing the well-being of the people was not possible. The vedas were also created by the divine power for the guidance of the people. The philosophy of the *Bhagawadgita* was handed over to Arjuna by Lord Krishna himself. These and some other evidences would suggest that the divine intervention was sought to make the worldly institutions everlasting and unquestionable.

The efficacy of divinity of political institutions may be explained in the light of the fact that in early India there was always a desire for righteous rule as it was instrumental in creating an atmosphere of peace and prosperity.[7] The development of art and culture was possible only when the ruler was pious and honest. Contrary to this a wicked rule was the cause of all miseries to its people. The concept of a *Dharmarajya* (righteous rule) is found in *Brahmanical* as well as Buddhist works.

The divine appointment of the ruler is evidenced by the *Rigveda, Satpathabrahmana,* the *Aitareyabrahmana, Ramayana* and the *Mahabharata.* The same is corroborated by the *Agnipurana.* It is stated in the *Mahabharata* that in the golden age there was no king. People protected one another by following *dharma,* but in course of time they began to commit violence against each other. As a result of anarchy, the Vedas were lost and unrighteousness prevailed. The gods requested *Brahma* to help. We are told that the king was appointed with the help of *Brahma* and *Vishnu.* Significantly enough, Prithu was instructed in *Rajadharma* by the *Rishis* and the gods. *Vishnu* himself entered the body of the king after confirming that no one should transcend Prithu.[8] Manu refers to the creation of the king by the Almighty with the help of the eternal particles of Indra, Vayu, Yama, Agni, Surya and Kubera, etc.[9]

Love for a Righteous Rule

The sources at our disposal suggest that the Indian mind always preferred good governance. It was generally believed that the conduct of the ruler affected the conduct of the people. It is stated in the *Mahabharata* that welfare, good rains, sickness, calamities and death among the people owe their origin to the king.[10] The righteous rule caused happiness to the people, whereas an unrighteous administration increased their plight. A righteous king meant a righteous and prosperous people while an evil king meant the reverse. All the spheres of life were affected by the conduct of the king. Due to the sinful acts of the king the virtue decreases considerably and sin begins to prosper. An unrighteous rule has a demoralizing effect on the people. It is from the sinfulness of kings that their subjects suffer from numerous evils. The Buddhist literature throws valuable light on this issue. It points to the fact that the nature helps in making people healthy and prosperous in the times of good rulers but during the rule of bad kings, it behaves otherwise. The *Jatakas* refer to Brahmadatta, the king of Banaras who came into contact with Bodhisattva. The latter told him that in times of unjust rulers oil, honey, molasses as well as wild roots and fruits loose their sweetness and flavour whereas these things become sweet and full of flavour when the rulers are just[12]. The *Mahabharata* holds that in fact the king is the cause of the era. It is the king that creates the *Krita*, the *Treata* or the *Dvapara* age. *Kali yuga* is also created by the king. A king of wicked deeds resides in hell for countless years. The idea is further elaborated in *Anguttara Nikaya*[13] leading to the conclusion that during the rule of unrighteous king, the whole administrative machinery such as ministers and other high officers along with *brahmanas*, the householders, townsfolk and villagers become corrupt. The sun and the moon go wrong in their courses. The seasons, winds and rains do not follow proper course and time. The crops ripen in the wrong season and the people who live on such crops are short-lived, weak and sickly. When the king is righteous the exact reverse occurs.[14] The spiritual power or glory of the king depended to a considerable extent on the righteousness of his rule. The spiritual merits that he accumulated from his subjects also helped in strengthening his government. The king was created out of the *Tejas* of different gods[15] but his own conduct decided the fate of his rule over his subjects. He had to perform his duties justly for the welfare of the people and also for safeguarding his own life and property[16]. The Indian mind always preferred a righteous and responsible government so that the people may follow the path of righteousness in the larger interest of society and the country as a whole.[17] The king in early India was greatly loved and favoured by the people but it was expected of him to rule in a just manner otherwise he would cause great loss to the society leading to the debacle of both, the ruler and the ruled.[18]

Love for Traditions and Culture

Our culture is deeply rooted in its traditions, norms, beliefs, ideas, customs and practices.[19] It has been my endeavour to have a clear perception of Indian mind as reflected in its culture system. Knowledge as an important instrument of social change has revolutionalised the thinking pattern in global context and India is no exception to it. In spite of the fact that there is a visible transforming of Indian mind, the traditional values still have tremendous appeal.[20] The advancement in the field of scientific and technical knowledge had led us to believe that the technical culture is distinct from the value culture. We find regular changes in the value system. The traditional values such as purity of heart, mind and soul, benevolence, mercy, liberality, humility and good conduct are universal, eternal and fundamental and may be differentiated from the functional values. Their relative significance may be ascertained only through objective mind. The *Mahabharata* refers to a dialogue between Duryodhana and Dronacharya which throws valuable light on the mind of the age in which the text was composed. The Kaurava army, led by Drona, suffered heavy losses and reversal at the hands of the Pandavas in the battlefield which surprised Duryodhana as he was aware of the fact that Dronacharya, being a skilled archer, had trained Arjuna and others in archery. He wanted to know as to why

Drona failed against the Pandavas in the battlefield? Drona assigned two main reasons for this. Firstly, the cereals consumed by him were that of a sinful state and secondly the Pandavas had spent 14 years in exile and suffered greatly. Adversity has made them strong enough to defeat their adversaries. In fact, adversity is the best teacher in this world. They have become invincible. The idea may be further elaborated by suggesting that the people of India were generally accustomed to bitter pills of life and hence they were not afraid of adversities. Rather they emerged stronger by learning a lesson from the adverse circumstances. This is corroborated by the historical facts. The invasion of Alexander, the Great on India in 326 B.C. and the enormous loss of life and property inspired the people to unite under Chandragupta Maurya for the welfare of the country. The invasions of the Indo-Greeks, Sakas, Parthians and the Kushanas paved the way for the rise of Samudragupta, the victor of a hundred fights. The Hunas were defeated by Skandagupta and subsequently by Prakashdharman and Yasodharman. The Pratiharas fought bravely against the Muslim invaders and thus protected the life and property of the people. The Indo-Greeks, Sakas, Pahlavas, Kushanas and the Hunas were assimilated in Indian culture. The rise of the Rajputs in India makes a new era known for its peculiar tradition, values, customs and convictions.[21] They had greater love for their country.

The foregoing discussion and evidence would suggest that the Indian mind concentrated mainly on the righteous governance, love for its tradition and culture, divine intervention and spirituality. In fact, divinity and spirituality may be called its soul.

REFERENCES

1. Basu, Jogiraj, *India of the Age of the Brahmanas,* Calcutta, 1969, pp. 139-40.
2. D.C. Sircar, *Inscriptions of Asoka,* Government Publication, Third Edition 1975, pp. 52-53.
3. It is stated in the *Bhagawadgita* (V. 2) that *Karmayoga* is more desirable than the *Karmasamnyasa* (detachment).
4. Mookerji, R.K., *Hindu Civilization,* (Fourth Edition), Bombay 1977, pp. 117-118.
5. Asoka prided himself on being called Devanampriya (dear to gods) a title which was continued by his grandson Dasaratha but it was abandoned in post-Mauryan times when the title Devaputra mentioned in Brahmi and Kharosthi inscriptions seems to have been popular with the Kushana rulers.
   Sharma, R.S., *Aspects of Political Ideas and Institutions in Ancient India,* (Second Edition.), Delhi, 1968, p. 227.
6. The king in ancient India could ill-afford to be an autocrat. He had to rule by right and morality and his wickedness could cause him life and throne.
   B.N. Puri, *History of Indian Administration,* Vol. I, Bombay, 1968, p. 18 and fn. 2.
7. The king was to be an embodiment not of protection alone but of love and care as well.
   B.N. Puri, *op. cit.,* p. 18.
8. The Chalukya king Kumarapala is described as an incarnation of God Hari, who had descended from heaven. E.I.I, p. 302.
   cf. Padma Udgaonkar, *The Political Institutions and Administration of Northern India during Medieval Times,* Delhi 1969, pp. 47-50.
9. Manu VII 4-5; V. 96.
   cf. J.W. Spellman, *Political Theory of Ancient India,* Oxford, 1964, pp. 30-31.
10. *Mahabharata,* Shanti Parva, 139.9.
11. *Mahabharata,* Vana Parva, 207.
12. *Rajovada Jataka,* No. 334.
13. *Anguttara Nikaya,* II, 74.
14. *Ummadanti Jataka,* No. 527.
15. *Manu,* VII. 11.
16. The *Arthasastra* of Kautilya (I. 4.) elaborates it as under:

"For punishment (*danda*) when rewarded with due consideration makes the people devoted to righteousness and to works productive of wealth and enjoyment; while punishment when ill-awarded under the influence of greed and anger or owing to ignorance excites fury even among hermits and ascetics living in forests not to speak of householders.

cf. Charles Drekmeier, *Kingship and Community in Early India,* Bombay, 1962, p. 202.

17. Asoka enunciates the paternal character of his government in his edicts. Beni Prasad, *Theory of Government in Ancient India,* Allahabad, Reprint 1974, p. 203. As compared to Darius I (the Achaemenian ruler) Asoka was more humane, diplomatic and devoted to his subjects.
R.P. Tripathi "Perspectives of Law and Justice as Gleaned from the Inscriptions of Darius I and Asoka" pp. 128-34 in *Dialogues Between Cultures: India and Iran,* A.K. Sinha and A.K. Singh, ed., Delhi, 2005.
18. "The Hindu king is the highest ideal of sacrifice on the part of the individual whose privilege it was to be the king of the Hindus." K.P. Jayaswal, *Hindu Polity,* Bangalore 1967, p. 340.
19. In ancient India values and social system were interrelated and hence the study of both in essential for the knowledge of the various stages of social formation vis-à-vis evolution of their value system.
20. The works which embody Hindu law and customs date back to very remote antiquity and embody customs and usages which have come down from a still remoter antiquity.
In fact the traditional values have a greater antiquity. Due to their love for traditions and culture, the Indian missionaries propagated their socio-religious and cultural ideas and beliefs to the people of Sri Lanka and South-East Asia in the remote past.
Cf. D.R. Bhandarkar, *Asoka,* Calcutta, 1969, pp. 122-151.
John F. Cady, *South-east Asia: Its Historical Development,* New Delhi, 1976, pp. 21-48, "Trade Patterns and the Process of Indianisation."
21. Cf. B.N.S. Yadava, *Society and Culture in Norther India in the Twelfth Century,* Allahabad, 1983, p. 203.

6. SOUL IN INDIAN PHILOSOPHICAL THOUGHTS

Rajjan Kumar

In India *Ātman* or soul is the most fascinating and debating metaphysical conception. Here, it is defined by different names viz. *Ātman, Puruṣa, Jīva, Brahmaṇ, Kṣetrajña,* etc. The basic property of *Ātman* is consciousness. However, to metaphysics conscious and unconscious are considered the two puzzling ends. The basic query of metaphysics is that who is conscious and who is unconscious? Is there any relationship between the two different entities? The Indian thinkers have their own interpretations and re-interpretations regarding conscious and unconscious, *cita* and *acita,* soul and non-soul, which vary from school to school.

Vedas and Soul

The Vedas are concentrated for worshipping different kinds of God by chanting *Mantras.* The concrete concept of soul as such describes by the Upaniṣads or later Indian philosophical schools are not found in the Vedas. However, the basic thoughts of Indian philosophy are borrowed from the Vedas. It is considered that the Vedas explain the different natural forces as personified Gods and these later on became mere forms of one personal and transcendental God, the custodian of the cosmic and the moral order, who himself, later on, passed into the immanent *Puruṣa*. Later on the Upaniṣadas developed this *Puruṣa* into *Brahmaṇ* or *Ātman*, which is both immanent, and transcendent. More or less it becomes the root source for the concept of soul from all other Indian philosophical schools.

The *Ātman* of the Vedas is conscious, real and *Puruṣaviśesa*. The *Ṛigveda* declares that the One Real, the wise, declare as many.[1] '*Puruṣa* is this, entire all that was, and all that shall be.'[2] 'The real essence of the Gods is One.'[3] 'The same Real is worshipped as *Ukthain* the *Ṛk* as *Agni* in the *Yajura* and as *Mahāvrata* in the *Sāma*.'[4] '*Aditi*, the Boundless is the sky, the air, the mother, the father, the son, all the Gods and all the men, all that is, all that was and all that shall be.'[5] 'He is the Custodian of the *Ṛta* (Truth), the binding Soul of the universe, the unity-in-difference in the cosmic and the moral order.'[6] The Gods also are the guardians of the Truth (*ṛtasya gopa*); even the rivers flow in this *Ṛta* (*ṛtamarpanti sindhavaḥ*).' 'Only the wise, the wide awake, the mindful, know the ultimate abode of the Lord.'[7]

Upaniṣads and Soul

Upaniṣadas are the most wonderful and trustworthy texts of India, which put remarkable mark to highlight the various Indian spiritual as well as material conceptions. It is Upaniṣadas who get the credit to make *Ātman* a rational form, which originally meant life-breath. In the Upaniṣadas there is an individual self and Absolute (soul). Individual self is a mixture of the real and unreal, a coupling of the true and the false. It is a product of ignorance. But its essence is the light of the Absolute. It is the highest thing that we know and it is the nearest approach to the Absolute, though it is not itself the Absolute.[8]

Ātman or the absolute or the true self is the ultimate subject, the fundamental postulate of all knowledge, the transcendental background of the empirical trinity of knowledge-known-known, the self-luminous and the self-proved pure conscious which manifests itself as the subject and the object, as the self and not-self and which at once over-reaches the division.[9] The ḍiscourses of *Prajāpati* and *Indra* explain the nature and form of true self, which is universal, immanent as well as transcendent. It is immortal self-luminous, self-proved and beyond doubts and denials. It is the ultimate subject which never becomes an object and which is to be necessarily presupposed by all knowledge.[10]

Nyāya-Vaiśeṣika and Soul

Vaiśeṣika are distinguished in the following manners: Soul is the known, doer, pleasure seeking, eternal, without organs, the subject of rebirth, distinct from body (unconscious), under the control of its own *karmaphala*—good or bad, beyond time and place, experienceable in body, infinite in number, who possesses the attributes—pain, pleasure, desire, hatred, endeavour and knowledge. Whenever soul possesses organs and body with one mind, consciousness of soul gets manifested. Soul is neither body, nor organs, nor mind.

The soul is a real substantive being having for its own qualities viz., desire, aversion etc. These are not the property of the material body. Consciousness is the very property of soul that is not materialistic by nature. If it were a property of the body, it would exist in the various parts of the body and its material constituents.[11] If the latter were also conscious, then we have to regard the individual consciousness as the combination of several consciousnesses produced by the different constituents. If body has consciousness, then an matter must have it, since it is of the same nature as the body. If beyond the body there is no soul, then the moral law would seem to be without any significance.[12] Since the body is changing from moment to moment, no sin can pursue us in subsequent lives.

Sāṁkhya-Yoga and Soul

Sāṁkhya-Yoga is important allies of Indian Philosophy. In many respect both have identical ideas. *Ātman* is one of them. Both are very much agreed that *Ātman* is the conscious entity and is known as *Puruṣa*. This *Puruṣa* is knower, inert (*niṣkriya*), free from the cycle of cause and effect, devoid of three *guṇas*, eternal, motivator, innumerable and enjoyer of *Prakṛti*. *Prakṛti* is an unconscious entity and is opposite of the *Puruṣa*.

To *Sāṁkhya Puruṣa* the soul, the self, the spirit, the subject and the knower. It is neither body nor senses nor brain nor mind (*manasa*) nor ego (*ahaṅkāra*) nor intellect (*buddhi*). It is not a substance, which possesses the quality of consciousness. Consciousness is its essence. It is itself pure and transcendental consciousness. It is the ultimate knower which is the foundation of all knowledge. It is the pure subject as such can never become an object of knowledge. It is the silent witness, the emancipated alone, the neutral seer, the peaceful eternal. It is beyond time and space, beyond change and activity. It is self-luminous and self-proved.

It is uncaused, eternal, and all pervading. It is the indubitable real, the postulate of knowledge, and all doubts and denials pre-suppose its existence. It is called *nistraigunya, udāsīna, akartā, kevala, mādhyastha, sākṣī, draṣṭā, sadāprakāśaswarupa* and *jñātā.*[13] In contrast it is postulated that all organic beings have a principle of self-determination to which the name of "soul" is generally given. It is further stated that in the strict sense of the word "soul" belongs to every being that has like in it, and the different souls are fundamentally identical in nature. The differences are due to the physical organizations that obscure and thwart the life of the soul.

Pūrvamīmānsā (*Mīmānsā*) and Soul

Soul (*Ātman*) is a substance (*dravya*)—the substratum of the accidental attributes and pure consciousness. Whenever *ātmā* comes in contact with mind and organs, consciousness appears in it. In the state of *susupti* and liberation, soul becomes free from all its attributes. Souls are eternal, self-luminous, subject, enjoyer of their *karmaphalas.* The significant characteristics of soul are pleasure, pain, desire, hatred, effort, *dharma, adharma, saṁskāra* and *buddhi.* To Prabhākara, in every knowledge, here is inevitably the knowledge of knower, knowable and knowledge, and to Kumārila, knowledge is the effect of soul. Whenever, I think of soul, I feel—'I am'. It is *ahaṁ-vṛtti* (self-consciousness). The soul of *Mīmānsā* is similar to the soul of *Vaiśeṣika* and *Jaina.* Everything in the universe, other than soul, is unconscious.

Uttaramīmānsā (*Vedānta*) and Soul

Brahmn itself is soul. There is nothing unconscious in the world really. Soul is pure consciousness. Similarly, in soul, there is existence and bliss also, i.e. soul is *sat-cit-ānanda.* For *Sāṁkhya,* it is *sat-cit,* and for *Nyāya-Vaiśeṣika,* it is only *sat,* while consciousness is its occasional quality. Soul is single, eternal and pure. But, it appears to be plural due to ignorance. Really, soul is not the enjoyer and agent.

It is inert, self-luminous, beyond time, place, causation, and the *Mīmāsakās* concept of *tripuṭi*—knower, knowable and knowledge. It is pure knowledge. *Ātmā* and *Brahman* are one and the same. Soul is absolute reality and *jīva* is relative reality. *Jīvas* are many in number, because of different *upādhi* (conditions or adjuncts). *Jīva* is subject, knower, enjoyer, eternal and the effect of reflection of soul on *māyā* (ignorance) with *buddhi*. Thus *jīva* is the appearance of soul. *Jīva* is agent, knower, enjoyer of vices and virtues, which are the results of *karmas*. *Brahman* (soul) is liberated and *jīva* is in bondage.

Īśvara is *Brahman* delimited by *māyā* (cosmic ignorance) and *jīva* is *Brahman* delimited by *avidyā* (individual ignorance). *Īśvara* is donor of *karmaphalas*, blissful, subject of *upāsanā*, free from *karmas*, eternal, omniscient, omnipresent, omnipotent, free from ignorance (*avidyā*), all powerful and the ordainer of *jīva*. Critics of the theory of reflection (*pratibimbavāda*) ask how reflection is possible in case of shapeless things (*Brahman and avidyā*). The theory of limitation (*avacchedvāda*), therefore, seems clearer than the theory of reflection.

Śaṁkara is firmed about the pure consciousness of *Ātman*. He said it is the self who is self-luminous and it also transcends the subject-object duality and the trinity of knower, known and knowledge, and all the categories of the intellect. Like *Brahman*, *Ātman* (pure) is considered unqualified Absolute. It is the only reality. Like *Brahman* it is everything and everything in it. There is no duality, no diversity at all. The self can never be denied. It cannot be doubted. It is self-proved (*svayaṁsiddha*). Though, everything is relative in this world, the self-alone is not relative. Therefore, it is self-proved.[14]

Rāmānuja, the preceptor of *Viśiṣṭādvaita* says that *Brahman* is the sum of three entities—*Īśvara*, *cit* and *acit*.[15]

Cit is *jīvātmā* and is conscious whereas *acit* is unconscious. Both *cit* and *acit* are dependent on *Brahman*. *Cit* of Rāmānuja is individual soul and is considered as attribute or mode (*prakāra*) of God and forms part of His body, yet it is also a spiritual substance in itself and is absolutely real. It is an eternal point of spiritual light. It is beyond creation and destruction. In the state of creation, it is embodied according to its *karmas,* while in the state of dissolution and in the state of liberation it remains in itself. But in the state of dissolution (*pralaya*), it is tinged with *karmas* so that in the next cycle of creation, it has to descend to the mundane life and to become embodied in order to reap the fruits of *karmas.* The relation of the soul and *karma* is said to be beginningless.

Rāmānuja describes three classes of souls.[16] To the first belongs the ever-free (*nityamukta*) soul, which was never bound. They are ever free from *karma* and *prakṛti* and live in *Vaikunṭha* in constant service of the Lord. They are Śeṣa, Garuḍa, and Viśvakṣena etc. To the second belong the Released or Liberated (*mukta*) souls who were once bound but who obtained liberation through their action, knowledge and devotion. To the third belong the bound (*baddha*) souls who are wandering in the *saṁsāra* on account of ignorance and bad *karmas.* These are further divided into four classes: superhuman or celestial, human, animal, stationary or immobile (*sthāvara*).

Āchārya Vallabh has repute for his thought known as *Śuddhādvaita* (pure monism) or pure non-dualism undefiled by *māyā*.[17] Like other *Vedāntin Brahman* in view of Vallabha is also signified as independent reality but is identified with Śri Krṣṇa. His essence is *sat* (existence), *cit* (knowledge), and *ānanda* (bliss). *Ātman* (soul) and *jada* (matter) are His real manifestation. They are His parts. He manifests Himself as many but this manifestation is neither an error nor an illusion. It is a real manifestation.

To Vallabha, the *jīva* has been revolving in this world due to 1. Ignorance of the real nature of the soul. 2. False identification with the body. 3. With the senses. 4. With the vital breaths. 5. With the internal organ. It (ignorance) follows the cycle of births and deaths of a soul. When knowledge downs ignorance vanishes and with it vanishes the *saṁsara*. But the world (*saṁsara*) continues because in view of Vallabha it is the real manifestation of God.

On the basis of above discussion the relevance of *Ātman* of *Vedanta* may be put forth as an ideals for commerating the various functions of human society. To some *Brahman* is the only absolute for others *Brahman* as well as its counterpart like *Ātman, Īśvara,* etc. are another realities too. Śaṁkara believes in *Brahman* as the only one reality. Soul and God are the part of the *Brahman*. For Rāmānuja, the soul, though different from God, is essentially identical with Him as forming His body. For Madhva, the soul, though a dependent part of God, is essentially different from Him. For Nimbārka, the soul is limited and dependent, is different from God, though as the power of God it is identical with Him. For, Vallabha, the soul as a part of God is identical with Him and appears as different on account of the limited manifestation of some divine aspects and obscuration of others.

Jainism and Soul

To Jaina, *jīva* (soul) is eternal and innumerable who resides in different things of the cosmos. Consciousness is the essential property of *jīva,*[18] whereas it is the accidental property of soul in *Nyāya-Vaiśeṣika*. Body is different from soul. Soul has free will to do good and bad deeds, and is responsible for its destiny accordingly. *Jīva* experiences the universe according to his *karmas*. He is self-luminous (*svayamprakāśa*)[19] *upayoga* is the property of *jīva* and is defined into two forms *sākāra* (corporeal) and *nirākāra* (incorporeal) known as *jñāna* and *darśana* respectively.[20] *Jīva* can attain four-fold path perfection—infinite knowledge, infinite faith, infinite power and infinite bliss in liberation. He can acquires body. The *jīvas* possess the shape of body. They do not acquire the place in matter. Hence, more than one *jīvas* can dwell in one place.

Bonded *jīva* is of two types—*sthāvara* (static or immobile) as earth, water, air, fire and plants, and *trasa* (mobile) as insects, birds, animals and men who have more than two organs. Consciousness in *jīvas* is not equal. It is maximum in liberated *jīvas* and minimum in *sthāvaras*.[21] The qualities of *jīvas* are different as well as non-different.[22] *Jīva* is recognized by its *guṇas* (attributes)—pain, pleasure, doubt, remembrance, perception etc., because, he is substratum of *guṇas*. *Jīva* (conscious) is the driver of body (unconscious). *Jīva* is the efficient cause and *pudgala* (matter or *jada* or unconscious) is the material cause of the universe.

Buddhism and Soul

In contrast with the eternal conceptions of soul of most of the Indian schools of Philosophy, Buddhism does not believe in as such concept of soul. Soul as is defined a conscious entity Buddha too believe in such kinds of conscious entity but it is ever of changing streams. Though it is not eternal it undergoes the law of rebirth. There is consciousness before birth and after death. According to Nagsena, soul (*ātman*) is the combination (*saṁghāṭa*) of five *skaṅdha*: *arupa, vedanā, saṁskāra* and *vijñāna*.

The Buddhist conception of consciousness as a stream is quite in agreement with his doctrine that all is momentary—*sarvam kṣaṇikaṁ*. It has often been rejected that if consciousness is simply a stream of moments and dying every moment. But these objections are not very valid and relevant because the stream of moments is, in fact, as good a permanent soul for all practical considerations. The only problem will be accounting for the emergence of new moments in place of old ones that are dying every moment. But then, it is a metaphysical problem, which is faced everywhere. A concept of permanent soul, too, has many problems to face.

Cārvāka and Soul

From the combination of four *bhūtas*—earth, air, fire and water—the unconscious (material) and the conscious constitute the world. Hence the consciousness is the product of accidental combination of four *bhūtas*. It is automatic and natural. Their answer to the question—how consciousness gets produced out of unconscious *bhūta* is 'Nature'. There is no purpose behind it. Therefore, Cārvāka is known as naturalistic and mechanistic. This consciousness is the attribute of body and the subject of perception. The consciousness is not different from body. The self (*ātmā*), according to them, is the conscious body. Cārvāka refutes the eternity of soul, its rebirth and God.

This view of Cārvāka is known as purely materialistic.[23] Cārvāka accepts only perception or visible things. In the world, there are so many invisible things. He (Cārvāka) cannot conceive the imperceptible or invisible things like soul, pain, pleasure, air, space, etc., which may be called metaphysical entities. Cārvāka view about consciousness (soul) is very similar to the modern view of science. Modern science, too, has so far not been able to establish consciousness as something quite different from the body; for science also, it is a quality of the body; it is created with the creation of body and is destroyed with the death of the body. Science has to know a lot about the consciousness and its attribute. In denying soul and rebirth, Cārvākas are nearer to modern Science. Denial of rebirth is a natural corollary of the denial of soul as an eternal entity.

REFERENCES

1. *Rigveda,* 1.164, 46; *ekam sad viprā bahudhā vadanti.*
2. *Ibid.,* X, 90, *Puruṣa evedaṁ sarvaṁ yad bhūtan yachcha bhavyaṁ.*
3. *Ibid.,* III, 55.
4. *Aitareya Araṇyaka,* III. 2.3.12.
5. *Rigveda,* I, 89, 10.
6. *Ibid.,* X, 190, I.
7. *Ibid.,* I, 22.21, *Visṇoryāt paramaṁ padaṁ.*
8. A Critical Survey of Indian Philosophy, C.D. Sharma, p. 19.
9. *Taitiriya Upaniṣad,* 3/1.
10. *Chāndogya,* VIII/3-12.
11. Indian Philosophy, I, Radhakrishanan, p. 146.
12. *Nyāya Bhāṣya* (N.B.) iii.i.4.
13. *Tasmāchcha viparyātsiddhaṁ saksitvamasya purusasya-Sāṁkhya Kārikā,* 19.
14. *Yaddhi anapekṣam tat svāt eva siddhaṁ, Kena-Vākya-Bhāṣya,* I, 3.
15. Relevance of Indian Philosophy to Modem Society, Tanaji Acharya, p. 148.
16. *Rahasutrayasara,* IV. Vide Indian Philosophy, II, Radhakrishanan, p. 695.
17. A Critical Survey of Indian Philosophy, Sharma, p. 377.
18. *Cetanālakṣaṇo jīvaḥ, Sarvadarsansaṁgraha,* p. 177.
19. *Syādvadṁañjari* (Mallisena), pp. 152-62.
20. *sa upayogo dwidhaḥ sākāro nākārāsca jñānopayogo darśanopayogscetyarthaḥ, Tattavārthavārtika,* 2-9.
21. *Bhāratīya Darśana Ki Ruparekhā,* Harrendra Sinha, pp. 144-47.
22. *Sarvadarsansaṁgraha,* p. 148.
23. *Bhasmibhūtasya dehasya punarāgamanaṁ kutaḥ,* Cārvāka Saṣṭi, p. 18.

7. THE *ARTHASHASTRA* TRADITION
A Study of an Alternative World View of Ancient India

Dinesh Kumar Ojha

By the end of the eighteenth century, it were the Europeans, mainly the Britishers, who initiated the process of unravelling the Past of India in a systematic manner. From the very outset the Indologists did not belong to a homogenous lot. It consisted of diehard utilitarians, the sentimental romantics, the pragmatic administrators and zealous evangelists. These diverse groups had equally diverse approaches towards the Indian Past. Thus, for the utilitarians the Indian society was stagnant, backward and unscientific, whereas romantics considered it to be characterized by harmony and absence of tension. Notwithstanding such divergence in opinion certain stereotypes dominated the writings of the imperialistic historiography of the nineteenth century. Perhaps the most prominent and long-lasting stereotype has been the notion that religion and metaphysics so dominated the psyche of ancient Indian people that mundane and this worldly affairs were not taken care of. Such a view is most profoundly expressed by the dictum of Max Mueller, where he observes "The Hindus were a nation of philosophers; their struggles were the struggles of thought;

their past, the problem of creation, their future, the problem of existence."[1]

The westerners took it as an axiom that ancient Indians were pre-occupied with spiritual and other worldly speculation. This world was considered to be transient and limited and hence the only worthy pursuit could be to transcend it rather than to comprehend it. Religion and philosophy thus were engrossed in finding paths to overcome the tyranny of time and often took shelter in abstract theorisations of the four *purusarthas. Moksha* was considered to be the highest goal and renunciation and asceticism the recommended means to achieve such goal. It was also assumed that neither history nor polity and political science could develop into an independent and worthy discipline. History is concerned primarily with the finite, limited and particular events that occurred in the determinate past and similarly polity too is related to those human actions which are thus worldly and are related to the general welfare of the society. A society which indulged in transcendentalism and spiritualism world have no inclination towards polity and history seems to have been a natural corollary. The general approach of Europeans is most beautifully reflected when Keith pronounces "the subtle and profound spirit of India which finds its fullest expression in the absolute idealism of the vedanta of Shankar and the skeptical nihilism of Nagarjuna is alien to the conception of man as a political organism......hence India offers nothing that can be regarded as a serious theory of politics in the wider sense of that term."[2]

The prevalence of such a stereotype among the westerners have been explained by many historians. Scholars like R.S. Sharma see it as a fallout of imperialism when he says "If Indians were essentially philosophers, absorbed in the problems of the spiritual world, it followed that their material world should be managed for them by their imperial masters."[3] Others have argued that it was mainly the rise of romantic movement, most notably among the Germans, which provided Europeans to look for an idyllic past. Romila Thapar writes "Indian society characterized by harmony and an absence of social tension was a utopian society."[4] Winternitz in his attempt to fathom the ancient Indian mindset remarks "sentimentality and natural feeling are equally characteristic of German and Indian poetry, whereas they are entirely unknown to Hebrew or Greek, poetry."[5]

The notion that ancient India was overwhelmed by religion and metaphysics has not been confined to the westerners only. Many Indians, mainly the nationalist historians too have been influenced by this stereotype. Though Indian scholars in general uphold that *Dharma* is a more comprehensive term than religion and is primarily ethical and practical in nature, they also underline that spiritualism and a constant pursuit for overcoming the bondage of this world and attainment of salvation has been a dominant feature of Indian philosophy and religion. Thus, the moot question pertains to the fact is that was the ancient Indian intellectual tradition confined to spiritualism and had an orthodox trajectory or some heretical, this worldly and material strains were also present. I understand that the Indian philosophy was never a monolithic and homogenous discipline but consisted of many parallel variants which would at times be contrary as well. Thus, besides spiritual, idealistic and other worldly speculations, there were always materialistic, realist and this worldly tradition as well. Such a parallel viewpoint had its origin in Vedic literature but became prominent in what is often termed as the heterodox school of philosophy. The secular this worldly and practical attitude is very vividly manifested in the manner in which polity is depicted in the *Arthasastra* tradition.

Existence of Heretical-Material World View

The beginnings of Indian thought can be traced to the *Ṛgvedic* period. Since then the antiquity of Indian philosophy is matched by its richness and variety. Practically speaking there is no shade of speculation which is not included within its ambit. From its early days, two divergent trends are discernible—one having its source in the Veda and the other independent of it. For want of any better characterization we call the former as orthodox and the latter as heterodox traditions. Beginning with the polytheism, supernaturalism and optimism of Veda, the orthodox school culminates into monism and idealism of *Vedānta*. The second school begins as a reaction against the Vedic orthodoxy and appears originally as critical and negative. But sooner than later it developed a constructive side with its own ontology and epistemology. Broadly speaking it is pessimistic and realistic.[6]

These two trends though distinct in their origin and spirit exhibit certain common features. The pursuit of *moksha* as the final ideal and the ascetic spirit of the discipline recommended for its attainment is common to all Indian thought. This peculiarity of Indian philosophy can be ascribed to the fact that unlike its western counterpart, it originated as a practical requirement to overcome the problem of physical and moral evil. Philosophy, as understood in India, is neither mere intellectualism nor mere moralism, but includes and transcends them both. In other words it aims at achieving more than what Logic and Ethics can. Though not an end in itself, Logic and

Ethics are must, for the former leads to *jñāna* or illumination and the latter to *vairāgya* or self-renunciation. Illustrating its significance Hiriyanna lays "they have been represented as the two wings that help the soul in its spiritual flight."[7]

The fact that all the schools of Indian thought which take *moksha* as the ultimate goal, have led many to believe that spiritualism is the very essence of Indian tradition. But from the very beginning itself there has been a parallel tradition which not only ridiculed and often opposed the vedas but also denied the existence of any transcendental reality. Taking this world to be real and material in origin the ideas of God and soul were refuted. The consciousness or the spiritual principle which is concomitant with the living being is explained to be a property of the physical aggregate of the body. In other words consciousness is the attribute of the body and disappears when the latter disintegrates. Such a viewpoint finds its fullest exposition in the *Chāravāka* tradition but its initial and obscure traces are found in the *Ṛgveda* itself and is explained to some extent in *Brāhamāṇas,* Upaniṣads and Epics.

The existence of heretical tendencies can be inferred from such allusions as 'haters of the veda' (*brahmadvis*), 'maligners of gods' (*devanid*), men of no principles (*apavrata*) which are found in the vedas itself. Similarly a hymn in the *Ṛgveda* ridicules the votaries of the veda by describing them as 'selfish prattling priests that go about self deluded.'[8] It continued in the post-vedic period wherein we find Buddhist and Jaina works referring to various philosophical schools other than the vedic, as having existed prior or contemporary to Mahavir and Gautama.[9] Among the *Brahmanical* sources, the *Mahabharat* refers to many teachers expounding heretical doctrines.[10] Yaska in his *Nirukta*[11] mentions one Kautsa, who criticizes the veda as either meaningless or self-contradictory, and *Kalpa-Sūtras* occasionally talk of infidels (*nāstika*)[12] putting them at par with sinners and criminals. The distinction between the twin traditions of *Brāhmanas* and *Sramanas* must have been the outcome of such heretical thought. Despite the fact that heretical doctrine was an important stream of thought, no detailed exposition of it is found in any part of early Sanskrit Literature. It is only in the *Mahabharat* and a few upaniṣads like *Śvetāsvatara Upanisad* wherein an inkling of the basic tenets of this tradition can be gauged.

The *Śvetāsvatara Upaniṣad* mentions nearly half a dozen views which are akin to heretical-material tradition, but two of them namely (a) accidentalism (*Yadrcchā-vāda* or *Animitta-Vāda*) (b) Maturalism (*Svabhāva-vāda*) were very important.[13] The former maintains that the world is a chaos and ascribes whatever order is seen in it to mere chance, the latter recognizes that 'things are as their nature makes them'. *Yadrcchā-vāda* denies causation altogether, *Svabhāva-vāda* acknowledges its universality, but regards all changes to be inherent in the things themselves. Everything is unique and it continues to be so throughout its existence. Hence according to *Svabhāva-vāda* the world is not lawless, only there is no external principle governing it. It is self-determined, not undetermined. So this doctrine, unlike the other, recognizes necessity (inherent in the very nature of a thing) as governing all phenomena. Despite these differences both the doctrines reject the existence of any transcendental being which controls the nature. Nor does either school seek for its view any supernatural sanction. Propounding such notions these schools differ from the supernaturalism of *Mantras* and the *Brahmanas* on the one hand and, on the other, from the metaphysical view of the upaniṣads. From different allusions in the *Mahabharat* and other philosophical works *Svabhāva-vāda* seems to have been an important school. Besides the positivistic character it was also marked for its denial of a transmigrating soul (although it might have admitted a self-lasting soul as long as life goes),[14] nor did it believes in the law of the *Karma* as commonly understood.

Arthashastra Tradition: An Alternative World View

The tribal way of life giving way to agrarian society organized on the principles of *varnaaṣrama* not only resulted into social diversification but economy and polity too became more elaborate and complicated. It appears that the conflicts and disputes among various social groups might have necessitated the emergence of state but it was the surplus production which paved the ground for its origin and development. The incessant struggle among new states enhanced the power and prestige of kingship and government. Such a situation may have called for greater interest in the affairs of state. It also facilitated the emergence of a group of people who advocated about the significance of state. This prepared the ground for the emergence of a band of thinkers who specialized themselves in the issues related to state policy and governance. The earliest references indicate that at least two different streams of thought namely *Dharmasastra* and *Arthasastra* showed interest in states and government. *Dharmasastra* through its *Rajdharma* section did speculate upon the polity but its tone and temper remained primarily ritualistic and idealistic. The *Dharmasastra* dealt more with the duties and obligations of King and endeavoured to establish the supremacy of law, which was supposed to be eternal and immutable. The followers of *Arthasastra* school were practical and realist. They espoused the cause of state power with great vehemence. It was clearly enunciated by this school that societal laws though important could not curtail the domain of state. Gradually the issues related to law and justice began to lose its central position and the King's power and prestige became the main focus of political speculation. This facilitated the school of *Arthasastra* to gain precedence over other streams of thought concerned with polity and administration.

Brahmanas through its various *Shrauta* sacrifices, especially those connected with the concentration rites, were the first to make an attempt to fathom the growing complexity of state organization and its management.[15] But the political issues still remained a part of the ritualistic tradition. During the post-vedic period when the notion of *varṇa, ashrama* and *purushartha* began to gain prominence the science of polity began to separate itself from the ritualistic tradition and acquire an independent status. Such an efflorescence of independent schools of thought was further facilitated by the rise of upanisads which began to replace vedic ritualism with seeds of questioning and seasoned enquiry. Such a phenomenon is described in the *Mahabharat* where it is stated that the science of polity which was created by *Brahma* got abridged successively by gods Shankara, Indra and finally by Brihaspati and Sukra. Similarly, Asvaghosa in *Buddhacharita* states that Sukra and Brihaspati, who were the sons of Bhrigu and Angira respectively, created the *Rajasastra*.[17] The fact that it was Brihaspati and Sukra who played a major role in giving shape to the science of polity and developing it into an independent status of a *shastra* was firmly embedded in tradition. Here it would be pertinent to point out that the families of Bhrigvangirasa played an important role in developing the *Itihasa-Purana* tradition during the later vedic period.[18] This *Itihasa-Purana* tradition, of which *Gatha* and *Narashainsis* were indispensable parts, was regarded as the product of mere human beings and as such much less sacrosanct than *rik* which were supposed to be divine and revealed. Perhaps more interesting is the fact that orthodox vedic schools regarded the families of Bhrigvangiras with disdain and suspicion.[20] It is tempting to suggest that the families of Bhrigu and Angira took the lead in initiating and giving shape to the study of lores and disciplines beyond the bounds of ritualistic traditions.[21] This brings to the fore the secular character of the *Arthasastra* tradition. The fact that the coming into being of the *Arthasastra* was the result of an attempt to separate the worldly human affairs from the clutches of ritualistic dominance gives it a unique character which was imbued with secular and this worldly mooring.

Kautiliya Arthasastra is replete with instances which establishes it secular, practical and this worldly approach. Thus the theory of divine origin of state is not given much credence and the primary duty of state was providing security and economic well-being of subjects. The text even though follows and vows to preserve the vedic way of life. It does not give undue importance to *Brahmins* and at the same time provides for *Sudras* certain rights and positions.

The *Arthasastra* states that Manu, the son of Vivasvat (the Sun) was the first ruler.[22] A little further it is said that kings occupy the position of Indra and Yama.[23] It may suggest that kings position was similar to that of God and thus must have been sacred. But a critical analysis of this passage makes it clear that it is not a fully developed theory of divine origin of king as is to be found in the *Manusmriti* where it is mentioned that King was created out of the essences of eight divinities and was declared to be a great divinity in human form.[24] Moreover it should also be borne in mind that these words are those of secret agents employed to impress on the people the necessity of being loyal to the ruling monarch. They do not necessarily reflect the author's own opinion on the question.

The *Arthasastra* does not contain any explicit reference to the source of authority wielded by the King. It can only be inferred from the various obligations of the ruler towards his subjects. True to the spirit of the *Arthasastra* this authority neither comes from divine sanction nor is conferred by any church or an association of *purohits*. The obligations of a ruler are mainly concerned with the economic and material well-being of the people. Though the primary duty of the ruler is the protection of person and property, often it is expressed not in terms of *raksana* or *palana* but in terms of ensuring *yogakshema*.[25] The concept of *yogakshema* involved besides the security of the idea of welfare and happiness. To accomplish the welfare the ruler was expected to undertake such *Karmans* or activities as *Sunyanivesana* (settlement on virgin land), *Setubandha* (building of dams, tanks and other irrigational works), *Vanikapatha* (opening trade routes and ensuring safety on them), *Khani* (working of mines) and so on. All such activities are economic in nature and are meant for material upliftment. The text emphasizes that the happiness of the people strengthens the stability and power of state. The *Arthasastra* says "in the happiness of subjects lies the happiness of the King, and in what is beneficial to the subjects his kown benefit etc.[26] Kangle is of the view that it is not a mere pious sentiment but a warning to the ruler that if subjects are not happy and content they might became disaffected towards the ruler and that might bring an end to his rule.[27] The fact that the ruler's authority is in the last analysis dependent upon the willing support of the ruled is further underlined by text when it announces "If the subjects become disaffected they may join hands with ruler's enemies or may rise in revolt and themselves slay him."[28] Thus the threat of the *Prakṛitikopa* or a revolt of the people was supposed to be a potent check on the wanton use of power by the king. Kangle opines "the subjects may have no voice in the choice of the ruler, but it is they who have, in the ultimate analysis, the power to allow him to continue or to remove him depending how he behaves."[29]

The Indian culture though marked by religion and philosophy was never bereft of materialistic and heretical views as well. Many schools of thought propagated parallel tradition. This is amply demonstrated in the basic tenets of the *Arthsashastra* tradition.

REFERENCES

1. Muller, Max, *A History of Sanskrit Literature,* London, 1960, p. 16.
2. Keith, A.B., in Foreword to N.N. Law's *Aspects of Ancient Indian Polity,* Bombay, 1921, p. V.
3. Sharma, R.S., *Aspects of Political Ideas and Institutions in Ancient India,* Delhi, 1968, p. 2.
4. Thapar, Romila, *The Past and Prejudice,* NBT, Delhi, 1975, p. 5.
5. Wintermitz, M., *History of Indian Literature* (trans. V. Srinivas Sarma, Motilal Banarasi Das), Delhi, 1981; Vol. 1, p. 6.
6. Hiriyanna, M., *Outlines of Indian Philosophy,* Bombay, 1932, p. 16.
7. *Ibid.,* p. 24.
8. *Ṛgveda,* X. 82.
9. Rapeon, E.J., *The Cambridge History of India,* Cambridge, Vol. 1, p. 150.
10. *Mbh.,* XII. 218, 4-5.

11. I, XV -XVI.
12. *Gautama Dharma Sutra* (Mysore Oriental Library Edn.), XV. 15.
13. 1.2 They are also found in later works, *cf. Kusumānjali,* 1-5 and *Animitta Vada* is referred in *Nyāyo-sutra* of Gautama, IV, 1.22-24.
14. See *Buddhist Philosophy* by A.B. Keith (Cambridge Univ. Press), p. 135 for the prevalence of such view in the period, CP also Katha UP (I, 1-20 ft).
15. Bhattacharya, S.C., *History of Science, Philosophy and Culture Civilization*, part II, PHISPC Publications, Delhi, p. 973.
16. *Santiparva,* Chapter 59.
17. *Buddhacharita,* 1-46.
18. Pathak, V.S., *Ancient Historians of India,* Asia Publishing House, Delhi, 1963, p. 4-14.
19. *Aitareya Brahmana,* VII. 18 (Keith, p. 309). *Katyayana Srauta Sutra,* XV, 156, *Visvarupa* on *Yajnavalkya* 1.45.
20. *Kathaka Samhita* (XIV.5) asserts that both *Gatha* and *Narasamsi* are baser kind of *Brahma* and hence false (anritam).
21. Bhattacharya, S.C., *op. cit.,* p. 976.
22. *Arthasastra,* I.13, 5-7.
23. *Ibid.,* 1-13.10-11.
24. *Manusmriti* 7.3-8, (*mahati devata hyesa nararupena tisthati*).
25. *Arthasastra,* 1.13.7.
26. *Ibid.,* I.19.34.
27. Kangle, R.P., *Kautilya Arthasastra,* Part III, p. 42.
28. *Arthasastra,* 7.5.27.
29. Kanlgle, *op. cit.,* p. 120.

8. GOLU DEVATA
The Mind and Soul of Kumauni People

C.M. Agrawal

Golu Devata, who is regarded as the God of Justice by the Kumauni people, needs no introduction. He is greatly popular, highly powerful and widely acclaimed deity. Though his temples are scattered all over the region, the most famous of them are located at Champavat, Chitai and Ghodakhal. His temple at Chitai, regarded as the 'Supreme Court', is one of the greatest religious shrines in Kumaun. Justice delayed or denied in human courts impels people in utter desperation to turn to this court to seek final judgment on their petitions not properly disposed of by the worldly courts of justice. It is believed that he not only fulfills all our spiritual needs but also frees us from physical and mental troubles and worries; none returns disappointed from there.

Not only the people of Kumaun, but people from different parts of the country also pledge *manautis* in the temple of Golu Devata for the fulfillment of their desires. Here appeals are also made in such cases where justice has been delayed or denied by the worldly courts. Thousands and thousands of bells hanging in the temple of Golu Devata at Chitai bear positive testimony to his popularity as a 'desire-fulfilling deity' and vouch for his greatness and people's faith and devotion to him. A large number of *manautis* written down on papers, stamped or ordinary, and pledged to Golu Devata describe him as the 'god of justice'. This affirms people's faith in his impartial justice. Though it is really next to impossible to say how many people get success in their *manautis* pledged to him, yet it can safely be concluded that thousands and thousands of people, who came here, did not return empty-handed; they at least achieved mental peace. Even idle and untrue, guilty and wrong, apprehending harsh and severe punishments at the hands of Golu Devata dare not commit crimes. Firm faith in Golu Devata boosts up one's morale. It is believed that if a *manautis* to Golu Devata is preceded by devotion and faith, is genuine and just and is followed by hard labour, it is certainly fulfilled. But such *manautis* as are pledged for harming anyone or are not in tune with the worth of the pledger remain unfulfilled as Golu Devata being a 'god of justice' always sides with the just. This is the reason why he is called 'the living god of justice' of Kumaun Himalayas. Golu Devata's power is universal and his knowledge all-pervading; he knows what is right and what is wrong. So none should place before him such demands only as are justified and reasonable. Golu Devata punishes them harshly whose demands are unjustified and punishes the wicked and the evil-doers. One who talks ill of Golu Devata or slights him has to suffer the punishments. The popularity and great importance of the temple of Golu Devata at Chitai is evident from the fact that even VIPs coming to Almora and its neighbouring places on official business, come here also without fail and offer worship to him.

Like any folklore, the origin of the story of Golu Devata is shrouded in obscurity. The local records tell us that

Jhalrai, the Katyuri Raja of Champavat, had seven wives but had no issue from them. For procuring a son though he worshipped various gods; took bath in holy rivers, gave charities, heard religious stories and did various acts, yet he did not get any issue. He summoned astrologers and *pandits* who going through his horoscope said that he should go in for the eighth marriage, as the eighth queen would give birth to a greatly illustrious and god-like son. In the midnight in a dream he saw a beautiful girl named Kalinka sitting on the peak of Neelkanth. He assembled his courtiers and told them about the dream. He then called a huge army and himself putting on royal dress, proceeded towards the peak of Neelkanth situated in the divine region. He crossed a number of forests and in the end reached Neelkanth. Years rolled on and the king roamed aimlessly in this divine region. At last he reached the place where Kalinka was engaged in severe penance. Raja met Kalinka and told her that he was the king of Dhauli Dhumakot and though he had seven wives yet had no issue, so he wanted to take her as his eighth wife. She asked him to go to the sages to beg that they would kill it but contrary to their expectations the child grew healthier day-by-day by drinking the milk of the cows. To deceive the mother they placed blood besmeared *sil-batta* (stone slab and muller) before her and removing the bandage from her eyes told her that instead of a child she had delivered the *sil-batta* which lay before her. When Kalinka saw it she cried bitterly and wept day and night and prayed God to end her life and went on fast unto death so that she might not show her face to any body. When the news reached the king that the queen had given birth to *sil-batta* he was sad.

Later on when the seven queens went to the *goth* to see the condition of the child there, they were greatly surprised to find that he was quite safe and sound in the midst of the cows and was licking and sucking his fingers. The co-wives again threw the child in the heap of *sisuna* (Scorpion grass) and covered him in it. When the child survived there also for seven days and seven nights the co-wives placed him in the heap of salt so that he might die there. But by the miraculous power of the child the salt turned into sugar and he grew healthier by eating it. Then the co-wives threw the child in the cattle-house of goats and buffaloes hoping that these ferocious cattle would certainly kill him either by trampling or piercing. But to their utter surprise they found that by the grace of the God the child was not harmed in the least, rather the goat named Lakha bore the child on his back. The seven queens who were bent upon killing the child any how did not stop making efforts to kill it. They put him in a basket and placed in a dense forest away from the capital to be devoured by evil spirits. But there also the child survived. Then they chalked out a new plan. They procured a very heavy iron box and inside lined with salt and placing the child in it flung it in the river Kali hoping that this time the child was sure to be killed. The box containing the child did not sink but continued flowing for seven days and seven nights and on the eighth day reached Gorighat and there it got stuck into the net of fisherman named Bhana. When the people removed the cover of the box they to their greater surprise forehand a newly-born babe weeping and looking towards them. Bhana who had no issue even after the lapse of twelve years of his marriage was damn pleased to see the child. Child's penetrating eyes, elevated forehead, white complexion and stout body revealed his relation with a royal family. In the meantime, his wife came. Bhana took her near the box and showing the child to her said, 'Baba

Kailash, (Shiva) has heard our prayer. See how a beautiful child has emerged from river Gori. Bhana's wife, being issueless, jumped with joy and hurriedly lifted the child from the box and she with the child in her lap and Bhana with box, net and fish on his back proceeded for their house. When the fisher-woman clasped the child milk began to flow from her breasts. They brought him up like their own son and named Golu. Golu's arrival made Bhana's house prosperous. The child who was fearless and highly intelligent grew fast. The neighbours regard him as the incarnation of God. Golu once in a dream saw his mother Kalinka, capital Dauli Dhumakot and his father Jhalrai. On the basis of this dream he told the fisherman that Halrai was his grandfather, Jhalrai his father and Kalinka his mother and his seven step-mothers to deceive his mother putting him in an iron box had flung him in the river Kali. But Golu with folded hands always said to them that they were their real parents as they had taken him out from the river and saved his life and he grew by drinking the milk of the fisherwoman. He asked them to be happy and any trouble to them would be averted if they remembered him. When Golu grew up he demanded a horse from them but on account of their acute poverty they could not manage a real horse for him; they only gave him a wooden horse. Wherever Golu had to go he went there riding on it. Once he took his wooden horse to make it drink water at a place where seven queens used to come to fetch water and take their bath. Golu regularly went to the place at a fixed time and asked the queens to vacate the place so that his horse might drink water there and also broke their waterpots with a *gulela* (Pallet). But he respected Kalinka who was his mother. One day the seven queens did not allow his wooden horse to drink water saying that it was impossible for a wooden horse to do so. Golu immediately replied, "If a woman can deliver a *sil-batta* certainly the wooden horse can drink water." At this statement the queens, apprehending the leakage of the conspiracy hatched by them, were greatly horrified. When the report of this event reached the ears of the king he summoned Golu and asked about the whole thing. Golu told him that not only great injustice had been done to his mother but the king himself had been deceived. The king did not believe his statement and asked him to produce evidence. Golu said that the eighth queen was his real mother and if she was brought there, milk would come out from her breasts and be transmitted into his mouth. The king did accordingly and milk flowing from the breasts of Kalinka directly entered into the mouth of Golu. There could be no greater evidence regarding the truth of Golu's statement. The king immediately accepted him as his son. The seven step-mothers of Golu were summoned. They came and fell at the feet of Kalinka and repented for their evil acts. King Jhalrai ordered his men to kill the seven queens by throwing them in a cauldron full of boiling oil and to escort Kalinka into the palace with full honour and himself begged pardon of her for his guilt committed unknowingly. But Golu, being kind-hearted, did not like this harsh decision in respect of his step-mothers and so he asked his father to take a liberal view in the matter. Jhalrai then left the decision on Golu who awarded them banishment with provision of their maintenance. According to another version they were reduced to the status of slaves in the palace.

Golu as a prince became well-known for his honesty and even-handed justice. King Jhalrai collected all his subjects and declared that he was going to give the kingship of Dhauli Dhumakot to Golu. People of

Champavat were damn pleased. Musical instruments began to be played and the sound of 'victory of Golu' reverberated in the atmosphere. In course of time the young prince succeeded his father. People respected Golu like a god as he carried on the administration with honesty and foresight. He became highly popular in his very life time.

To sum up, we can safely conclude that Golu Devata is the most powerful and respected deity of Kumaun Himalayas and its tremendous impact on the social, cultural, religious and psychological outlook and practices of the people is really great and praiseworthy. In fact, he can be safely termed as the 'Mind and Soul of the Kumauni people'.

REFERENCES

Agrawal, C.M. *Golu Devata, The God of Justice of Kumaun Himalaya.*
Atkinson, E.T., *The Himalayan Gazetteer*, Vol. II, Part II.
Prasad, Jagedishwari, *Kumaun ke Devalaya.*
Shah, G.R., *Abode of Gods, Uttarakhand.*
Pande, B.D., *Kumaun Ka Itihasa.*
Sankrityayan, R., *Kumaun.*
Joshi, P., *Kumauni, Loka Gathayen.*
Ashoka, Y.D.V., *Kumaun ka Loka Sahitya.*
Belavala, M.D., *Gwel Devata*
Walton, H.G., *Almora Gazetteer.*
Dabral, S.P., *Uttarakhand ka Itihasa.*
Joshi, K.N., *Kumaun Ka Loka Sahita.*

9. HUNGER, GREED, AND THE 'FALL' OF MAN

Prashant Srivastava

The aim of this paper is to delve into the Indian mind, and try to find out what kind of relationship it conceived between hunger, greed, and the 'fall' of man; an attempt shall also be made to compare this Indian theme with the Judeo-Christian theme of the sending forth of Adam from the garden of Eden. The meaning of 'fall' of man shall become clear as I proceed.

According to the Judeo-Christian belief, God planted a garden in Eden, and made grow all kinds of trees, including the tree of life and 'the tree of knowledge of good and evil'.[1] He then placed man (Adam) in the garden of Eden,[2] and permitted him to eat the fruit of all the trees, except for that of the tree of knowledge.[3] God also created woman (Eve) from out of a rib of Adam,[4] and they started living like man and wife. Both Adam and Eve were naked, but were not ashamed of their nakedness.[5] Eve was beguiled by a serpent to partake of the forbidden fruit of the tree of knowledge, and she also made her husband eat it.[6] On eating the fruit of the tree of knowledge, Adam and Eve realized that they were naked, and ashamed of it. They hid when the Lord came to them.[7] When God saw them hiding, He could, at once, understand that the two must have eaten the forbidden fruit. As punishment, He drove Adam and Eve out of the garden of Eden, and cursed them to 'till the ground'.[8] From this Biblical creation of myth, we learn that man initially possessed innocence, and was not ashamed of his nakedness. On eating the fruit of the tree of knowledge, Adam realizes his nakedness, and becoming ashamed of it, hides from the Lord; his Maker. This implies the loss of innocence of man. He was sent forth from the garden of Eden, where food was readily available to him, and he had, thenceforth, to labour to feed himself.

Now, let us notice an Indian theme. According to the *Ahirbudhnyasaṁhitā*,[9] an eighth century A.D. text, knowledge became a cow, and milk flowed from her. The Manus, who possessed omniscience, 'drank' that milk, and lost their knowledge. This is regarded as an 'immediate reversal' of the Judeo-Christian theme,[10] mentioned above. But, is it an 'immediate reversal'? It is true that, in the Judeo-Christian theme, Adam and Eve, who were earlier innocent, on eating the fruit of the tree of knowledge, *gained knowledge*, and comprehended their nakedness. On the contrary, in the Indian theme, the Manus, who were earlier omniscient, on drinking the milk of knowledge, *lost knowledge*. But the ultimate result of both, the gain and loss of knowledge for man, is the same. In case of the Judeo-Christian theme, by gaining knowledge, man loses his innocence, is turned out of the garden of Eden, where food was readily available to him, and has to labour to feed himself. In the case of the Indian theme, by losing knowledge, man loses his virtue. For, knowledge makes a man virtuous, and loss of knowledge leads to loss of virtue. Thus, the ultimate result, in both the cases, is the 'fall' of man, and the ultimate cause, in both the cases, is man's hunger—for the forbidden fruit in the Judeo-

Christian theme; for the milk of knowledge in the Indian theme.

I would digress here to cite an example, which, I feel, is a better example of an 'immediate reversal' of a Judeo-Christian motif. It is told in the *Exodus*, Chapter 14, that the 'children of Israel', pursued by the Pharaoh, reached the sea. The Lord instructed Moses to lift up his rod, and stretch his hand over the sea, and divide it.[11] Moses did so, and the Lord caused the sea to go back by a strong east wind all that night, and made the sea dry land.....[12] The 'children of Israel' crossed the sea, walking upon the dry ground, 'and the waters were a wall unto them on their right hand, and on their left'.[13] When all the Jews had crossed the sea, Moses, on the instructions of the Lord, again stretched his hand over the sea, and the waters joined, drowning the pursuing Egyptians.[14] Thus, in this Judeo-Christian motif, the waters of the sea went against their nature, and parted to provide a dry, safe passage to the 'children of Israel'.

In India, in the *Rāmāyaṇa*, we find Rāma requesting the ocean to provide passage to his army to Laṅkā.[15] But, even when Rāma threatened to dry up the ocean with an arrow,[16] the ocean refuses to part, saying that the elements—earth, air, ether, water, and fire, cannot go against their nature.[17] To reach Laṅka, Rāma, on the advice of the ocean himself,[18] had, perforce, to construct a bridge;[19] to return from there, he had to fly on board the Pushpaka.[20] This is what, in my opinion, would be termed an 'immediate reversal' of a Judeo-Christian motif in India.

Another instance of the hunger and greed of man, leading to his 'fall', is to be found in the *Mahābhārata.* At the beginning of time, man lived in the sky and moved about freely in the air. The earth was sweet and delicious like honey. Man came down to the earth to 'taste her', although he did not need to eat. Then, he became greedy, and started taking 'more than a taste'. Consequently, his body became solid and heavy, and he was unable to fly.[21] Being unable to fly, man could no longer live in the air, and became earthbound.[22] Thus, once again, hunger and greed lead to the 'fall' of man.

In the Indian mythology, there are a number of instances, when hunger and greed lead man to commit sin(s).[23] In the *Śatapathabrāhmaṇa,* we are told that the creatures, on being created, ate the barley of Varuṇa. For this sin, Varuṇa seized them, and made them swollen. Prajāpati freed them from the *pāśa* of Varuṇa, and healed them. He also created an abundance of food for his creatures.[24] Hunger led the creatures of Prajāpati to steal, as it were, the food grain belonging to Varuṇa. They had sinned, and were punished by Varuṇa.[25] Prajāpati intervened, and also created an abundance of food, so that his creatures did not have to take recourse to theft to assuage their hunger.

The *Ṛgveda* states: "The gods did not give us hunger as an instrument of slaughter; for various deaths overcome one who has eaten."[26] When man is hungry, he might slaughter other creatures, thus committing the sin of violence. In vedic literature, hunger is often associated with evil and sin. It is said that the demons created hunger as a weapon.[27] The *Śatapathabrāhmaṇa,* while describing Indra's victory over Vṛtra, informs us that the demonic half of Vṛtra became the stomache of man.[28] The same text also states: "Whenever there is drought, then the stronger seizes upon the weaker..."[29] Drought means lack of food, resulting in hunger. This state leads to what is called *mātsyanyāya* in the Indian tradition.[30] The situation is beautifully summed up in the *Vishṇupurāṇa,* which says that anger and the *rakshasas* (representing evil) were born of hunger.[31]

The *Mahābhārata*[32] tells us of a great 12 year drought, during which people started devouring each other. The sage, Viśvāmitra, saw a dead dog, and tried to steal it to satiate his hunger. An outcaste tried to dissuade him from this sinful act of eating a dead dog. But the sage went ahead, and devoured it. Thus, hunger turned the common man into a cannibal.[33] But that was not all. Even learned men were not left unsullied by the evil effect of hunger, and we find a *ṛshi* committing the sins of theft and eating a dead dog. It is another matter that the sage's sins were, later on, burned away by the performance of asceticism. The *Devībhāgavata* speaks of a 15 year long drought, a later one than the 12 year drought mentioned above. During the course of this 15 year drought, men not only ate animals like horses, but also dead human beings. Hunger drove mothers to devour their sons and husbands, their wives.[34]

An interesting account is given in the *Padmapurāṇa*.[35] The Goddess created goddesses to defend the gods against the demon, Ruru. When these goddesses had killed Ruru, they became hungry. Rudra offered them food, which they refused as they regarded it as defiled through contact with pregnant women, women prone to weep all the time, and newborn children. Rudra then offered them his testicles as food. The goddesses ate them with delight. In this account, hunger is born of violence, and is, itself, the root of sin. Although Rudra himself had offered his testicles as food to the hungry goddesses, the act of the goddesses in eating them is tantamount to castrating Rudra, a god known for his virility.[36] Thus, hunger leads to sin, not only among the mortals—both ignorant and learned, but also among the immortals.

A primitive myth may here be recounted with benefit. Among a certain central Indian tribe, it is believed that, in the beginning, human beings had no sexual organs. Whenever a man saw a beautiful woman, he desired to swallow her, as he could derive pleasure only by this kind of union. Mahādeva then made sexual organs for man and woman, and saved the world.[37] Hunger, here, takes the place of sexual desire, in the absence of the ability to engage in sexual intercourse due to the lack of sexual organs. This leads to the killing of women, in itself an evil. It also threatened the survival of the world in the long run, and the deity had to intervene to save the world.

Instances abound in the Purāṇas, in which hunger and greed lead to the 'fall' of man. According to the *Mārkaṅḍeyapurāṇa*, the wish-fulfilling tree emerged from the liquid, which fell from the sky. This tree was the source of shelter and food. Man became greedy, and fenced in the tree. The tree vanished. Man became hungry. He built cities.[38] With the wish-fulfilling tree providing shelter and food, man did not have to labour for sustenance. But he became greedy, and fenced in the tree, thereby declaring his ownership of it. When the tree consequently vanished, he had to build cities for shelter, and labour to obtain food.[39] The *Vāyupurāṇa* also says that, when the wish-fulfilling tree disappeared, man had to take recourse to property and clothing.[40] The building of cities, the taking recourse to property and clothing, all this implies the beginning of civilization, which is regarded as the source of 'further greed and sin';[41] the beginning of civilization marks the end of the innocence of man.[42] According to the *Skaṅdapurāṇa*, when the wish-fulfilling tree disappeared, man became subject to 'passions'.[43] When man became greedy, the wish-fulfilling tree vanished.[44] Since the wish-fulfilling tree was the source of food, besides other desirables, its disappearance led to hunger. We are faced, thus, with a vicious circle—hunger and greed of man leading to the disappearance of the wish-fulfilling tree, which, in its turn, creates scarcity of food, that is hunger.

Now, let us recall to mind the behaviour of the seven sages and Arundhatī, in the face of hunger during a 12 year long drought. The group searched the whole earth for food, but in vain. In their despair, when they saw a dead boy, they decided to boil and eat his corpse. They were, however, dissuaded from committing this sin by a king, Vṛishādarbhi by name. The king offered them riches, which they refused.[45] Hunger had driven them to the verge of devouring a dead boy. But they were not greedy and did not accept the gifts offered by the king, and, for this virtue, were rewarded with immortality or heaven.[46]

REFERENCES

1. *Genesis* 2. 8-9.
2. *Ibid.*, 2. 15.
3. *Ibid.*, 2. 16-17.
4. *Ibid.*, 2. 21-22.
5. *Ibid.*, 2. 25.
6. *Ibid.*, 3. 1 ff. 'And when the woman saw that the tree was good for food, and that it was pleasant to the eyes, and a tree to be desired to make one wise, she took the fruit thereof, and did eat, and gave also unto her husband with her; and he did eat.' *Ibid.*, 3.6.
7. *Ibid.*, 3. 7-11.
8. *Ibid.*, 3. 23-24.
9. *Ahirbudhnyasaṁhitā* VII. 59b-63a.
10. W.D. O'Flaherty, *The Origins of Evil in Hindu Mythology*, (Delhi, 1976), p. 32.
11. *Exodus* 14. 16.
12. *Ibid.*, 14. 21.
13. *Ibid.*, 14. 22.

14. *Ibid.*, 14. 26-30.
15. *Rāmāyaṇa* (Gītā Press Edition, Gorakhpur, 2006) VI. 21.
16. *Ibid.*, VI. 22. 1 ff.
17. *Ibid.*, VI. 22. 26-28.
18. *Ibid.*, VI. 22. 46.
19. *Ibid.*, VI. 22. 47ff.
20. *Ibid.*, VI. 122-127.
21. William Buck, *Mahābhārata* (Berkeley, 1973); p. 318. See W.D. O'Flaherty, *op.cit.*, p. 29.
22. A similar motif is seen in the Buddhist text, *Dīghanikāya, Aggaññasuttanta* XXVII. 10 ff.
23. A number of such instances have been noticed by W.D. O'Flaherty, *op.cit.*, *ad passim.*
24. *Śatapathābrahmaṇa* II. 5. 2. 1-3; V. 2. 4. 1-2; V. 1. 21; *Kaushitakībrāhmaṇa* V. 3.
25. The punishments meted out by Varuṇa usually take the form of diseases, like tuberculosis (*Ṛgveda* I. 122. 9), deformity (*Ṛgveda* I. 122. 5-8), etc. There is a suggestion (Sukumari Bhattacharji, *The Indian Theogony*, Cambridge, 1970, p. 32) that 'an offence against the god of the norm is punished by a disease which is abnormal'. In the present case, to punish the thieving creatures, Varuṇa makes them 'swollen'. This is commonly taken to mean dropsy (W.D. O'Flaherty, *op.cit.*, pp. 21-22). This might be due to the close association of Varuṇa with water, which is seen since vedic times. He brings rain by his *māyā* (*Ṛgveda* V. 63. 3). He is the lord of the waters (*Taittirīyabrāhmaṇa* I. 1. 3. 8). He determines the courses of rivers (*Ṛgveda* VII. 34.11; X. 75. 2). This association with water becomes more pronounced in epic-puraṇic mythology. Varuṇa is the lord of the sea (*Rāmāyaṇa*, edited by G. Bhatt, Baroda Oriental Institute, 1960, VI. 6. 26), and the lord of the waters (Salilarāja, *Rāmāyaṇa*, edited by G. Bhatt, Baroda Oriental Institute, 1960, VI. 51. 32). All the gods (*Mahābhārata* IX. 46), or Śiva alone (*Mahābhārata* XII. 122), made Varuṇa the lord of the waters. His abode is in the waters (*Atharvaveda* V. 24; VII. 83. 1; *Rāmāyaṇa* (Gītā Press, edited by G Bhatt, Baroda. Oriental Institute, 1960, III. 60. 18; *Rāmāyaṇa* (Gītā Press Edition, Gorakhpur, 2006) VI. 22. 30; etc. *cf Harivaṁśa* II. 102. 33).
26. *Ṛgveda* X. 117. 1. *cf. Bṛhadāraṇyakopanishad* I. 2.
27. *Taittirīyabrāhmaṇa* I. 6. 7. 2.
28. *Śatapathabrāhmaṇa* I. 6. 3.

29. *Ibid.*, XI. 1. 6. 24.
30. See D.W. O' Flaherty, *op.cit.*, pp. 23-24.
31. *Viṣṇupurāṇa* I. 5. 41-43.
32. *Mahābhārata* XII. 139. 13-92.
33. The *Devībhāgavata* (XII. 9. 1-10) also speaks of a 12 year long drought, during which men killed and devoured each other, and also animals like elephants and horses.
34. *Devībhāgavata* (XII. 9. 1-10).
35. *Padmapurāṇa* V. 26. 91-125.
36. Mahādev Chakravarti, *The Concept of Rudra-Śiva Through the Ages* (Delhi, 1994), pp. 108ff.
37. Verrier Elwin, *Myths of Middle India* (Oxford, 1949), p. 261.
38. *Mārkaṇḍeyapurāṇa* XLVI. 1-35. *cf. Kūrmapurāṇa* I. 28. 15-40.
39. This reminds one of Adam, who had to 'till the ground', when he lost his innocence, and was turned out of the garden of Eden (above).
40. *Vāyupurāṇa* I. 8. 77-88.
41. W.D. O' Flaherty, *op.cit.*, p. 24.
42. See *Dīghanikāya : Aggaññasuttanta* XXVII. 1 10 ff; *Sumaṅgalavilāsinī* of Buddhaghoṣa III. 865; *Visuddhimagga* XIII. 49.
43. *Skandapurāṇa* I. 20. 14. 173-185.
44. *Liṅgapurāṇa* I. 39. 23-56; *Skandapurāṇa* I. 20.14. 173-85.
45. There are several versions of this episode in the various Purāṇas and the *Mahābhārata.* See *Skandapurāṇa* VI. 32. 1-100; *Padmapurāṇa* V. 19. 210-391; *Mahābhārata* XIII. 94. 3-44; XIII. 95. 1-86. In the *Padmapurāṇa* version, there are certain variations; for instance, the name of the king is not mentioned.
46. *Skandapurāṇa* VI. 32. 1-100; *Padmapurāṇa* V. 19.210-391; *Mahābhārata* XIII. 94. 3-44; XIII. 95. 1-86.

10. THE MIND OF PRIMITIVE MAN

Anil Kumar

The earth on which we live is nearly 4.5 billion years old. In the early period of its existence, the earth was in a hot fluid state, a burning ball in the solar system. Slowly the crust of the earth cooled. The present shape of earth is a result of long process of cooling and consolidation. Gradually, the dense clouds of gases of earth cooled down. Water vapours at that time began to condense into drops and fell as rain.

Around 3000-2000 million years ago life appeared in the water. However, it is difficult to explain how life appeared. The first form of life on earth may have been microscopic single called organism known as unicellular organisms. The life on the earth developed in different period. The Geological era on the earth are divided into four periods—the Pre-Camberian, the Palaeozoic, the Mesozoic and the Cenozoic. The Cenozoic era is further sub-divided into the Tertiary and the Quaternary. The tertiary period is of great importance because human evolution took place at the end of it. The quaternary period (Charlesworth, J.K., 1957; Flint, R.F., 1957) is concerned with the major activities of positive man. It is also sub-divided into two phases the Pleistocene and the Holocene.

Man is an animal of vertebrate group and belongs to class of mammals (Issac, G.L., 1989). He is bipedal using only his hind legs for locomotion. The man, monkey and apes are very similar in the details of their anatomy. It is customary to group them together as an order the primates.

When we talk about the evolution of the human mind, it is unclear what this means. There are two schools of thought who present their views on this issue. According to one school, the human mind works as a 'general-purpose information processor' with intimate connections between all the distinctly human cognitive processes (Piaget, 1960). The other school views the mind as a series of modules, each evolved for specific work (Cosmides and Tooby, 1987), for to be different types of intelligences, such as those for language, mathematics, social science and music (Gardner, 1983). The views of the evolution of human mind indicate that it evolved not as a 'general-purpose computer' but as having evolved to solve a specific type of problems faced by hominids in their evolutionary environments. The archaeological materials recovered during excavations from the pre-historic period appear to provide greater support to the gradual creep of mind as a series of modules rather than first view that is mind as one general-purpose information processor of cognitive evolution.

Basically pre-historic archaeology is concerned with the origins and development of early human culture between the first appearances of man as a tool-using mammal (Johnson, A.W. and T. Earle, 1987). Throughout the Palaeolithic period, man was a food-gatherer, depending for his subsistence on hunting wild animals and birds, fishing and collecting wild fruits, nuts and berries (Zvelbil, M., 1986). For doing these activities many applicable tools, made of stone, bone, perhaps woods have been used by early human. In general, these materials develop gradually from single to all-purpose tools, each designed to serve in connection with a specific function. Indeed, it is a process of increasingly more complex technologies, each founded on a specific tradition, which characterizes the cultural development of Palaeolithic times (Wymer, J., 1982). In other words, the trend was from simple to complex, from a stage of non-specialization to stages of relatively high degrees of specialization, just as has been the case during historic times.

Evolution of Primitive Man

The history of the emergence of man and its evolutionary processes originated from a group primates (Mark, J., 1992; Delson, E., 2000). The earliest primates are classified as *prosimians* (Delson, E., 1985). The hominid that closely related to humans only evolved at the end of Pliocene period (Potts, R., 1988). These are called *Australopithecines* and it is from them that the first member of the genus *Homo* merged at the beginning of the quaternary period (Leakey, 1964; Brain, C.K., 1958; Crooke, H.B.S., 1958; 1962). *Australopithecus* means 'southern ape'. This name is used because the first fossils were found in South Africa. Dr. Raymond Dart, Professor of anatomy at Witwatersand University in Johannesburg, was the first to study these fossils. In 1924, at Taung in South Africa, Dart discovered a fossil skull consisting of a full face, teeth and jaws, and an endocranial cast of the brain size was 410 cc. Dart was convinced that some teeth were man-like and thus concluded a transition between apes and man. Although modern scientists do generally accept that *Australopithecines* had a generally upright gait and human-like posture, this notion has not gone uncontested.

In three million years, the genius, Homo passed through three successive stages of evolution, each characterized by a new species (Butzer, K.W., 1975)—*Homo habilis* (handy man), *Homo erectus* (upright man) and *Homo sapiens* (intelligent man). *Homo sapiens* formed two distinct sub-species during this evolution—*Homo neanderthalensis* and *Homo sapiens sapiens*. The modern man evolved from *Homo sapiens sapiens*.

Evidence of fragmented pieces of skull of *Homo habilis* was found in 1959 by Mary Leakey and dated at about 1.8 million years old. Louis Leakey also accepted his existence when it appeared to be stone tools were found near the site of *Homo habilis*. The bones of many of these animals revealed that they had been butchered and deliberately broken for their marrow. Leakey decided, on the basis of this evidence, that his fossil had been a tool-maker and thus called his *Homo habilis* or 'handy man'. Most other investigators, however, were not comfortable with such as extremely primitive beast being a toolmaker.

In July 1984, a nearly complete fossilized skeleton of 12 year old boy was discovered at Lake Turkana in Kenya. It is the most complete fossilized skeleton todate to be included as a *Homo erectus*. The boy stood 160 cm. (5' 3") tall and had a brain capacity of 880 cc. In general, the cranial capacity of *H. erectus* is 1000 cc. Similarly, from other parts of the world many fossilized skeleton have been found time to time. The remains of *Sinanthropus pekinensis*, known as Peking Man and dating back to 400,000 B.C., were excavated in 1923 at Zhoukoudianzhen near Peking (now Beijing), China. An almost complete skull cap was discovered in 1929 in a filled-in limestone cave near Peking. Peking Man was of *Homo erectus* species. According to current evolutionary theory, the earliest specimens of *H. erectus*, found in 1891-92 near

Trinil on the Indonesian island of Java (thus called Java Man), are about 700,000 years old. The teeth of Java Man, found separately and which are now thought to belong to an orangutan, were said to be remarkably like those of *H. habilis* of eastern Africa, suggesting that '*H. erectus* might have evolved from *H. habilis*'. *Homo erectus* was an advanced hominid who first appeared around 2 million years ago.

Neanderthal Man (*Homo neanderthalensis*) was the first 'ape-man' found (Howell, F.C., 1958; Maitland, A., 1973). In 1856, in the Neander Valley near Dusseudorf of Germany, a school teacher, Johann Fuhhott, found a fossilized skeleton that consisted of a skullcap, thingbones, part of a pelvis, some ribs, and some arm and shoulder bones in a small cave at Feldhofer. The lower left arm had been broken and as a result the bones of the left arm were smaller than those of the right. A careful examination and description by Professor Schaafhausen reported them to be human. Two years later, two similar skulls were found in Belgium. Subsequently, over 60 parts of skeletons were found in eleven different countries. His cranial capacity was in between 1300 cc and 1750 cc and the average cranial capacity was 1400 cc. They used animal skin for clothing and dwelling. Fishing and hunting of birds or small animals are added other modes of living. *Neanderthal* race of mankind disappeared around 35,000 B.C.

The new hominid who appeared around 40,000 B.C., were known as *Cro-Magnon* man. They replaced *Homo erectus* in the Upper Palaeolithic period which continued upto 10,000 B.C.

Stone Age Cultures and Primitive Man

Stone Age is first stage of the history of mankind. It is

further sub-divided into three periods (Braidwood, R.J., 1960)—Palaeolithic period, Mesolithic period and Neolithic period. On the basis of tool-typology and economic activities of man, the Palaeolithic period is also divided into three phases—Lower Palaeolithic period, Middle Palaeolithic period and Upper Palaeolithic period.

The Palaeolithic period ranges from 4.4 million to 10,000 B.P. *Austrolopithecus* was ape-like and was the first tool-user animal. *Homo erectus* was adapting to life in warm and arid climatic in Asia. *Homo erectus* succeeded by more complex tools based on large bifacially flaked implements as handaxes and cleaver, although eastern Asia dominated by chopper-chopping tools. The *Homo erectus* were the first to live in caves. He was specialized in hunting of big animals as is evident from the discovery of skeletal remains found from their dwelling sites. He also learnt how to use and control 'fire'. Fire provided them warmth during the cold seasons and protection from wild animals. *Homo erectus* is concerned with Lower Palaeolithic period.

A new race of man known as *Neanderthal* appeared on the earth in the Middle Palaeolithic period. He was the next ancestor after the *Homo erectus*.

In the manufacture of the stone implements, four fundamental traditions were developed by the Palaeolithic peoples—pebble-tool traditions, bifacial-tool or handaxe traditions, flake-tool traditions and blade-tool traditions. In general, however, there is an overall trend in the order as given above, starting with simple pebble-tools that have a single edge sharpened for cutting or chopping. By far the outstanding feature of the Palaeolithic period was the evolutionary of the human species from an ape-like animal or near human, to true *Homo sapenians*. This development was exceedingly slow and continued through the three successive divisions of the period—the Lower, Middle and Upper Palaeolithic. The most abundant remains of Palaeolithic cultures are a variety of stone tools whose distinct characteristics provide the basis for a system of classification containing several tool-making traditions or industries.

The oldest recognizable tools made by early human are simple stone-chopper and chopping. These tools may have been made or used by *Australopithecus*, ancestor of modern man. Lower Palaeolithic stone industries—the *Clactonian*, *Abbevillian*, *Achculian* and *Levalloisian* were represented at various sites in Europe, Africa and Asia. Stone tools of this period are of the core type, made by chipping the stone to form a cutting edge or of the flake type fashioned from fragments struck off a stone. Hand axes were the typical tool of these early hunters and food-gathers. The Middle Palaeolithic period includes the Mousterian culture, often associated with *Neanderthal* (Borders, F., 1961, 1968). Stone tools of this period are of the flake tradition, and implements, such as needles, indicate that some sort of sewn skins of animals were used as body coverings. Since the dead were painted before burial, a kind of primitive religion may have been practiced. In Upper Palaeolithic period *Neanderthal* disappears and is replaced by a variety of *Homo sapiens* such as *Cro-Magnon man* and *Grimaldi man*. In Europe many cultures came in existence, viz., *Aurignacian*, *Gravettian*, *Solutrean* and *Magdalenian* with their characteristics artefacts, mainly tool types which were highly refined and varied and livings.

Mesolithic period is in between the end of the Palaeolithic period and at the beginning of the Neolithic period which began with the end of the last glacial period over around 10,000 years ago and evolved into the

Neolithic period. This change involved the gradual domestication of plants and animals and the formation of settled communities at various times and places. Mesolithic cultures represent a wide variety of hunting, fishing and food-gathering techniques. The variety may be the result of adaptations to changed ecological conditions. Characteristics of the Mesolithic period were hunting and fishing settlements along rivers and on lake shores. Microliths, the typical stone implements of the period, are smaller and more delicate than those of the late Palaeolithic period.

The term Neolithic is used, especially in archaeology, to designate a stage of cultural evolution or technological development characterized by the use of polished and grounded stone tools, the existence of settled villages largely dependent on domesticated plants and animals, and the presence of such crafts as potter and probably weaving. The time period and cultural content indicated by the term varies with the geographic location of the culture considered and with the particular criteria used by the individual scientist. The domestication of plants and animals usually distinguishes Neolithic culture from earlier Palaeolithic or Mesolithic hunting, fishing and food-gathering cultures. In Neolithic period stone tools include celt, adze, chisel, pick, sling ball, quern, muller. All these tools made on fine-grained stone with the technique of grinding and polishing. Mostly Neolithic tools were used in domestic work suitable for contemporary climate. Along with stone, bones were also an important raw material according to their availability. Sedentary way of life was salient feature of Neolithic culture supported by findings of different pattern of dwellings—huts, pit dwelling etc. Neolithic art is best illustrated by the decoration of pottery. Pots (handmade, but in late phase wheel-made) were painted either pre-firing or post-firing.

Stone Stage Technology and Tools

It is not known how stone tool technology was discovered, although it is very possible that the earliest stone tool-making developed as a by-product of some other activity, such as hammering nuts or either offensively or defensively throwing stones that cracked against a hard surface, and then investigating the new properties of the resultant sharp edges. The earliest stone tools were usually made of relatively coarse-grained volcanic and metamorphic rocks common in much of Africa, such as lavas, quartzite or quartz, although some were made of finer-grained siliceous rocks such as chert. Over time, more selection is seen in the choice of stone materials for many tools, with greater use of obsidian or volcanic glass and fine-grained cherts in some regions, as well as transport of materials over greater distances.

Experimental investigations of stone technology involve replicating stone tools found at pre-historic sites, especially investigating the techniques and procedures evident, and also exploring the possible uses of stone tools for different activities. Ultimately, archaeologists wish to know not only information about pre-historic stone technologies, but also how tools in stone and other materials fit into the lives and adaptations of pre-historic peoples. Questions of interest to many experimental archaeologists today embrace the entire stone technology system of pre-historic societies, including their acquisition of stone raw materials, initial working of the core, shaping of finished tools, discard of manufacturing by products or debris, duration and transport of raw materials and tools, reshaping and retouching of tools, and their ultimate discard or abandonment. Through experiments and studies investigating such problems, archaeologists have gained a great deal of insight into pre-historic stone technologies, particularly how stone tools were made and how they would have been used by pre-historic ancestors and have thus become better able to interpret the evidence found at archaeological sites. These study also reflecting the development of human mind along with technological expertise.

The findings of stone tools from all over the world, a framework of stone tool-making technology has been drawn by many pre-historians. According to them stone tools technique was gradually developed in different stages which reflects the capacity of human mind thinking. Firstly, in Stage 1, stone tools were made on core and identified as chopper-chopping. In Stage 2, technology of tool-making emerges with the appearance of bifacial handaxes and cleavers at more or less the time of the emergence of a larger-brained, larger-bodied hominid, *Homo erectus*. Stone tool-making technology in Stage 3 was concerned with the Middle Palaeolithic period as Flake-tools types. Scrapers, bores and points made on flakes were major tool types of this stage.

Starting 40,000 to 30,000 years ago, Stage 4 of blade technology pre-dominates during the period known as the Upper Palaeolithic period in which many other tools made on bone and antler also become common (Braidwood, R.J., 1961). Microliths of Mesolithic period of the Stage 5 of the development of stone tool-making technology. Along with Microliths other artefacts and tools such as bone harpoons and shell beads were the findings of this stage. Stage 6 is characterized by ground and polished stone tools, viz., celts, adzes, chisels, picks, mullers, querns etc. This technique represents a significant investment of time and energy in tool-making, but produced tough, stable-edged, long-lasting tools. Ground and Polished stone tools are commonly found among many early food-producing societies, known as Neolithic period.

Transition phase appears in Middle and Upper Palaeolithic periods, when we find widespread changes in the archaeological record that may reflect the appearance of fully modern man cognition, the appearance of new technologies and of symbolic artefacts, increased rate of culture change (Mellars, 1973, 1989). Middle and Upper Palaeolithic transition is most clearly defined with the replacement of *Neanderthals* by *Homo sapiens*. A series of distinct artefacts types such as scrapers, points, blades and body ornaments as crude beads have been important changes with previous phase (Bordes, 1968; Mellars, 1989, 1991).

Comparative studies of *Neanderthals* and modern man has been seen as reflecting cognitive differences between the two hominid types (Mellars, 1991). Cognition of modern man allowing him to hunt more efficiently, cope with environmental fluctuations and attain greater behavioural flexibility which reflect in the extension use of visual symbolism in the form of cave or rock art and sculptures (Davidson, 1991). For many art traditions, the information being stored may be purely symbolic, but in other cases, ecological knowledge may also be stored within the art. If we examine the imagery of the cave paintings and mobility art in detail, we can identify a series of references to the process by which hunter-gatherers acquire information from their environments. These references probably acted as cues to the recall of information from memory that containing information about past events, rather than general knowledge. Hunter-gatherers are always acquiring information and storing it in long-term memory (Mithen, 1990). But, the problem they face is the recall of relevant information when a particular problem arises. Upper Palaeolithic art with its series of recall cues is likely to have facilitated such information retrieval, probably at times of substantial change in hunting strategies (Mithen, 1988).

The above evidences clearly indicate that in prehistoric period human mind capacity, physical appearance and technologies have gradually developed. In this context, climatic conditions played greater role. Selection of material (mostly types of rocks) for making implements, animals and plants for domestication and habitation pattern according to their surrounding environment are important features reflect cognitive capacity and its advancement. Art in the form of paintings or ornaments is the prominent evidence of cognition of human mind.

REFERENCES

1. Bordes, F., 1961, 'Mousterian Cultures in France', *Science* 134.803-10.
2. Bordes, F., 1968, *The Old Stone Age*, London.
3. Braidwood, R.J., 1960, 'Levels in Prehistory : A Model for the Consideration of the Evidence' in S. Tax (ed.), *Evolution After Darwin*, Chicago, University of Chicago Press, Vol. 2, pp. 143-51.
4. Braidwood, R.J., 1961, *Pre-historic Man*, Chicago.
5. Brain, C.K., 1958, 'The Transval Ape Man Being Cave Deposits', *Transvaal Mus. Mem*, 11, pp. 32-48.
6. Butzer, K.W., 1975, *After the Australopithecus*, The House Mouton.
7. Charlesworth, J.K., 1957, *The Quaternary Era*, Vol. 2.
8. Cosmides, L. and J. Tooby, 1987, 'From Evolution to Behaviour; Evolutionary Psychology as the Missing Link', in J. Dupre (ed.), *The Latest on the Best; Essay on Evolution and Optimally*, Cambridge, pp. 277-306.
9. Crooke, H.B.S., 1958, 'Observation Relating to Quaternary Environments in East and South Africa', *Geol. Soc.*, South

Africa, Vol. 40.
10. Cooke, H.B.S., 1962, 'The Pleistocene Environment in South Africa', in D.H.S. Davis (ed.), *Ecology of South Africa*, Amsterdom.
11. Davidson, I., 1991, 'The Archaeology of Language Origins- A Review', *Antiquity*, 65 : 39-48.
12. Delson, Eric (ed.), 2000, *Encyclopaedia of Human Evolution and Prehistory*, London.
13. Flint, R.F., 1957, *Glacial and Pleistocene Geology*, New York.
14. Gardner, H., 1983, *Frames of Mind: The Theory of Multiple Intelligences*, London.
15. Howell, F.C., 1958, 'Upper Pleistocene Man of the Southwest Asian Mousterian', in *Neanderthal Centenary*, Kemink, pp. 185-98.
16. Issac, G.L., 1989, *The Archaeology of Human Origin*, Cambridge.
17. Johnson, A.W. and T. Earle, 1987, *The Evolution of Human Societies*, Standford University Press, U.K.
18. Piaget, J., 1960, *The Psychology of Intelligence*, Totowa.
19. Marks, J., 1992, 'Chromosomal Evolution in Primates', *The Cambridge Encyclopedia of Human Evolution*, S. Jones, R. Martin and D. Pilbeam, (eds.), Cambridge University Press, Cambridge.
20. Maitland, Aedey, 1973, *Early Neanderthal*, Netherland.
21. Meller, P., 1973, 'The Character of the Middle/Upper Plaeolithic Transition in Southwest France', in C. Renfrew (ed.), *The Explanation of Culture Change*, London, pp. 255-76.
22. Meller, P., 1989, 'Major Issues in the Emergence of Modern Humans', *Current Anthropology*, 30: 349-85.
23. Meller, P., 1991, 'Cognitive Changes and the Emergence of Modern Humans in Europe', *Cambridge Archaeological Journal*, 1: 63-76.
24. Mithen, S., 1988, 'To Hunt or to Paint? Animals and Art in the Upper Palaeolithic', *Man*, 23: 71-95.
25. Mithen, S., 1990, *Thoughtful Foragers: A Study of Pre-historic Decision Making*, Cambridge.
26. Potts, R., 1988, *Early Hominid Activities at Olduvai*, New York.
27. Wymer, J., 1982, *The Palaeolithic Age*, London.
28. Zvelbil, M. (ed.), 1986, *Hunters in Transitions, Post-Glacial Adaptation in the Temperature Region of the Old World*, Cambridge.

11. REVISITING THE ARCHAEOLOGICAL LANDSCAPE OF UTTAR PRADESH

R.C. Thakran

The state of Uttar Pradesh presents very interesting natural and archaeological landscapes. The former is covered by the Ganga plains, which is broadly divided into the Upper and Middle Ganga Plains. The Upper Plains covers its western parts, while the latter envelopes the eastern ones, though its southern parts are dotted with the Vindhyan ranges. The entire landscape of Utter Pradesh is dissected by a number of tributaries of the Ganga which join it from different directions. This produces four types of contrasting landscapes the Bhangar, the Jhaddar, the Tarai region and the Vindhyan upland zone. These very landscapes both posed challenges and offered opportunities to be harnessed by the mankind according to its differential working capacity at different stages of social developments through history. Its archaeological landscape needs to be contextualized and viewed afresh in this light.

The archaeological landscape is equally interesting and it is broadly arranged into two categories along the geographical sub-divisions—the archaeological landscapes of the Upper and Middle Ganga Plains. These two present contrasting trajectories of the beginning and development of human activities overtime and space. These offer very significant insights, when viewed both independently and collectively, into the ongoing debates on the antiquity of human life, migration and movement of people along with their expertise, the introduction of cultivation and domestication of plants, the knowledge and application of metal tools (iron) into the productive activities and their contribution in shaping the very process of social development. All these issues deserve appropriate treatment.

Let us first begin with the Upper Ganga Plain. In this area, especially the western parts, the history of human activities travels back to the uppermost levels of the mature Harappan phase as revealed at the famous sites of Alamgirpur,[1] Baragaon[2] and Hulas[3] in this part. About 43 other sites (11 in Muzaffurnagar and 32 in Saharanpur district) have produced such remains.[4] This was followed by the late Harappan phase and remains of this have been reported so far from 70 settlements.[5] This brings the combined strength of the Harappan remains to 113 (43 + 70) settlements. This growing number of habitations shows that more and more new areas were brought under human influence in their advance movement beginning about 2000 BC. Around this time period only these areas seem to have been occupied by another cultural group, popularly known as Ochre Coloured Pottery (OCP) with a strength of 118 settlements with their ever-eastward orientation to rope in more pristine areas into their fold.[6] In this cultural milieu we also find, though in a highly sparse manner, presence of Black and Red Ware (BRW) which appears to have been strictly confined to only the southern parts.[7] Still more interesting is the fact that all the three traditions arrived to this zone from the areas situated west of the Yamuna.

A novel tradition known as Painted Grey Ware (PGW) succeeds the preceding cultural deposits after a stratigraphical break. Over two hundred settlements of this group have so far been reported over this landscape.[8] The movement of people is oriented to the east and in the process it reached upto the eastern most limit of this zone by incorporating more pristine areas in the fold of human activities. Like the preceding cultural traditions this also came to this area from that situated west of the Yamuna with progressive reduction in time. This was followed by another cultural tradition represented by the RW/NBPW. During this phase what we witness is a stratigraphical continuity with PGW deposits, further increase in the number of sites to 297 and size along with enrichment of their cultural achievements.[10] Some of the settlements were also transformed into urban centres in due course, this, of course, took cost 1500 odd years after the introduction of human life in this zone. It was not that the natural conditions were not favourable right from the beginning of human life in this area nor was there any major transformation into the realm of the natural properties. Instead what underwent a huge change during the said period is the working capacity of the people to harness better the extant natural resources, which seems to have proved a fountainhead of such transitions. Although this point is being questioned in the name of other contributing factors, yet it generates more information and brings further refinement in academic discourse.

This, however, brings us to the Middle Ganga Plains and we would like to begin with the Vindhyan region first for obvious reasons. Here the history of human presence goes back to Palaeolithic levels.[11] The area of human interaction strictly remained confined to the

Vindhyan ranges and naturally so primarily because the raw material, in the form of stones, was available in these areas only for their tools and more so this was being part of their ongoing forward movement from the central to the peripheral Vindhyas. These were the areas where their hunting-gathering mode of subsistence was also quite successful. So much so during this very period human beings strongly inclined to transcend the limits of the mountains, this was, of course, in tune with the pattern of human behaviour the world over, but the limits of their working capacity precluded them from going completely beyond their primary resource zones. Nevertheless the tangible impact of this tendency is visible only during the succeeding Mesolithic phase. However, we need to remember that the antiquity of this phase is not comparable with that of the general time span it represents, instead it is late.[12]

In the suceeding Mesolithic period what we witness is a big increase in the overall numerical strength of the (500) seasonal settlements in the northeastern Vindhyas and the Middle Ganga Plains. Over two hundred of these sites are located in the Middle Ganga Plains of Uttar Pradesh.[13] Of them thirteen have been excavated by colleagues from Allahabad University.[14] These include Morna Pahar, Chopani Mando in the Vindhyas and Sarai Nahar Rai, Mahadaha in Pratapgarh district. While Lahariyadih in Sonbhadra district was excavated by colleagues from Banaras Hindu University.[15] Most of these sites are located on high levels/sandy cliffs, along horse-shoe lakes, small water courses in general. The spur in the movement of the people towards the plains appears to have been inspired by multiple factors. One of these factors that seemed to have played heavily on their mind was the availability of a new raw material in the form of animal bones for making their tools free from any geographical limit. The sharp reduction in the size of the microlithic tools would have demanded less of raw material on the one hand and also this could have facilitated to carry them along in a good number without much of a problem for considerable distance. Moreover there appears to have emerged some kind of specialized groups involved in the production of these specialized tools in large number if the quantity of debitage at Mesolithic sites, especially Baghor-II in Sidhi district of Madhya Pradesh[16] is any pointer. Further the small size, composite nature and the sophisticated functions involved less of human labour and time in carrying out the job at hand, which speak themselves of the changing of working capacity of the people. These enabled them dare venture but in the open landscape of the Middle Ganga Plains, of course, initially along the margins of the Vindhyas and later in due course inroad in the hinterlands as well. Among the excavated sites we may add Chopani Mando,[17] Mahagara,[18] Koldihwa,[19] Jhusi[20] in Allahabad district, Damdama,[21] Mahadaha[22] and Sarai Nahar Rai[23] in Pratapgarh district and Lekhahia in Mirzapur district.[24]

Neolithic remains succeed the Mesolithic in the area as well and evidence of Neolithic period comes from Braunha[25] and Manigara[26] in the Vindhyas, Tokwa[27] at the confluence of the Belan and Adwa rivers, in Mirzapur district, Koldihwa[28] and Mahagara[29] in the Belan area of Allahabad district. These remains are dated around 5000 B.C. on the basis of C-14 dates,[30] though can be placed between the last quarter of the third millennium B.C. to the middle of the second millennium B.C. on the basis of C-14 dates as well as the circumstantial evidences in the form of wheat, barley, lentil crop remains of the northwestern parts of the Indian subcontinent.[31]

Now we can move on to the plains of the Middle Ganga Valley. Here we are primarily concerned with the areas situated between the Vindhyas and the Himalayas. In this zone we do not have any evidence of human presence in Palaeolithic as well as Mesolithic levels. Only during the succeeding Neolithic period we get remains of human presence for the first time in some form at Lahuradeva,[32] Sohgaura[33] near the Rapti and Amin rivers, Imlidih Khurd,[34] Khairadih[35] among others. This sequence is extended further east by the discovery of these remains at Chirand[36] and Senuwar[37] in Bihar.

The important points that come out distinctly from the exposed cultural sequence at the aforesaid sites are the use of handmade as well as wheel thrown ceramic wares, of diverse shades, in succession, especially the cord impressed wheel made pottery in the upper levels, the occurrence of varied crop remains, etc., which clearly point towards the late arrival of the first settlers of these areas. This is being placed between seventh-sixth millennium B.C., though their date does not go beyond the first half of the second millennium B.C.

The cultural sequence further continued in the succeeding Chalcolithic phase at the above settlements in addition to the others. During this phase we notice the use of Black and Red Ware, plain as well as painted with white colour. This has been recovered from Narhan[38] for the first time and later from Imlidih Khurd[39] in Gorakhpur district, Bhunadih,[40] Waina[41] and Khairadih[42] in Ballia district, Ganwaria[43] in Basti district, Prahladpur[44] and Rajghat[45] in Varanasi district, Sringaverpur[46] in Allahabad district, Malhar[47] in Chandauli district and Agiabirpur[48] in Mirzapur district. This sequence is further extended to the eastern parts of the Middle Ganga Plains at Taradih,[49] Senuwar[50] and Sonpur[51] (in the hilly areas), Oriup,[52] close to Patharghat hills, in Bhagalpur and Vaishali in the same district of Bihar.[53] Besides these excavated sites, there are a large number of explored sites also, which are dispersed over the length and breadth of this vast geographical expanse.

This was succeeded by the NBPW cultural deposits. During this phase what we mark is the use of NBPW and the associated redware in profusion. The numerical strength of sites goes to over five hundred in the area under study.[54] These remains have been uncovered from all the pre-NBPW settlements without any stratigraphical interruption. Besides an increase in the size of the settlements, their cultural deposits, assemblage and living standard is distinctly conspicuous. This signifies greater production and consumption patterns induced by the higher working capacity of the people.

Locational Analysis

The locational analysis of archaeological settlements is very interesting aspect. This relates to the choice of site-selection and evaluation of the risk factor/s involved in exercising their preference for particular locus in the light of their working capacity and the extant natural conditions. By taking into account the exact locations of sites during different cultural periods we get information on properties of the natural surroundings. But in regard to the actual working capacity of the people we get information from the tools they used, from the crop remains they produced and from the locations they preferred with varying frequency of occupancy. The preference for particular locations is the natural outcome of their understanding of the intensity of the risk factor involved. This points towards the interplay of the growing level of awareness about the landscape, the crops and their seasonal potential and the working capacity of people. None of the constituents, of course, has been static, instead they constantly change overtime and space. When we view the location of settlements in the light of the above what we experience is that people in the ancient past opted spurs, high sandy cliffs on river confluences and ox-bow lakes for their residential purposes[55] rather than being aligned with mighty perennial rivers only. The emerging settlement patterns are not linear in any manner albeit they present a dispersed order. The big water courses appear to have worked as a deterrent rather than being any big attraction for making their settlements, for the risk factor involved being very high in terms of intractable sudden floods, thick growth of vegetation infested with dangerous wild animals, coupled with the deficient working capacity. This approach was not unique in any manner to this area alone as this was also true in the case of Indus system.[56] So much so neither the rivers were nor are present even here over the Landscape nor was ever their water accessible to the majority of the settlements even for drinking purposes, let alone the other requirements.[57]

Subsistence Patterns

To understand the sequence of changes overtime and space we may begin by discussing the archaeobotanical evidences from the excavated settlements in the same order we followed in the preceding paragraphs. In the areas of the Upper Ganga Plains the primary mode of subsistence was based on agriculture. We have evidence to this effect in the form of domesticated barley from Hulas,[58] Lal Qila[59] and Atranjikhera;[60] wheat, gram, millet, big millet from Hulas,[61] rice remains from Hulas,[62] Un,[63] Lal Qila[64] and Atranjikhera.[65] In addition to the cereal remains, there are evidences of lentil (*Lens culinaris*), horse gram (*Dolichos bifflorus*), common/garden pea (*Pisum sativum Linn*), field pea (*Pisum arvense Linn*), cow pea (*Vigna ungiculata Linn*), lobia (*Dolicos sinsinis Linn*), chaunla (*Vigna sinsinis Save*) and grass pea (*Lathyrus sativus*) all from Hulas.[66] The list of leguminous plants is further enlarged with the addition of green gram/mung (*Vigna radiata*) from Hulas[67] and Atranjikhera,[68] black gram/urad (*Phaselus mungo/Vigna mungo*) from Hulas.[69] Besides evidence of cotton, a source of oil and yarn, also comes from Hulas itself.[70] This composition of crops suggests the practice of two crops—rabi and kharif—in one harvest year was well established in this part and its antiquity travels back to the areas situated west of the Yamuna. These crops were raised in the given landscape, which is considered better than that of the areas west of the Yamuna, in terms of its natural properties, with the help of the available copper-technology. More or less the same crop composition continued in the subsequent levels of PGW[71] and NBPW[72] in addition to the introduction[73] and greater use of iron tool-technology[74] in the respective levels, in combination with the application of paddy transplantation.[75] Thus, the combination of better natural conditions, crops and cropping systems with that of the more effective iron tool-technology accelerated production (agricultural as well as artisanal) and thereby development of urban centres.

On the contrary, the mode of subsistence in the Mid-Ganga plain during the Palaeolithic and Mesolithic periods was hunting and gathering. We do have indirect evidence of the processing of wild plant food with the help of querns, grinding stones, hammer stones from these (Mesolithic) sites. Also, perhaps harvesting of some wild grain, bearing grasses, is suggested by the composite cutting tools of this period. We are also informed of the presence of the wild perennial rice (*Oryza rufipogon*) in the form of husk impressions or imprints on clay lumps or in the sections of brittle potsherds from the late Mesolithic levels at Chopan Mando[76] in Allahabad district. A sole carbonized grain is said to have been reported from Damdama[77] in Pratapgarh district. However, we do not have any direct and conclusive evidence to prove the very knowledge of this variety of rice during these levels except the said sole carbonized grain and such stray evidences do not support such a major conclusion. We also do not have any evidence whatsoever about the other known wild species of annual rice, i.e., *Oryza nivara* and *Oryza perennis* from here. Their absence is also very crucial for ascertaining the knowledge, cultivation and domestication of rice at the local level.[78]

Remains of the cultivated rice (*Oryza sativa*) are said to have been gathered from the Mesolithic levels at Lekhahia as suggested by Saraswati[79] and Lekhahia rock-shelter in Mirzapur district,[80] and Damdama in Pratapgarh district as Pant quotes Saraswat.[81] However, this was controverted by Kajale[82] and thus the question of domesticated rice remains open to doubt until clinching evidence is uncovered. Further, this is being dated to 5000 B.C., though the overwhelming data speak otherwise.[83]

However, the question of the beginning of cultivation is settled in the Neolithic and Neolithic-Chalcolithic levels. We have evidence of rice species of perennial (*Oryza rufipogon*), annually (*Oryza nivara*) and *Oryza perennis*, though their distinguishing features have not been mentioned. Secondly the perennial variety is said to have been more pervasive as its remains come from Koldihwa and Mahagara in district Allahabad, Braunha and Manigara in the Vindhyas, Chirand and Senuwar in the eastern plains. Does it have any relevance with the course of its movement? We do not know. However, this surely calls for an exhaustive stratigraphic index and grain profile. The third variety—*Oryza perennial*—reported from only Chirand in Saran district of Bihar. This being in the eastern part of the plains may offer some significant inputs to its trajectory of expansion.

A good amount of information on cultivated variety of rice (*Oryza sativa*) is obtained from Koldihwa,[84] Mahagara,[85] Tokwa,[86] Braunha,[87] Manigara,[88] Lahuradeva,[89] Oriup,[90] Chirand,[91] Taradih[92] and Senuwar.[93] Its remains are coming in both, husk as well as grain forms. These are coupled with remains of barley, wheat, lentil, black pea, chick pea, field pea, grass pea, gram etc. from Chirand, Taradih, Sonpur, Narhan, Imlidih Khurd in pre-NBPW levels.[94] Also remains of millet, big millet and pearl millet come from pre-1000 B.C. levels at Imlidih Khurd.[95] Saraswat suggested the presence of fully domesticated rice in the assortment of wild rice and foxtail grasses. He further suggested the beginning of cultivation and domestication of rice in the 9th-8th millennia B.C. in the opening phase of occupation at the site. He placed the upper levels of this phase in the first half of 3rd millennium B.C. on the occurrence of barley. The presence of dish-on-stand in these levels is placed in the middle phase of this millennium. And further the presence of dwarf wheat, bread wheat[96] and lentil is placed around the turn of the millennium,[97] while Tewari assigns it a time-bracket between 6th to 5th millennium B.C. on the basis of two C-14 dates of 5298 + 160 and 4161 + 90 B.C. from Period IA at Lahuradeva.[98] Saraswat has rightly pointed out that the presence of these was the result of either direct or indirect interaction between the people of the Indus and the Ganges systems. But he seriously missed the fact that this interaction was not with the people of the trans-Indus and Indus zones, rather it was with the people of the Indus system living in the western areas of the Upper Ganga Plains around the turn of the third millennium B.C. only, for their being closer to the Middle Ganga people both in terms of time and space. Its feasibility appears to be quite strong in the light of both the zones being contiguous, the former being endowed with a large number of Harappan settlements and these also contain grain remains of wheat, barley lentil, green gram, black gram, rice,[99] etc. This seems to have facilitated the mutual exchange of these grains between the two people—wheat, barley, lentil along with other legumes travelled to the Middle Ganga and rice came to the Upper Ganga in a two way traffic movement. The time period of this interaction coincides well with the upper limit of the earliest habitations in the Upper Ganga zone. If we try to push the date around 9th to 3rd millennium B.C., it would pose a serious problem of the non-presence of contiguous settlements as envisaged by Sharma[100] and the lack of supporting antecedent Chrono-cultural evidence in the Mid-Ganga Plains also, for the Neolithic and Neolithic-Chalcolithic settlements in this part of the land do not represent independent development, instead they are very much integral to the evolving cultural process of the Vindhyan region.

In the foregoing paragraphs what we experience in the field of subsistence is a sequential transition from the hunting-gathering mode upto the Mesolithic period to the incipient agriculture in the Neolithic period. This seems to have further graduated to a stage of primarily subsistence mode in the Neolithic and Neolithic-Chalcolithic phase and finally it attains the status of a surplus agricultural economy in the NBPW phase. This brings us to the question of as to how did these transitions take place over time and space? This question, obviously, can be addressed to by taking into account the changing tool-kit and the cultural deposits during the period in the following lines.

In the upper Palaeolithic levels the tools were made of stones and these were primarily consisting of limited types of blades and burins among others. Naturally these could generate a limited working capacity to harness the natural resources. The composition of the tools is changed in a big way during the succeeding Mesolithic period where we discover use of Microliths and their composite tools of a variety of stones. This was, of course, combined with bone-tools and their consequent effect is noticed in terms of tremendous increase in the working capacity of the people, which, in fact, propelled them to venture out in the alien open terrain of the Middle Ganga Plains. This promised a better life but only to be realized in due course. In the Neolithic period still better tools of stones, bones, antlers were produced that contributed towards the beginning of animal and plant husbandry, sedentary way of living and potters craft among others.

During the succeeding Chalcolithic phase, the use of copper is strictly restricted at almost all the excavated settlements. The overwhelming number of tools is of bones, antlers and stones of course, the order is reversed from stones to bones. This prompted Sharma to propose even a new term of 'Osteolithic' than Chalcolithic for this phase. Bone-points and arrow-heads abound in Narhan, Khairadih, Maner and Champa.[101] Copper tools are very few in Narhan, Prahladpur, Taradih and Maner,[102] they comprise of knives, spear-heads and arrow-heads. Two socketed arrow-heads, one each of bone and copper came from Khairadih.[103] The knowledge of socketing was better than hafting and may have prepared the way for socketing of the iron share into the wooden plough in succeeding NBPW levels.[104] This period is marked by the use of black and red ware, painted with white colour and came first from the site of Narhan[105] and these are decorated with incision, applique and painted designs profusely. Iron objects are absent from these levels though one arrow-head is said to have been recovered from the uppermost levels of this phase at Prahladpur,[106] another arrow-head from lower levels of period I at Dadupur and a fishing-hook impression with iron-rust grains on a mud clod from Narhan period I.[107] Among the agricultural tools, an iron plough-share comes from the uppermost levels of period I, pre-NBPW phase at Ganwaria.[108] These cultural remains from these levels are termed as Chalcolithic for general absence of iron objects. But Rakesh Tewari has argued in favour of naming these remains as 'early iron age'[109] on the basis of the above objects as well as the occurrence of iron objects from period-II at Raja Naī Ka Tila, district Sonbhadra,[110] period-II at Malhar, district Chandauli[111] and period-I of Dadupur, district Lucknow.[112] He is also placing it between 1700-1300 B.C. on the basis of C-14 dates, archaeological context and circumstantial evidences, which are seriously vulnerable to any scientific scrutiny of the whole range of available data. Without going into these details what we observe is that the pre-NBPW archaeologocial complex deserve a serious re-look. However, the number of iron objects, including agricultural tools such as shares, sickles, edges, knives, etc., goes substantially up during the succeeding NBPW levels.[113] And this change enhanced the working capacity of the people through the sequential stages of developments, which is so distinctly visible in the depositional patterns at the excavated sites and the happening of the 2nd urbanization in NBPW levels. This bring us to the question of as to what was the prime moving force in this case, the natural or social forces. We know that the natural forces have broadly been constant with minor oscillation well within their broad contours while the social forces underwent a range of transitions from the stone tool technology to the iron-technology with intervening stages of bone and copper applications. Interestingly in the Ganga Plains all these were at work at one stage or the other. The copper technology was with the Harappan people in the Upper Ganga as well as with the Chalcolithic people in the Middle Ganga Plains. In the case of the former, it failed to arrest the declining process of the Harappa civilization, while in the case of the latter it equally was unable to accelerate the pace of growth pattern beyond a limit despite the fact that in both the regions the natural landscape was very conducive, especially in comparison to the Indo-Gangetic Divide in the west. People also remained unsuccessful in realising the full potential of this favourable landscape even immediately after the introduction of iron objects on a limited scale in the early stages, rather it could become a reality only after greater application of these tools in the NBPW levels, especially from the middle levels onwards.

REFERENCES

1. *IAR*, 1958-59, p. 52.
2. *Ibid.*, 1965-64, pp. 53, 99; 1979-80, p. 82.
3. *Ibid.*, 1965-66, p. 44.
4. *Ibid.*, 1952-53; 1962-63, p. 34; 1966-67, p. 33; 1970-71, p. 37; 1984-85, pp. 86-88.
5. *IAR*, 1970-71, p. 37; 1974-75, pp. 42, 45; 1985-86, p. 79; 1986-87, p. 77; 1982-83, p. 99; 1991-92, p. 104.

6. *Ibid.*, 1958-59, p. 52; 1962-63, pp. 31, 34, 70; 1963-64, pp. 43-44, 91; 1964-65, pp. 42, 76; 1965-66, p. 42; 1966-67, p. 33; 1970-71, p. 37; 1974-75, p. 42; 1975-76, pp. 45, 50-51; 1978-79, p. 101; 1982-83, p. 99; 1986-87, p. 80; 1991-92, pp. 97, 104.
7. *Ibid.*, 1978-79, p. 58.
8. *Ibid.*, 1964-65, p. 76; 1965-66, p. 41; 1966-67, pp. 41-43; 1971-72, pp. 79-80; 1974-75, pp. 42-43; 1991-92, p. 104.
9. Vibha Tripathi 'A Macro Level Study of PGW Culture' *Pragdhara*, I, 1990-91, p. 93.
10. *IAR*, 1965-66, p. 41; 1966-67, pp. 41-43; 1972-73, pp. 79-80, 1974-75, pp. 42-43; 1977-78, p. 51; 1981-82, p. 100.
11. Colleagues from Allahabad University and BHU, Varanasi have done commendable research work in this context and they have published their data in *IAR*, *Pragdhara* and other publications. According to them, the history of mankind begins sometime in Palaeolithic Stage.
12. There is a very interesting debate on this issue in the light of new researches and this should continue for further refinement. Usually the process of development has not been uniform and we witness differences in time scale from one region to the other. The archaeological data need to be situated in their contexts.
13. V.D. Misra, 'The Mesolithic Cultures of the Vindhyas with Special Reference to Environment and Archaeology', in B.M. Khanduri and Vinod Nautiyal (eds.), *Him-kanti* (Prof. K.P. Nautiyal Felicitation Volume), Book India Publishing Co., Delhi, 1977, pp. 41-42.
14. Purushottam Singh and Ashok Kumar Singh, *The Archaeology of Middle Ganga Plain*, Aryan Books International, New Delhi, 2004, p. 7.
15. *Ibid.*
16. D.K. Chakrabarti, *India: An Archaeological History*, OUP, New Delhi, 1999, p. 102.
17. *IAR*, 1966-67, p. 38; 1977-78, pp. 51-52; 1978-79, pp. 56-57.
18. *Ibid.*, 1971-72, p. 44; 1973-74, pp. 45-47.
19. *Ibid.*, 1977-78, pp. 54-56; 1978-79, p. 57.
20. V.D. Misra, *et.al.*, 'A Preliminary Report of the Excavation at Jhusi, 1995', *Pragdhara*, Lucknow, 1996, pp. 63-66; idem 'Further Excavation at Jhusi (1998-1999)', *Pragdhara*, 10, Lucknow, 2000, p. 28.
21. *IAR*, 1982-83, pp. 99-100; 1983-84, pp. 90-92.
22. *Ibid.*, 1977-78, pp. 58-59; 1978-79, pp. 59-60.

23. *Ibid.*, 1969-70, pp. 43-44; 1971-72, pp. 48-49; 1972-73, p. 35.
24. *Ibid.*, 1962-63, p. 37; 1963-64, pp. 51-53.
25. *Ibid.*, 1983-84, p. 149. Anil Kumar and P.C. Pant, 'Economy of the Neolithic Cultures of Southern Uttar Pradesh and Western Bihar,' *Puratattva*, 30, New Delhi, 1999-2000, pp. 25-29.
26. *IAR*, 1989-90, pp. 102-05; 1981-82, p. 106; 1983-84, p. 149.
27. V.D. Misra, *et al.*, 'Excavation at Tokwa: A Neolithic-Chalcolithic Settlement,' *Pragdhara*, II, Lucknow, 2001, pp. 59-72; J.N. Pal, 'A History of the Development of Human Cultures in the Tons Valley' in K.K. Chakrabarti and G.L. Badam (eds.), *River Valley Cultures of India*, Aryan Books International, New Delhi, 2005, pp. 35-37.
28. J.N. Pal, *Archaeology of Southern Uttar Pradesh: Ceramic Industries of Northern Vindhyas*, Allahabad, 1986, pp. 133, 66; *IAR*, 1971-72, p. 44.
29. D. Mandal 'Cultures of the Vindhyas: Excavations at Mahagara in the Belan Valley' in V.D. Misra and J.N. Pal (eds.), *Indian Pre-history*, University of Allahabad, Allahabad, 1977, pp. 163-74.
30. There is a need to review the date in the light of fresh information. R.C. Thakran 'Early Food Production Activities in Punjab,' *Social Science Probings*, December 2004, pp. 1-22.
32. R. Tewari *et.al.*, 'Excavation at Lahuradeve, District Sant Kabir Nagar, Uttar Pradesh,' *Puratattva*, 32, New Delhi, 2001-02, pp. 54-62.
33. *IAR*, 1974-75, pp. 46-47.
34. *Ibid.*, 1991-92, pp. 107-09; 1992-93, pp. 92-93.
35. *Ibid.*, 1982-83, pp. 92-94; 1983-84, pp. 86-87.
36. *Ibid.*, 1981-82, pp. 13-14; Purushottam Singh, *The Neolithic Origins*, Agam Kala Prakasham, New Delhi, 1991; R.S. Sharma, *The State and Varna Formation in the Mid Ganga Plains*, Manohar, New Delhi, 1996, p. 28.
37. *Ibid.*
38. *IAR*, 1984-85, pp. 89-91; Purushottam Singh, *Excavations at Nurhan* (1984-89), B.H.U. and B.R. Publishing House Corporation, Delhi, 1994.
39. *IAR*, 1991-92, pp. 107-09; 1992-93, pp. 92-93.
40. Singh and Singh, *op.cit.*, 2004, pp. 12-13.
41. *Ibid.*
42. *IAR*, 1982-83, p. 93.
43. Sharma, *op.cit.*, 1996, p. 68.

44. *IAR*, 1962-63, p. 41; A.K. Narain and T.N. Roy, *Excavations at Prahladpur, March-April 1963*, B.H.U., Varanasi, 1968.
45. *IAR*, 1961-62, p. 57; 1962-63, pp. 41-42.
46. *Ibid.*, 1978-79, p. 57; 1982-83, pp. 91-92; 1983-84, pp. 84-85; 1984-85, pp. 85-86.
47. R. Tewari, *et al.*, 'Excavation at Malhar, district Chandauli (U.P.) 1999: A Preliminary Report', *Pragdhara*, 10, Lucknow, 1999-2000, pp. 69-98.
48. Singh and Singh, *op. cit.*, 2004.
49. *IAR*, 1983-84, p. 12; 1984-85, p. 10; 1985-86, p. 8.
50. Sharma, *op. cit.*, 1996, p. 29.
51. B.P. Sinha and B.S. Verma, *Sonpur Excavations* (1956 and 1959-62), Directorate of Archaeology and Museums, Bihar, Patna, 1977. Sharma, *op. cit.*, 1996, p. 29.
53. *Ibid.*, p. 36; Singh and Singh, *op. cit.*, 2004, p. 12, They have listed a number of sites of this period.
54. Sharma, *op. cit.*, 1996.
55. *Ibid.*, Singh and Singh, *op. cit.*, 2004.
56. R.C. Thakran, *Kya Harappa Sabhyata Saraswat Thi*, New Delhi, 2002; Idem. 'The Myth of Saraswati Civilization: Locational Analysis of Harappan Sites, *PIHC*, Bhopal, 2002, pp. 945-64.
57. R.C. Thakran, 'Recent Archaeological Explorations along the Ghaggar in Rajasthan', *PIHC*, 2006-07, pp. 92-1000.
58. K.S. Saraswat 'Crop Economy of Late Harappans at 'Hulas', *Puratatttva*, 123, New Delhi, 1992-93, pp. 1-12.
59. G.M. Buth and K.A. Chaudhary 'Plant Remains from Atranjikhera, Phase III (1200-600 B.C.),' In *Botanist*, XX, 3, 1971.
60. *Ibid.*
61. Saraswat, *op.cit.*, 1992-93.
62. *Ibid.*
63. *Ibid.*
64. *Ibid.*
64. *Ibid.*
65. *Ibid.*
66. *IAR*, 1993-94, p. 144.
67. *Ibid.*
68. Buth and Chaudhary, *op. cit.*, 1971.
69. Saraswat, *op. cit.*, 1992-93.
70. *Ibid.*
71. *Ibid.*
72. *Ibid.*

73. *Ibid.*
74. Sharma, *op. cit.*, 1996, pp. 32-68.
75. *Ibid.*, p. 68.
76. V.D. Misra, 'Origin, Chronology and Transformation of the Mesolithic Culture in India', in V.D. Misra and J.N. Pal, (eds.), *Mesolithic India*, Allahabad, 2002, p. 458.
77. M.D. Kajale, 'Some Initial Observations on Palaeo-botanical Evidence for Mesolithic Plant Economy from Excavations at Damdama, Pratapgarh, Uttar Pradesh,' in N.C. Ghosh and S.C. Chakrbati (eds.), *Adaptation and Other Essay*, Visva Bharati, Santiniketan, 1990, pp. 98-102.
78. This needs to be further explored.
79. *IAR*, 1983-84, p. 178.
80. M.D. Kajale, 'Current Status of Indian Palaeobotany: Introduced and Indigenous Food Plants,' in Jane Renfew (ed.), *New Light on Early Forming*, Edinburgh, 1991, p. 164.
81. P.C. Pant, 'Indus Civilization *Versus* Mahagara Neolithic Culture: A Note on Acculturation,' *Paravritta*, 1, 2001, p. 69.
82. Kajale, *op. cit.*, 1990, pp. 98-102.
83. Thakran, *op. cit.*, 2006-07.
84. G.R. Sharma, *et al.*, *Beginning of Agriculture*, Abhinava Prakashan, Allahabad, 1980.
85. *Ibid.*, Mandal, *op. cit.*, 1977, pp. 163-74.
86. V.D. Misra, *et al.*, *op. cit.*, 2001.
87. K.S. Saraswat and Anil Kumar Pokharia, 'The Emerging Trends of Early Agriculture Economy in Middle Ganga Plain, with Special Reference to Lahurageva in South Asian Context', in Abstracts of the International Seminar on *First Farmers* in *Global Perspective*, Organised by the Directorate of Archaeology, Department of Culture, Government of Uttar Pradesh, Lucknow, January 18-20, 2006, p. 16.
88. *IAR*, 1981-82, p. 106; 1983-84, p. 149.
89. Rakesh Tewari, *et al.*, *op. cit.*, 2001.
90. Kajale, *op. cit.*, 1991.
91. Vishnu Mittre 'Neolithic Plant Economy at Chirand, Bihar', in *The Palaeobotanist*, 21, Lucknow, 1972, pp. 17-22; *IAR*, 1976-75, p. 78.
92. Kajale, *op. cit.*, 1991, p. 172.
93. Pratap Singh, 'Stages of Culture Development in the Middle Ganga Plains—A Case Study of Senuwar', *Pragdhara*, II, 2001, pp. 109-18.
94. Sharma, *op. cit.*, 1996, p. 68.

95. *Ibid.*
96. Saraswat and Pokharia, *op. cit.*
97. *Ibid.*
98. Rakesh Tewari and Pokharia, *op. cit.*
99. The history of their domestication is very old and associated with West Asia.
100. Sharma, *op. cit.*, 1996, p. 29.
101. *Ibid.*
102. *Ibid.*, p. 32.
103. *Ibid.*
104. *Ibid.*
105. Singh, *op. cit.*, 1991.
106. Sharma, *op. cit.*, p. 68.
107. Rakesh, *et al.*, *op. cit.*, 2001-02, pp. 113-14.
108. Sharma, *op. cit.*
109. Rakesh and Srivastava, *op. cit.*, 1996-97.
110. *Ibid.*
111. Rakesh, *et al.*, *op. cit.*, 1999-2000.
112. Rakesh, *et al.*, *op. cit.*, 2001-02
113. Sharma, *op. cit.*, 1996, p. 68.

12. *Dharma, Artha* and Politics in Ancient India

Aparna Mathur

(I)

Values, traditions and institutions are indicators through which one can have an insight into the mind and soul of any culture.[1] They can be used as sources to illustrate the accurate representation of the legacy that a particular culture owes in various spheres. Indian culture also laid emphasis on certain values which are responsible for the emergence of a peculiar kind of value-system[2] distinguishing Indian way of life from other ancient societies. All notions, beliefs, terms, concepts and institutions etc., developed in ancient India, are influenced directly or indirectly by the value-system.[3]

Polity also emerged in India, in consonance with the prevailing value-system which is manifested through a combination of four-fold values popularly called *Purusartha-Catustaya*[4] or human ends. This scheme of four-fold values is a synthesis of material, moral and spiritual values. They are included in it as *Dharma, artha, kama* and *moksa.* In these four values *kama* and *moksa* are the extrinsic values or 'goals' to be achieved and aims towards the attainment of satisfaction temporal and transcendental respectively. *Dharma* and *artha* on the other hand are included in this scheme as intrinsic values or 'means' which help in the realization of *kama* and *moksa*. The end which polity has to promote ultimately formed the part of this scheme of four-fold values, but "the direct objective of its policy were defined as *dharma* and *artha*."[5] Thus both these values, meant for the righteous things and well-being of humans, played a significant role in the development of political philosophy of ancient India.

Most of the available sources on polity reveal that the guiding principles of the polity were based on these two ideals only and they give birth to two different schools of political philosophy namely the *dharma* and the *artha* schools. While the former school is manifested in the laws of *Dharmasastras*, in the *Rajdharma* section of *Mahabharata* and in the *Smrtis*, the latter one is manifested chiefly in the *Arthasastra* of Kautilya. The aim of the present paper is to seek relations between these two schools of Indian polity and analyze their influence on the socio-political developments in ancient India.

(II)

Dharma is the core concept of Indian political theory profound in its implication and subject to varied definition.[6] Radha Krishnan regards it as "the most important concept in Indian thought."[7] Etymologically the word is derived from the root '*dhr*' meaning "to be firm or support."[8] By usage, the term is employed in many senses. To the ancient Indian, this word had different meanings in different contexts. In its various meanings, it stands for ordinance, usage, duty, right, justice, virtue, religion, good work, functions, innate propriety of thing, moral precepts and righteous course of conduct.[9]

Scholars have tried to interpret the term from various

angles and as a result we have a variety of definitions. For Zimmer it means "the fixed order of heaven and earth",[10] to Macdonell[11] "it is law or custom covering both criminal and civil law and morality"; Keith equated it with custom, law and righteous conduct;[12] to Hopkins it means "ethical good usage";[13] Mckenzie argued that term covers not only conduct but the whole conglomeration of forms of conduct that were settled or established.[14] Bhagwan Das denotes it as an ethico-religious conception,[15] while Radha Krishnan opines that *dharma* is the stable condition, capable of giving perfect satisfaction to man and of helping him in the attainment of happiness and salvation.[16] Kane interprets it as "the mode of life or a code of conduct";[17] Sinha opines that it may "bear the interpretation of customs and usage both sacred and secular in society."[18] G.H. Mees defines it as "the fundamental force in the life of man as a social being";[19] and so on. Above discussion is sufficient to show that scholars tried to interpret the term from various angles. In this context we can also argue that in the *Mahabharata*[20] term has been defined as which bears (maintains) society (people by establishing) order. So the conception of *dharma* was a far reaching one embracing the whole life of man. It regulated a man's work and activities as a member of society and as an individual and was intended to bring about the gradual development of a man and to enable him to reach what was deemed to be the goal of human existence.[21] In the realm of polity, *Dharma* stands in a manner reminiscent of Plato for justice as well as for the social allocation of role and duties. *Rajdharma* as political obligation is part of *dharma* in the wider sense and as constituted by the duty of conforming to and supporting in traditionally conceived socio-ethical order.[22] Around 4th century B.C. the tribal set up of ancient India was losing its relevance due to new agrarian, commercial and political developments. To sustain new ideology, new codes of political behavior were required and that appeared on scene in the form of *Dharmasutras* which later on reconstituted in the *Rajdharma* section of *Mahabharata* and in *Smrtis* with more profound ideology.

(III)

Artha which occupies an important place in the Indian scheme of four-fold values, has been treated in the scheme of *Purusartha* as a material-empirical value which is instrumental to achieve *kama*.[23] But in a wider sense it is a name for all values belonging to the empirical life.[24] *Artha*, for example, in the *Rgveda*, is generally used in empirical or material sense. It denotes the wish,[25] goal,[26] aim,[27] gain,[28] end,[29] wealth,[30] object,[31] purpose,[32] limit,[33] etc. In fact, all those object of wealth and prosperity which man wishes to achieve for the fulfillment of his material and empirical needs, either through his labour, earning or barter are *'artha'*; the pleasure and joy which he gets through the satisfaction of his desires is also included in *'artha'*.[34] Vatsyayana said in his *Kamasutra* that *artha* "is the acquisition of arts, land, gold, cattle, wealth and friends. It is also the protection of what is acquired and the increase of what is protected."[35] Literally, *artha* stands for an object, a thing or a referent or a substance.[36] In the *Amarkosa* it is used in the sense of wealth purpose, object or prohibition.[37] Zimmer has pointed out that the term "comprises a whole range of tangible objects that can be possessed, enjoyed and lost, and which we require in daily life, for the upkeeping of a household, raising of a family and discharge of religious duties, all that is necessary for the virtuous fulfillment of life's obligation."[38]

It also signifies that objects through which pleasure can be achieved. The word *'artha'* thus, "connotes the attainment of riches and worldly prosperity,[39] material advantage, wealth and all that which concern commercial life, business matter, business affair, work, price, etc. and in the sphere of law it means plaint, action, petition,"[40] in the politics it is interest of state. In life, in general, it is utility, i.e. what is useful.[41] With reference to the external world, *'artha'* in its widest connotation signifies that which can be perceived; an object of senses, with reference to the interior world of psyche, "end and aim, purpose, object, wish, desire, motive, cause, reason, interest, use, want and concern."[42] The term, thus, as pointed out by Zimmer bounds together all the meanings of:—

1. The object of pursuit
2. The meaning of this pursuit
3. The needs and the desires suggesting this pursuit.[43]

Potter has suggested that *artha* indicated for Indian "an attitude of minimum concern towards those things which are manipulated in making of a living."[44]

Kautilya in his *Arthasastra* defines *artha* technically as the livelihood *(vrittih)* of man and inhabited land and *Arthasastra* as the science of maintaining and protecting that earth.[45] His treatise gave rise to a new line of thoughts in the brahmanical ideology. This ideology emphasized on *artha* as strategy of state. The reasons were inherent in the socio-political sphere of the age. This was an era which witnessed the setting up of state on firm footing in the form of Mauryan Empire.[46] As, according to tradition, Kautilya was the teacher as well as prime minister of Candragupta Maurya, the founder of Mauryan dynasty, therefore, the problem before Kautilya was to manage the state affairs and protect this newly founded kingdom, so he wrote a practical testimony to guide emperor in every situation.[47] Up to the age of Kautilya king had been considered responsible for everything, beneficial or unbeneficial, that occurred in his kingdom.[48] The prime responsibility of king was to maintain law and order in the society so that their remain peace and harmony and people could earn their riches easily.[49] The Kautilyan concept of *artha* can be understood only by relating it to the state and politics. This notion of *artha* includes in itself both manpower and inhabited land or earthly resources. Both were essential for state because these two elements constitute the backbone of the state economy.[50] As Kautilya was realist in approach, he was well aware of the importance of both these resources in the development of country.[51] This unparallel importance of these resources was already realized in the later Vedic period when the tribal states were transformed into territorial.[52] This also indicated that the people of those states had developed skill in agricultural activities for which they needed more and more land for cultivation, hence an agriculture-based society was being emerged slowly and slowly.[53] With an increase in the importance of land[54] as the main source of prosperity imperialist tendencies grew that resulted in the development of sixteen Mahajanapadas in the age of Buddha and finally in the unification of country under the rule of imperial Mauryas. According to Kautilya livelihood of man is "'*artha*' because without it survival of life is not possible. It is *vritti* through which men earned their riches.[55] Kautilya is of the view that the root of *artha*-benefits is *vritti*.[56] It is related intimately with *Varta*[57] which as a totality of the agriculture, cattle-rearing and trade and commerce, is highly important for state for the development of a sound economic system to fulfill the basic requirements of its subjects and also for developing into a prosperous state.

(IV)

The idea of polity was developed for the smooth functioning of the society and simultaneously for the well-being of its members. Passages in different texts—Brahmanical, Buddhist or Jain—refers to a golden age in which without any political relationship and obligations everyone was living happily and peacefully.[58] In other words, we can submit that in all above mentioned sources there are references to a pre-state society where humans were living peacefully without any sufferings and troubles. But somehow this golden age ended and era of chaos and anarchy prevailed.[59] In this age all social interests and values were degraded. People faced problems and the smooth functioning of the society was affected.[60] To get rid from this uncomfortable situation, for the well-being of the individual and society, for protecting their interests and values polity was emerged.[61] Therefore polity in India was expected to promote public good and happiness through the adoption of a policy ultimately backed by force *(danda)* but in accordance with right *(dharma)*.[62] *Rajdharma* as political obligation is part of *dharma* in the wider sense and is constituted by the duty of conforming to and supporting the traditionally conceived socio-ethical order. *Artha* stands for interest and utilities, for power and good. Although objectively seen, the contents of *dharma* and *artha* would seem to overlap. Their distinction arises from the way in which each is given to us. *Dharma* is transcendently given. It cannot be apprehended by mere instinct, perception or reason. *Artha* on the other hand, to what is desired. *Dharma* as the Law is primarily revealed but practically known through tradition. *Artha,* comprising economic and administrative affairs is known through the imperial sciences of *varta* and *dandaniti.*[63] Their influence varied from time to time, with one on the other gaining importance in deciding the state policy. However, many a times, perhaps often expediency and exigencies of circumstances determined the state policy.

The goals of the state according to both the schools are the same, i.e. to preserve and maintain the society in a way that the ends of human existence could be pursued by all without any kind of hindrance—internal or external. In essence, it is so preserve the social order establish peace and promote such activities as to help all to achieve the goals of life.[64] Both the schools further agree that the way in which the state could work for the above end is through the proper exercise of *danda* (punishment), hence the term *dandaniti* is to be seen common to both. It is only with reference to the method of operation and the degree of freedom allowed to the state to use the power of *danda* that the schools vary.[65]

Dharma as conceived in the *Rajdharma* section of the *Mahabharata* is concerned with the social as well as individual good. According to the *dharma* school protection and establishment of *dharma* has been proclaimed to be an important function of state. *Mahabharata* in the "Shantiparva" gives extraordinary importance to *dharma* and goes to the extent of saying that it is for the cause of *dharma* that sovereignty exists.[66] For the realization of this function, a state is given the right of exercising *danda* (coercion). *Danda* was regarded to be capable of restraining[67] the natural turbulence and depravity of men which led them to violate different rules and regulations. It was *danda* which made them follow *dharma.*[68] In the absence, chaos prevailed and people did not do their duties.[69] Manu very clearly states that people become righteous only due to the fear of danda.[70] In its absence vices creeps in, hence *danda* is *dharma.*[71] According to *Mahabharata,* it is the duty of a King to punish the wicked and the unrighteous people[72] and establish *dharma* thereby. Manu insisted that if King does not punish such persons, he earns infamy and goes to hell.[73] Like any person, the King too is bound to operate within the limits of *dharma* associated with kingship. A King becomes unworthy and liable to be deprived of kingship if he does not carry out his duties within the framework of *dharma.*[74] This *dharma* is the established code of social conduct enshrined in the traditional scriptures. Even the King's inclination too cannot over- ride the precepts of the *dharma* virtually it means under normal circumstances he could hardly exercise his discretion. His conduct, too, is bound by *dharma*. Thus the *dharma* school curbs the growth of any type of authoritarians and totalitarian state.[75]

The *artha* school on the other hand, provides extra ordinary powers to the King. Kautilya asserts that there are four legs of law, namely *dharma* (sacred law), *Vyavhara* (contract), *Charita* (custom) and *Rajasasana* (royal decree). Each succeeding one of superior validity than the one previously named.[76] Hence while the *dharma* occupies the last place, royal decree is made the ultimate authority, though neither Kautilya nor those who followed him give any theoretical basis for this exalted position of ruler. But Kautilya's work being more a Manual of statecraft, its assertions is supposed to be for practical use than for theoretical explanation.[77] Kautilya supported the idea of monarchy. That is the only type of state which Kautilya upholds, as can be seen in his merciless views on republican state, which is clearly in contrast to the views of the *dharma* school, in which the state governing the people in the *dharma* way is more important that the type of state.[78]

While the fulfillment of the goal of state is most important for the *dharma* school, by way of proper protection of *dharma* through the means of *danda,* the *artha* school shifts its emphasis from *dharma* to the wielder of *danda.* It is the resources and strength of the state in a way the King himself who ensures these in his state, that can ensures achievement of the state objectives.[79] This shift brings in a sea-change in the nature of the state. War and conquest becomes an essential part of state's operation which a king has to conduct for acquiring land, wealth and allies, so that the security of the state is strongly maintained. This school also emphasizes the complete control on the economy of state which is an essential requirement for the proper functioning of the state. The king exercising his authority has to bestow his attention on all types of measures required for ensuring the increase of wealth in his territory by providing proper support to such activities as wealth and agriculture. A sound system of administration has to develop to exercise control over all aspects of trade, commerce and other activities so that the treasury is always replenished well from time to time. This control is equally important according to the *Arthasastra,* to safeguard the people at large from exploitation by those enraged in economic operations.[80]

(V)

From the above discussion it is quite clear that both *Arthasastra* and the *Rajdharma* have virtually the same nature, involving in either case the art of government in a state. The *Arthasastra* however confines itself exclusively to the investigation of the phenomena of the state while *Rajdharma* deals with the same as an incident in a comprehensive scheme of duties. *Arthasastra* lacks the positive character attaching to the *Rajdharma* by virtue of the latter's association with the great concept of *dharma.* Since *Rajdharma* is equivalent to the whole duty of the King, its rules are determined by the ideal of the highest good of this individual. *Arthasastra,* on the other hand, avowedly for its end the security and prosperity of the state. Accordingly its rules of kingly conduct are determined primarily with reference to the interests of the state alone. In conflicting situations both these schools propagate their own objective *artha* school subordinate *dharma* principles to justify its views and *dharma* school does the vice-versa.

NOTES AND REFERENCES

1. Mukherjee, R.K., *The Destiny of Civilization,* Bombay, 1964, pp. 31-32; Devraj, N.K., *Samskrti Kai Darsanika Vivecana,* Lucknow, 1972, pp. 171-72; Hiriyana, M., *Indian Conception of Values,* Mysore, 1975, p. 5; Sinha, A.K., "On the Problem of Cultural Identity with special reference to Ancient Indian and Greek Cultures," in U.P. Arora (ed.), *Graco-Indica Demetrius Galanos Memorial Volume,* Delhi, 1989, pp. 280-81.
2. Pande, G.C., *An Approach to Indian Culture and Civilization,* Varanasi, 1985, pp. 20-22; Mukherjee, R.K., *op. cit.,* pp. 22-24; Radha Krishnan, S., *Indian Philosophy,* Vol. I. London, 1929, pp. 24-25.
3. Mukherjee, R.K., *op. cit.,* pp. 31-32; Sinha, A.K., *op. cit.,* pp. 280-81.
4. Das, Bhagwan, *Purusartha,* Varanasi, 1966, p. 47; Tripathi, P.V., *Purusartha Catustay,* Varanasi, 1970, p. 5; Pandey, R.B., *Hindu Dharma Kosa* (IInd ed.), 1988, p. 409; Lal, Kanvar, *The Cult of Desire* (3rd ed.), Delhi, 1982, p. 9; Devaraj, N.K., *The*

Mind and Spirit of India, Varanasi, 1967, p. 96; Murty, Satya, K., *Indian Heritage and Culture*, p. 75; Hiriyana, M., *op. cit.*, pp. 6-7; Pande, G.C., *Mulya Mimamsa*, Jaipur, 1973, p. 259.

5. Pande, G.C., 'The Conception of Ancient Indian State' in *Vajpeya*, Prof. K.D. Bajpai Felicitation Volume, p. 373.
6. According to Van Buitenen, "*dharma* is all that activity that a man if he to live fittingly is required to contribute to the fixed order of things to the norms of the universe, which is good and not to be altered."— Buitenen, J.A.B. Van, 'Dharma and Moksa' in *Philosophy: East and West*, Vol. 7, No. 1-2, 1957, p. 36, downloaded from www.jstor.org. on 14/3/11; Tripathi, P.V., *op. cit.*, pp. 30-31.
7. Radha Krishnan, S., *op. cit.*, p. 52.
8. Kane, P.V., *History of the Dharmasastra*, Vol. 1, Poona, 1968, p. 1; Dasgupta, Surama, *Development of Moral Philosophy in India*, Bombay, 1978, p. 5.
9. The term Dharma cannot be taken as an equivalent to English Religion. "*Dharma* is neither religion, nor philosophy, nor culture exclusively, it is all the three rolled into one." Harsh Narayan, "The Dharmic Outlook in Studies" in Madhu Sen (ed.), *Religion and Change*, Delhi, 1985, p. 5; Zimmer, H., *Philosophies of India*, p. 163, as quoted by Organ, T.W., *The Hindu Quest for the Perfection of Man*, p. 131; For different meanings of *dharma* see, Kane, P.V., *History of Dharamsastra*, Vol. I, pp. 1-4.
10. Zimmer, H., *Altindischen Leben*, Berlin, 1879, p. 180, as quoted by Salatore, B.A., *Ancient Indian Political Thoughts and Institutions*, Bombay, 1963, p. 11.
11. Macdonell, A.A. and Keith, A.B., *Vedic Index*, Vol. 1, London, 1912, pp. 390-98.
12. Keith, A.B., *A History of Sanskrit Literature*, Oxford, 1928, pp. 92, 450-67.
13. Hopkins, E.W., *Ethics of India*, New Haven, 1924, p. 92.
14. Mckenzie, J.S., *Hindu Ethics*, Oxford, 1922, p. 51.
15. Das, Bhagwan, *The Science of Social Organisation*, Madras, 1910, p. 7.
16. Radha Krishnan, *op. cit.*, pp. 501-506.
17. Kane, P.V., *op. cit.*, Vol. II, Poona, 1941, p. 2.
18. Sinha, H.N., *Sovereignty in Ancient India*, London, 1938, p. 27.
19. Mees, G.H., *Dharma and Society*, Preface, p. xii, as quoted by Jauhari, M., *Politics and Ethics in Ancient India*, Varanasi, 1968, p. 74.

20. *Mahabharata,* 'Kama,' 69.58.
21. Kane, P.V., *op. cit.,* No. 17.
22. Pande, G.C., *op. cit.,* No. 5.
23. Mathur, A., *The Arthasastra Tradition and Ancient Indian Value-System,* Delhi, 2009, p. 104.
24. *Ibid.,* pp. 40-41.
25. *Rgveda,* 1.102; 105.2.
26. *Ibid.,* 1.38.2; 2. 30.2; 3.53.5; 6.1.3; 6.32.5; 7.18.9, 63.4; 10.51.4,73.5, 143.1.
27. *Ibid.,* 1.158.6; 7.63.4.
28. *Ibid.,* 1.113.6
29. *Ibid.,* 1.130.5, 158.6
30. *Ibid.,* 3.11.3; 8.69.17.
31. *Ibid.,* 4.13.3, 10.27.20.
32. *Ibid.,* 1.124.1; 2.39.1.
33. *Ibid.,* 10.184.
34. *Ibid.,* 5.53.5.
35. Vatsyayana's *Kamasutra,* Chokhamba Series, Varanasi, 1.1.
36. Sinha, A.K., *Readings in Early Indian Socio-Cultural History,* New Delhi, 2000, p. 48.
37. *Amar Kosa,* 3.3.86.
38. Zimmer, H., *Philosophies of India,* Campbell, J. (ed.), New York, 1953, p. 35.
39. Gupta, Shantinath, *The Indian Concept of Values,* Delhi, 1978, p. 48.
40. Pant, A.D., *A Critical Study of Arthasastra Tradition in Ancient Indian Political Thought,* (Unpublished D.Litt. Thesis) Allahabad, 1966, pp. 139-40.
41. Gokhale, B.G., *India Through Ages,* pp. 54-55.
42. Pant, A.D., *op. cit.,* p. 140; Gupta, S.N., *op. cit.*
43. Zimmer, H., *op. cit.,* pp. 35-36.
44. Potter, K.H., *Presuppositions of India's Philosophies,* New Delhi, 1965, as quoted by Pant, A.D., *op. cit.,* p. 140.
45. *The Kautiliya Arthasastra* 15.1; Jayswal, K.P., *Hindu Polity,* Part I, p. 5; Kangle, R.P., *The Kautilya Arthasastra: A Study,* Part III, p. l.
46. Roychowdhary, H.C., *Political History of Ancient India,* Calcutta, p. 263.
47. Sharma, R.S., *Aspects of Political Ideas and Institutions in Ancient India,* p. 22.
48. The Phrases like *Raja Kalasya Karanam,* etc. are frequently used in the *Mahabharata* and some other texts. Santi Parva,

67, 72, 73, 79, 91.6, 9, Udyoga Parva 132, 16; Sukranitisara 4.1.60; Kamandikiya Nitisara, 5.82.83; Kane, P.V., *History of Dharamsastra* (Hindi Tr.), Part II, Lucknow, 1972, pp. 601-04, 655.

49. *Arthasastra,* 1.3, 16-17; Altekar, A.S., *State and Government in Ancient India,* pp. 48-49.
50. *Arthasastra,* 13.4.5.
51. Sinha, A.K., *op. cit.,* p. 53.
52. Roy, B.P., *Later Vedic Economy,* pp. 118-19.
53. Srimali, K.M., *The Age of Iron and Religious Revolution,* New Delhi, 2007, pp. 10-12.
54. Verma, Jaya, *Pracina Bharata mein Mulya Cetna aur Artha,* New Delhi, 2001, p. 53.
55. *Ibid.,* p. 145.
56. *Canakya Sutra,* 1.88, as quoted by Verma, Jaya, *op. cit.,* p. 147.
57. P. Masson Oursel said that *Vrtti* which is the basis of *Varta* refers to the whole human activity; *artha* raises the questions of ends, *Varta* that of means.—Masson, Oursel P., *Ancient India,* p. 106 as quoted by Sinha A.K., *op. cit.,* p. 59, fn. 60.
58. *Markandeya Purana,* Ch. 49; *Vayu Purana,* i, Ch. 8; *Kurma Purana,* Ch. 29; *Visnu Purana,* Bk. I, Ch. 6; *Brahmanda Purana,* Chs. 29-31; *Padma Carita,* Ch. 3; *Digha Nikaya,* Aggann Sutta; Mahavastu, I, 340-48; *Santi Parva,* Chs. 59, 67, 69 and 206.
59. *Satapatha Brahmana,* 11. I.6-24; *Arthasastra,* 1.4.13-14; *Manu,* 7.3.20.
60. Sharma, R.S., *Aspects of Political Ideas and Institutions,* Delhi, 2009, pp. 50-51.
61. *Ibid.,* pp. 54-55.
62. Pande, G.C., *op. cit.,* pp. 373-74.
63. *Ibid.*
64. Jauhari, M., *op. cit.,* pp. 60-64.
65. *Ibid.,* pp. 56-59.
66. *Mahabharat,* Santi Parva, 90, 3, 14.
67. *Mahabharat,* Santi Parva, 122, 56.
68. *Ibid.,* 121, 36.
69. *Ibid.,* Adi Parva, 41, 27-31; Santi Parva, 15, 41-45; 121, 37-39.
70. *Manu,* VII, 22.
71. *Ibid.,* VII, 24; VII, 18.
72. *Mahabharat,* Santi Parva, 121, 8.
73. *Manu,* VIII, 128.
74. For details, see Jauhari, M., *op. cit.,* Chs. 4 and 5.
75. Nagaraju, S., 'Dharma and Artha School in Indian Political

Philosophy' in *Krishnabhinandana,* New Delhi, 2008, pp. 338-39.

76. *Ibid.*
77. Murty, K.S., *Readings in Indian History, Politics and Philosophy,* London, 1967, p. 133.
78. Nagaraju, S., *op. cit.,* p. 339.
79. *Ibid.*
80. Murty, K.S., *op. cit.,* p. 134.

13. इतिहास में मानवीय मानस
खोज एवं संभावनाएं

विभा उपाध्याय

19वीं शताब्दी के उत्तरार्द्ध के यथार्थवादी युग में अनेक परिवर्तन हुए। एक ओर वैज्ञानिक चिंतन पद्धति ने डार्विन के विकासवाद के माध्यम से जीव विज्ञान में ऐतिहासिक परिवर्तन की अवधारणा पुष्ट की तो दूसरी ओर मानव ज्ञान के ऐतिहासीकरण की संभावनाएं प्रकट हुईं। एनी बेसेंट के पदचिह्नों पर चलने वाली Helena Petrovna Blavatsky ने 1888 में पुस्तक लिखी *The Secret Doctrine* और तभी वैज्ञानिक नियमों को चुनौती देते हुए मानव अस्तित्व को महत्वपूर्ण बताया। उन्होंने पुस्तक की भूमिका में लिखा : "The aim this work may be thus stated to show that nature is not a fortutious concurrence of atoms and to assign to man his rightful place in the scheme of universe"..... इस प्रकार के लेखों ने बुद्धिवादी वर्ग में एक चेतना का विकास किया। 19वीं शताब्दी की बौद्धिक क्रांति ने एक ओर वैज्ञानिक पद्धति के माध्यम से मानवीय अध्ययन का प्रयास आरंभ किया तो दूसरी ओर मनुष्य का समाज के सदस्य के रूप में अध्ययन करते हुए समाजशास्त्र का सहारा लिया गया। मनुष्य और समाज के अध्ययन के लिए आर्थिक कारणों की मदद ली गई तो मनोवैज्ञानिक विश्लेषण से ऐतिहासिक परिवर्तनों को पढ़ने का प्रयास किया गया। इसी पृष्ठभूमि में इतिहास अध्ययन की कई अवधारणाएं प्रचलित हुईं। आधुनिक विश्व में परिवर्तन की प्रक्रिया का आरंभ मनुष्य की आत्म संचेतना के विकास से आरंभ होता है। देकार्त ने सर्वप्रथम कहा कि मानव वह प्राणी है जो न केवल सोच सकता है बल्कि अपनी सोच के बारे में भी सोच सकता है जो प्रेक्षण की प्रक्रिया में खुद अपना प्रेक्षण कर सकता

है। इस प्रकार मनुष्य अपने विचार और विचार का कार्यान्वयन दोनों ही है। लुई नेमियर ने मानव की भूमिका पर विशेष बल दिया, कालिंगवुड ने मानव के संपूर्ण ज्ञान के स्त्रोत के रूप में इतिहास-ज्ञान के महत्व को उचित ठहराया। स्पेंगलर और टॉयनबी ने मानव सभ्यताओं से इतिहास की पहचान की।

आधुनिक यूरोप में 20वीं शताब्दी के आरंभिक वर्षों में एक नया दृष्टिकोण उभर कर आया *'The New History'* जिसने मानव की सभ्यता के उदय, विकास और विकास की प्रक्रिया से संबंधित मानव शास्त्रीय, नृतत्वशास्त्रीय, आर्थिक, मनोवैज्ञानिक, सामाजिक, वैज्ञानिक, पुरातात्विक आदि-आदि सभी अवशेषों के अध्ययन का मार्ग प्रशस्त किया, जिससे भूत से परिचय तो हो सके साथ में समकालीन समय में उसके योगदान को भी समझा जा सके। इसी संदर्भ में आर्थिक इतिहास, सामाजिक इतिहास जैसी विधाएं विकसित होती चली गईं।

18वीं शताब्दी से ही ऐसे लेखन आरंभ हुए (उदाहरण के लिए 'Elie Halevy' का The English people in 1815)। इसमें सबसे महत्वपूर्ण योगदान माना गया फ्रांस के Marc Bloc का जिसने लिखा Original Character of French History 1931 और एक महत्वपूर्ण पत्रिका निकाली जाने लगी Annals of Economic and social History और इसे मानव को समझने के लिए एक मील के पत्थर के रूप में मान्यता प्राप्त हुई। इस लेखन की परंपरा ने धीरे-धीरे समाज के सभी वर्गों के रीति-रिवाज, विश्वासों आदि का भी अध्ययन कर सामाजिक इतिहास के विकास को पढ़ा और New History को Total History के रूप में जाना जाने लगा। कई पद्धतियां अपनाई गईं जन मानस को पढ़ने के लिए, मानव की समाज में घटित होने वाले सभी गतिविधियों का अध्ययन किया जाने लगा। मानव के व्यवहार को उसकी गतिविधियों के माध्यम (Mentality) से मानव विशेष और समाज के सामान्य अंग के रूप में पढ़ा गया। विश्व की विभिन्न जातियों के आचार-व्यवहार, रीति-रिवाज, विश्वास और अंधविश्वासों के माध्यम से जनजातियों की मानसिकता को कई बार अध्ययन का विषय बनाया गया। History of mentalities नामक कई ऐतिहासिक लेखन की परंपरा ने मानव विशेष के मानस में हो रही उथल-पुथल के प्रभाव के रूप में ही विश्व की कई बड़ी-बड़ी घटनाओं की व्याख्या की। उदाहरण के लिए, फ्रांस के राजा 'Charls V' के द्वारा अंतिम समय में मृत्यु शैय्या पर करों की माफी के संदर्भ में उसके मन में उठते उस नरक के भय को[1] पढ़ा गया। राजनीतिक सिद्धान्तों के पीछे व्यक्ति विशेष की मानसिक परिस्थितियों को उत्तरदायी मानते हुए आधुनिक विश्व की कई घटनाओं की व्याख्या की गई। लगभग आधुनिक

उदाहरण के माध्यम से यह सिद्ध करने का प्रयास किया कि मानवीय मानसिकता बहुत बार नियमों और सिद्धांतों के विपरीत भी काम करती है।

किंतु प्रश्न यह है कि History of Mentality क्या History of mind soul के संदर्भ में समझी जा सकती है। बहुत वाद-विवादों के बाद अंग्रेजी (Latin) भाषा के क्रमशः विकास में इसे (Mind) से संबद्ध किया गया। Mind से अतिरिक्त Mental से भी संबंधित कर इसका मानवीय मानसिकता विशेष और सामान्य दोनों के संदर्भ में अध्ययन किया गया। Lock (1632-1704) ने 'Theory of Mind' में प्राकृतिक विज्ञान की पद्धति से मानवीय प्रकृति को पढ़ने का प्रयास किया। Collingwood की मान्यता थी कि 'Mind' के अध्ययन के लिए ऐतिहासिक पद्धति ही अपनाई जानी चाहिए क्योंकि इतिहास 'विचारों का इतिहास' ही होता है। उदाहरण के लिए, यूनान में नगर राज्यों के उत्थान एवं पतन के पीछे मानव मन एवं मस्तिष्क के क्रियाकलापों की व्याख्या की जा सकती है। Thomas Reid (1710-1796 में 'An inquiry into Human Mind on the Principles of Common Senses' के माध्यम से मानव मन की खोज का संदेश दिया था और तभी से अंग्रेजी और स्काटिश परंपरा का आरंभ हुआ, वह थी 'Philosophy of Human Mind'। यह कहा गया कि यह विचार फ्रांसीसी Voltaire (1694-1778) के द्वारा Essai Sur L'Histoire Generale Sur Les Moeurs Et L'espirit des Nations (1756)* में सर्वप्रथम रखा गया। क्रमशः इस अध्ययन ने मानवीय मन की उथल-पुथल को धर्म, रीति-रिवाजों के माध्यम से समझना शुरू किया गया। मानवीय मन की आध्यात्मिक तड़प को History of Ideas के रूप में समझा गया और सामान्य जन के मन को उसके क्रियाकलापों, उसके बनाए गए उपकरणों के माध्यम से समझने का प्रयास किया गया।

आधुनिक समय में यह अध्ययन संभव हो सकता था, जहां विभिन्न जन-जातियों के जाति नियम, विश्वास और उपकरण सभी उपलब्ध थे।[2] इस प्रयास में कई बार इतिहासकार को मनोविज्ञान के क्षेत्र में भी प्रवेश लेना पड़ता है। मानवीय मन को समझने के लिए उसकी जीवनियां भी सहायक हो सकती हैं। उदाहरण के लिए, हिटलर अथवा मार्टिन लूथर हो या गांधी और नेहरू ही क्यों न हो। किंतु व्यक्ति विशेष के आधार पर अनुमान से समूह के कार्यों का विश्लेषण दुरूह ही है।

* Essay on the Morals and Character of the Nations from Charlemagne to Louis XIII.

उदाहरण के लिए, प्रथम विश्वयुद्ध की पूर्व संध्या पर यूरोप के समाज में दिखने वाली युद्ध की इच्छा का अध्ययन मनुष्य की आक्रामक प्रकृति के अध्ययन के प्रकाश में हुआ। किंतु तत्कालीन समय में खेतिहर समाज के नगरीकरण का इतिहास, लोकप्रिय साहित्य, संगीत गृहों के गीत, विरोध प्रदर्शन के गीत के माध्यम से युद्ध की सम्मानित व्याख्या अपेक्षित थी।

यह सब उस समय के लिए संभव है जब इतिहासकार के पास मानव मन को पढ़ने या समझने के तथ्य हो। प्राचीन समय में जबकि पुरातात्विक, जैविक, प्राणीशास्त्रीय साक्ष्य तो है, पर उनसे मानव मन को कैसे समझा जाए? इसके भी प्रयास हो रहे हैं। फिर भारतीय संदर्भ में इसे कैसे पढ़ा जाए। क्या यह केवल पाश्चात्य प्रणाली या पद्धति है जिससे मानवीय मन और आत्मा को समझा जा सकता है। ऐसा नहीं है। प्राचीन भारत में यह प्रयास तो वैदिक युग से ही दिखाई दे रहे हैं।

भारतीय ऐतिहासिक संदर्भ में 'Mind and Soul' को ढूंढ़ने के लिए दो माध्यम हैं एक तो इतिहास की व्याख्या अथवा परिभाषाओं में इतिहास का अध्ययन क्या सभ्यता, संस्कृति, आदि-आदि के साथ मन को भी सम्मिलित करता है। दूसरा भारतीय ऐतिहासिक लेखन अथवा भारतीय साहित्य अथवा भारतीय परंपरा में मन के विषय में क्या मिलता है।

इतिहास शब्द वैदिक है और सर्वप्रथम अथर्ववेद में प्रयुक्त हुआ। इति+ह+आस। भाष्यकार इति का अर्थ प्रायः गति बताते हैं वह भी विशिष्ट प्रकार की। कुछ-कुछ स्थानों पर वांछित अर्थ के प्रति होने वाली मानसिक गति का सूचक भी इति है, तवमर्थभिव त्वमित्यै, (*ऋग्वेद*, 1:11:3-6) इति वा इति में मनो (*ऋग्वेद*, 10:119:1)। अन्यत्र अति मानसिक अंतर्जगत की गति के लिए इति शब्द का प्रयोग हुआ : आ सूर्येव विधतो रथं गातृत्वेषप्रतीका नभसो नेत्या (*ऋग्वेद*, 1:167:5) अर्थात इति आंतरिक गति है और इस पर आसीन होना ही इतिहास है।

परंपरा के अनुसार इतिहास, धर्म, अर्थ, काम और मोक्ष का प्रदाता है और पूर्व कथा एवं वृत का संगम है। अर्थात इतिहास लौकिक और पारलौकिक दोनों पक्षों का उद्घाटन करता है—

धर्मार्थ काम मोक्षाणां उपदेश समन्वितम
पूर्व वृत्तं कथ युक्तं इतिहास प्रचक्ते।।[3]

इतिहास में मानव और लोक परिवेश दोनों का सामंजस्य है। वस्तुतः विश्व चक्र की मौलिक एकता में मन, प्राण और भूत तीनों में सृष्टा और सृष्टि का तारतम्य

विचारणीय है एवंन्मयो व अयमात्या वाङ्मयो मनोमयः प्राणमयः।[4] इसी सूत्र को रूपांकित करने के कारण ऋषि-मुनियों ने वाङ्मय में मन की संवेदनशीलता का महत्व दिया। विगत पीढ़ियों के असंख्य मानवीय विचारधारा, पुरुषार्थ व निष्ठाओं से युग महात्म्य बनता है और यही युग महात्म्य इतिहास का विषय है।[5]

वेदों की इतिहास विद्या "गाथा" इस विद्या का नाम है, जिसे यदि राजनैतिक इतिहास का साधन माना जाता है तो वहीं यह मनुष्य के आध्यात्मिक जगत की घटनाओं का भी प्रतीक शैली में वर्णन करती है। अथर्ववेद की इंद्र गाथा मनुष्य के भीतर होने वाले दाशराज्ञ युद्ध का वर्णन ब्रह्मरूपी यक्ष के सायुज्य संदर्भ से करती है। दूसरे शब्दों में, ब्रह्मात्म सायुज्य डूबा हुआ शुद्ध आत्मा गाथी है–

यदिन्द्रादो दाशराज्ञे मानुषं वि गाहथाः।
विरूपः सर्वस्मा मधवन्नभ्रं मर्याकरो इति।
त्वं रोहिणं व्यास्यो वि वृत्रस्या भिनच्छिरः।।
यः पर्वतान् व्यदधाददद यो अपो व्यगाहथाः
इंदो यो वृत्रहान्महं तस्मद्रिन्द नमो ऽस्तु ते।[6]

इसी प्रकार पुराण भी सृष्टि की उत्पत्ति के साथ-साथ आत्मा, वासना, ज्ञान आदि की भी चर्चा करते हैं। पुराणों के लक्षणों की चर्चा करते हुए उसके दस लक्षण बताए गए–सर्ग, विसर्ग, वंश, मन्वतर, वंशानुचरित, स्थान–ब्रह्मांड, पोषण–धर्म, उति–जीवों की कर्मवासना, निरोध–,आत्मसंयम के नियम, मुक्ति एवं आश्रय–ज्ञान, योग, आश्रय–भक्ति। अर्थात यह सब इतिहास के विषय हैं।

वैयक्तिक जीवन में समाज और राष्ट्र में इतिहास की उपयोगिता स्थापित करते हुए वेद व्यास लिखते हैं--

इतिहास प्रदीपेन मोहावरण धातिना,
लोक गर्भगृहं कृत्स्नं यथावत् स प्रकाशितम्।[7]

यहां लोक गर्भगृह का तात्पर्य लोक मानस रूपी गर्भगृह में स्थित वृत्तियों तथा रुचियों को केवल इतिहास रूपी प्रदीप ही प्रकाशित कर सकता है।

अर्थात भारतीय इतिहास का विषय तो आरंभिक काल से मानवीय चेतना रहा है। इसलिए पाश्चात्य अवधारणाओं पर निर्भर होने की आवश्यकता नहीं है।

अब यदि इतिहास में मानवीय मानस या आत्मा को पढ़ना है तो उसके साक्ष्य या तथ्य भी संकलित करने पड़ेंगे। पर इस अभ्यास से पूर्व Mind का हिंदी रूपांतर भी समझना पड़ेगा। वैदिक काल के महान महीषियों ने जगत की उत्पत्ति जड़

पदार्थ (प्रकृति) और चेतनतत्व (पुरुष) के संयोग से उत्पन्न मानी है। यह अष्टधा प्रकृति पृथ्वी, जल, अग्नि, वायु, आकाश; पंच महाभूत और मन, बुद्धि और अहंकार में विभक्त स्वयं कृष्ण की प्रकृति है। जो मानवीय वातावरण की द्योतक है। पंचमहाभूत जीव या मानव का बाह्य स्वरूप है तो मन, बुद्धि और अहंकार आंतरिक स्वरूप है। मन को चित्त का पर्याय भी माना गया है। अर्थात Mind का अर्थ मन, चित्त, बुद्धि और अहंकार को यदि लिया भी जा सके तो Soul क्या भारतीय परंपरा की आत्मा है जो अकर्त्ता भी है, ज्ञेय भी है। सत्य भी है, शाश्वत भी है। ऐसे में बाह्‌य उपकरणों से आत्मा को समझना दुरुह लगता है। समन्वयात्मक दृष्टि से यदि मन, बुद्धि, प्रकृति आदि को मानव के इतिहास में चिंतन के इतिहास की दृष्टि से पढ़ा जाए तो यह अध्ययन कुछ आसान हो सकेगा।

इस पद्धति में भारतीय इतिहास में दोनों प्रकार के साक्ष्य हैं साहित्य और पुरातत्व। साहित्यिक साक्ष्यों में तो लोकप्रिय महत्वपूर्ण साक्ष्य है भगवद्‌गीता में कृष्ण के उपदेश और अर्जुन की प्रतिक्रिया। अर्जुन का युद्ध-क्षेत्र में विषाद, युद्ध त्याग का विचार, श्रीकृष्ण के द्वारा अर्जुन का विभ्रम दूर करना, अर्जुन के द्वारा वासनाओं को समझना, उसकी आत्मानुसंधान की योजना आदि-आदि प्रक्रियाओं से निकलते हुए गांडीव उठाने तक अर्जुन के मन, आत्मा, योग, दर्शन, संन्यास सभी का विशद विवरण किसी भी मानवीय प्रवृत्तियों को प्रकट करने का एक पुष्ट साक्ष्य है। महाभारत का रचयिता मानवीय मन की दुर्बलताओं से परिचित हैं और उससे निकलने का मार्ग भी कृष्ण के उपदेश के माध्यम से दिखाता है। वह इतिहास के परम उद्देश्य से भी परिचित है और आने वाली अनेक पीढ़ियों के लिए मार्गदर्शक का काम करता है।

इसी संदर्भ में भगवान बुद्ध का व्यक्तित्व भी मानवीय मनोविज्ञान को समझने में भारत में ही नहीं समस्त विश्व में एक अमूल्य उदाहरण है। जो बौद्ध धर्म के प्रणेता के साथ समाज-सुधारक, मनोवैज्ञानिक चिंतक के रूप में तत्कालीन समय में लोकप्रिय हुए। उन्होंने समकालीन जन की चेतना को अपनी संवाद की शैली से प्रभावित किया। शिष्यों को भी अपने उपदेशों से क्रमशः प्रभावित कर उनके मन को समझा-बुझा कर दीक्षित किया न कि अपने विचारों को थोपा।[8]

इन्हीं उदाहरणों की परंपरा में अशोक प्रियदर्शी का उदाहरण विश्व के इतिहास में अन्यत्र उपलब्ध नहीं हो सकता। जिसके द्वारा स्वयं के मन के साथ तो अभ्यास किया ही गया और साथ ही राज्य कर्मचारियों और प्रजा के भी चिंतन को क्रमशः

प्रभावित किया गया। अशोक किसी भी धर्मलेख में ओदश न देकर (इच्छांकिति) इच्छा प्रकट करता है और मनोवैज्ञानिक तरीके से स्वर्ग और राज्य-कृपा का लोभ भी कर्मचारियों और प्रजा के मन में स्थापित करता है।[9] अशोक के अभिलेख राजा की प्रकृति के साथ सामान्य जनमानस की प्रकृति समझने में सहायक सिद्ध होते हैं।

(कौटिल्य) कौटिल्य जैसे कूटनीतिक राजनीतिक, विचारक तक कूट मनोवैज्ञानिक तरीके से चैत्यों और मंदिरों के नायकों के मन के लोभ को जानने का मार्ग प्रशस्त करता है।[10]

इसके अतिरिक्त भी जनमानस को पढ़ने के कई दृष्टांत भारतीय वांङ्मय में उपलब्ध है। कालिदास से लेकर रवींद्रनाथ टैगोर तक ऐसे असंख्यों साक्ष्य उपलब्ध हो जाएंगे।

जहां तक प्रागैतिहासिक मानव के मन और विचारों को समझने अथवा ऐतिहासक क्रम में उसके महत्व को स्थापित करने का प्रयास है, तो उसका सह विकास उसके द्वारा निर्मित उपकरणों के माध्यम से पढ़ा जा सकता है। यह उपकरण सुरक्षा की भावना, जीविकोपार्जन, तकनीकी विकास, उसके नैतिक नियमों का निर्धारण करते हैं। बहुत से ऐसे पुरास्थल प्राप्त हुए हैं जहां के क्रमिक उपकरणों के विकास के उदाहरण, मानवीय विचारों के क्रमिक विकास को उचित ठहराते हैं। उसकी आवश्यकताओं ने क्रमशः उसके उपकरणों के प्रारूप में भी परिवर्तन किया। यह परिवर्तन उसकी मानसिकता के परिवर्तन का द्योतक प्रतीत होता है। आज के मानव के द्वारा जटिल मशीनों का उपयोग उसकी तर्क बुद्धि का पर्याय है तो प्रागैतिहासिक मानव के भी उपकरण उसकी तर्क बुद्धि के उपयोग के द्योतक हो सकते हैं। पुरातात्विक अध्ययन में एक नई विद्या का प्रचलन हो गया है 'Ethno-Archaelogy'। जिसमें जीवित सभ्यता और संस्कृति एवं पुरातात्विक संस्कृतियों के बीच संबंधों को खोजा जा रहा है।[11]

एक मार्ग और प्रतीत होता है प्राचीन भारतीय मन को पढ़ने का। जहां आधुनिक जनसमूहों के अध्ययन के द्वारा प्राचीन इतिहास और पूर्वजों की परिस्थितियों का अध्ययन भी किया जा सकता है। यह सामान्य सिद्धान्त सबसे पहले 1877 में मोरगन[12] ने प्रतिपादित किया जिसने अपना अधिकांश समय अमरीकी आदिवासियों के साथ बिताया था। उनका अनुमान है कि आर्यों के प्राचीन पूर्वज उन्हीं अनुभवों से गुजरे जो आज के आदिवासियों या वन्य जाति के थे। इसी दृष्टि से देवी प्रसाद चट्टोपाध्याय[13] का यह आग्रह महत्वपूर्ण है कि छांदोग्य उपनिषद के प्रथम अध्याय के बारहवें खंड में श्वानों के उद्गीथ के पीछे

मर्म को समझने के लिए जनजातियों में गीत और संगीत की भूमिका को समझना पड़ेगा। वसुधारा व्रत में वर्षा के लिए गाए गए गीत व्यर्थ नहीं हैं। ग्रीष्म ऋतु के मध्य में पड़ने वाला यह सूखा काफी लंबे समय तक चलता है और किसानों के लिए घोर परीक्षा की घड़ी होती है। किसान इन गीतों में जलमग्न पृथ्वी के दृश्य की कल्पना करते हैं जो भले ही भौतिक सत्य न हो पर मनोवैज्ञानिक सत्य हो सकता है। इस तुलनात्मक अध्ययन में प्राचीन मानव के मन को पढ़ने की पद्धति और मार्ग दोनों ही प्रशस्त किया। शुनःशेष की कथा में पिता के द्वारा पुत्र को सौ गायों के लिए बेचने पर शुनःशेष के द्वारा निर्मित श्लोक नई सत्ता अथवा व्यवस्था के द्योतक हैं।

पुरातत्व विज्ञान के क्षेत्र में भी काफी प्रगति हो चुकी है और लिखित इतिहास की प्रागैतिहासिक नींव के पुनर्निर्माण की संभावनाएं बढ़ चुकी हैं। पुरातत्व से प्राप्त भौतिक अवशेषों का जाति विज्ञान की मदद से अध्ययन किसी भी प्राचीन जाति अथवा मानव के मन, विश्वास, विचारों आदि-आदि के अध्ययन का सुलभ बनाएगा।

यह अवश्य है कि मानव या व्यक्ति विशेष के मन चित्त की अभिव्यक्ति, दर्शन, कला, विचारों के माध्यम से पढ़ना संभव है तो मानव सामान्य या समाज के विचारों को समाज या राज्य में घटित होने वाली घटनाओं के माध्यम से समझा जा सकता है।

इस अध्ययन से सजगता की आवश्यकता है कि कहीं इतिहासकार का मानस इस अध्ययन को प्रभावित न करने लगे।

* कृतज्ञता ज्ञापन : लेख के उत्साहवर्धन और लेख के संवर्धन के लिए मैं अपने विभाग की अग्रजा डॉ. रेखा दासवानी जी की आभारी हूं।

संदर्भ एवं टिप्पणियां

1. विस्तार से देखें Historiography, *Critical Concepts in Historical Studies*, Edited by Robert M Burm. New York. 2006, Vol. II, 33, p. 331, Mentalities A New field for Historians, Jacques Le Goff; Primitive Mentality, Levy Bruhl, 1923; *Man in India*, Journal of Royal Asiatic Society.
2. इसी तरह का तुलनात्मक जनजातीय आचार-व्यवहार के माध्यम से जनजातीय सभ्यता के अध्ययन के तरीके निकाले गए। देखें *Patterns of Culture* by Ruth Benedict, Pub. by New American Library, VIII edn., 1951.

3. विष्णु पर्व 3/15, हिंदू संस्कृति अंक, कल्याण, वर्ष, 24, संख्या 1, पूर्ण संख्या 278, जनवरी 1950, पृ. 301
4. शतपथ, 44 : 3 : 10
5. इतिहास दर्शन, गणेशी लाल वर्मा, इतिहास दर्शन, सम्पादित ओमप्रकाश, दिल्ली, 1990, पृ. 73
6. अथर्ववेद, शौनक 20 कांड, सूक्त 128:12:14, पृ. 436, दयानंद संस्थान, नई दिल्ली
7. चंद्रकांत बाली, इतिहास दर्शन, इतिहास दर्शन संपादित ओमप्रकाश, दिल्ली, 1990, पृ. 44 पर वर्णित
8. विस्तार के लिए देखें—लामा अंगारिक गोविंद, *द साइकोलोजिकल एटीट्यूड ऑफ अरली बुद्धिस्म*, लंदन, 1969, रीप्रिंट; आर.के. मुखर्जी, मेन एंड थॉट इन एनशियंट इंडिया, बॉम्बे, 1957, दूसरा एडीशन।
9. 13वां शिलालेख, शहबाजगढ़ी प्रति, हिस्टोरिकल एंड लिटरेरी इंस्क्रिप्शंस, चौखंबा वाराणसी, डा. राजबली पांडेय, 1962, पृ. 14, विस्तार के लिए अशोक के अभिलेखों का अध्ययन वांछनीय है।
10. कौटिल्य अर्थशास्त्र, अनुवाद आर. शामशास्त्री, मैसूर द्वितीय प्रति, 1961, प्रथम बुक, अध्याय 10, पृ. 15
11. गुजरात के गुंडियाली और लोदै (कच्छ) के पुरातात्विक अवशेषों का अध्ययन, सीताबंगा और जोगीमरा गुफाओं के चित्रों के अध्ययन ने प्रोगैतिहासिक मानव के विचारों, क्रियाकलापों और भावनाओं को पढ़ने के प्रयास किए जा रहे हैं : अर्चना चौकसी, सिरेमिक बेसेल्स, देयर रोल इन इल्यूमिनेटिंग पास्ट एंड प्रजेंट सोशल एंड इकानामिक रिलेशनशिप, मेन एंड एन्वायरमेंट, 1995, 20(1), 87-108: के.के. सुबय्या, एथनो आर्किलॉजिकल स्टडी, द ट्राइबल ऑरिजिन ऑफ मेगालिथ्स, गौरवम्, बी.के. गुरुराज राव फेलिसिटेशन वाल्यूम, दिल्ली, 1996
12. एल.एच. मोरगन, एंशिएंट सोसायटी, कलकत्ता
13. लोकायत, *प्राचीन भारतीय भौतिकवाद का अध्ययन*, देवी प्रसाद चट्टोपाध्याय, हिंदी अनुवाद, बृज शर्मा, राजकमल प्रकाशन, 2005, पृ. 61

14. बसोहली कलम : विषयवस्तु एवं शैलीगत परिशीलन

हरि नारायण दुबे

17वीं शताब्दी में मुगल सम्राट औरंगजेब की कला-उपेक्षा तथा तत्कालीन राजनीतिक अशांति के कारण मुगल दरबार में आश्रय का अभाव अनुभव करने वाले चित्रकारगण कलाप्रेमी आश्रयदाता नरेशों की खोज करते-करते हिमालय की सुरम्य उपत्यकाओं में जाकर बसने लगे। धीरे-धीरे इन कलाकारों को जम्मू, चम्बा, गुलेर, बसोहली, नूरपुर, कांगड़ा, सुकेत मंडी, कुल्लू, नाहन, सिरमौर तथा गढ़वाल आदि रियासतों में राजकीय आश्रय प्राप्त होता गया। पहाड़ी परिवेश में बस जाने के उपरांत उक्त कलाकार मुगल दरबार से हटकर काव्यात्मक सृजन की एक नई सांस्कृतिक एवं सामाजिक संचेतना प्राप्त करने लगे। फलतः उपर्युक्त रियासतों में उनके द्वारा बनाए गए चित्र मुगल चित्रशैली से सर्वथा भिन्न नई-नई शैलियों अथवा कलमों के साथ उच्चित्रित होने लगे। इन्हें हम मोटे तौर पर पहाड़ी चित्रकला के नाम से संबोधित करते हैं। पहाड़ी कला अपने विकासक्रम में मुख्य रूप से तीन दिशाओं में विशेष उन्मुख हुई—जिन्हें बसोहली, कांगड़ा एवं गढ़वाल चित्र-शैली के नाम से पहचाना जाता है। इनमें जैसा कि अजित घोष का मानना है। बसोहली कलम सबसे पुरानी है। इस पहाड़ी शैली के अधिकांश उल्लेखनीय चित्र सत्रहवीं एवं अठारहवीं शताब्दियों में उच्चित्रित किए गए।

बसोहली वर्तमान जम्मू-कश्मीर प्रांत के जनपद जसरोटा की बसोहली तहसील के रूप में रावी नदी के तट पर आज भी विद्यमान है। 17वीं-18वीं शताब्दी में बसोहली कुल 74 गांवों की एक छोटी सी पर्वतीय रियासत थी। यहां की घाटी बड़ी उपजाऊ है तथा इसकी प्राकृतिक सुषमा अत्यंत मनोहारी है। 1030 ई. में जे.सी. फैंच ने बसोहली के कलाकारों की खोज करने के लिए इस घाटी की यात्रा की थी

तथा उसका अपनी पुस्तक 'हिमालय आर्ट' नामक पुस्तक में बड़ा ही रोचक वर्णन किया है।[1] तबारीख-ए-राजपूताना के लेखक तथा बसोहली राज्य के इतिहास के मर्मज्ञ ठाकुर काहन सिंह बलोरिया के उल्लेखानुसार यहां के राजमहल सुंदर भित्तिचित्रों से सुसज्जित थे जिनमें नायिका तथा अन्य शृंगारिक विषयवस्तु को लेकर चित्र अंकित किए गए थे।[2] उचित रख-रखाव की कमी के कारण ये भित्तिचित्र अब लगभग नष्ट हो चुके हैं।

बसोहली 16वीं-17वीं शताब्दियों में एक प्रमुख व्यापारिक नगरी बन चुकी थी। बलोरिया राजवंशों के शासनकाल में यह नगर पश्मीनी वस्त्रों के निर्माण का प्रमुख केंद्र था। यहां पर कश्मीर तथा अन्यान्य नगरों के ऊनी कपड़ों के निर्माता जुलाहे एवं कारीगर भारी संख्या में आकर बस गए थे। बसोहली की प्रारंभिक नृपतिगणों ने मुगल शासकों से घनिष्ठ संपर्क स्थापित कर रखा था। 1590 ई. में यहां के राजा कृष्णपाल के सम्राट अकबर के दरबार में अनेक भेंटों के साथ उपस्थित हुए। उसका पुत्र भूपतपाल (1598-1635) बड़ा पराक्रमी था। डोंगरा आर्ट गैलरी जम्मू में रखे गये एक चित्र में उसे मुगल सम्राट! शाहजहां को सम्मानित करते हुए अंकित किया गया है। भूपतपाल का यह चित्र बसोहली कलम में आंका गया है। भूपतपाल की मृत्यु के उपरांत उसका पुत्र संग्राम पाल बसोहली का राजा मनोनीत किया गया। वह अप्रतिम सुंदर राजकुमार था तथा उसे मुगल बादशाह शाहजहां के अतिरिक्त शाहजादियां भी बहुत पसन्द करती थीं। इसी राजा के शासनकाल में बहुतेरे चित्रकार दिल्ली से बसोहली आकर बस गए। संग्रामपाल के उपरांत उसका अनुज हिंदपाल राजगद्दी पर बैठा, जिसका एक चित्र प्राप्य है। हिंदपाल की मृत्यु के बाद उसका पुत्र कृपालपाल (1678-1693 ई.) बसोहली का राजा मनोनीत हुआ। इसी राजा के शासनकाल में बसोहली कलम अपनी स्वतंत्र पहचान बनाने में सफल हुई। उसके कला-प्रेम एवं राज्याश्रय से आकर्षित होकर अनेक चितेरे दिल्ली दरबार से चलकर बसोहली आकर बस गए। कतिपय कला-समीक्षक इस मत के पोषक हैं कि बसोहली चित्रांकनों में बेलबूटों को बनाने संबंधी आलंकारिता मुगल चित्रकला के प्रभाव को इंगित करती है। इतना ही नहीं, बसोहली चित्रों में सुनहरे रंग का प्रयोग भी मुलतः मुगल चित्रकला की ही देन प्रतीत होती है।

कृपालपाल की मृत्यु के उपरांत उसका ज्येष्ठ पुत्र धीरजपाल 1693 ई. में राजा बना। अपने पिता की भांति धीरजपाल भी कला-प्रेमी एवं साहित्यानुरागी था। दुर्भाग्यवश 1725 ई. में चम्बा के राजा के साथ युद्ध में वह मारा गया। उसकी मृत्यु के पश्चात उसका पुत्र मेदिनीपाल (1725-1736 ई.) बसोहली का राजा मनोनीत

हुआ। उसके भरपूर प्रश्रय एवं राज्याश्रय के फलस्वरूप बसोहली कलम का पर्याप्त विकास हुआ। मेदिनीपाल के बाद उसका पुत्र जीतपाल (1736-1757 ई.) राजा हुआ। उसके शासनकाल के अंतिम चरण में बसोहली कलम पर कांगला चित्र शैली का प्रभाव पड़ने लगा। इस बात की संपुष्टि पंजाब संग्रहालय, पटियाला में सुरक्षित राजा जीतपाल के एक चित्र से होती है, जिस पर कांगड़ा कलम का स्पष्ट प्रभाव परिलक्षित होता है।

जीतपाल की मृत्यु के उपरांत अमृतपाल (1757-1776 ई.) बसोहली का शासक हुआ। वह कलात्मक अभिव्यक्ति में स्वतंत्र चित्रांकन तथा पोषक तथा स्वयं कलाप्रेमी राजा था। उसके संरक्षण में बसोहली कलम का तेजी के साथ विकास हुआ। बसोहली कला में इसी काल में नायिका-चित्रण की ओर कलावंतों का विशेष आग्रह मिलने लगता है। बसोहली के चित्रांकनों में नायक-नायिका संबंधी चित्रों का सबसे बड़ा संकलन बोस्टन म्यूजियम ऑव फाइन आर्ट्स तथा अहमदाबाद स्थित 'कस्तूर भाई लाल' भाई का संकलन है। परंतु यहां एक बात की ओर विद्वानों का ध्यान आकृष्ट किया जाना अपेक्षित प्रतीत होता है कि बसोहली कलम पर कांगड़ा कलम का प्रभाव इस काल से उत्तरोत्तर बढ़ता जा रहा थ। इस तथ्य की संपुष्टि डोंगरा आर्ट गैलरी, जम्मू में सुरक्षित बसोहली नरेश के राजवैद्य के वंशज पाधा कुंजलाल के द्वारा संकलित चित्रों कर कांगड़ा कलम का स्पष्ट प्रभाव देखा जा सकता है। इतना ही नहीं, राजा अमृतलाल तथा उनकी राजरानी का एक चित्रांकन उक्त गैलरी में विशेष द्रष्टव्य है, जिस पर कांगड़ा कलम का विशेष प्रभाव परिलक्षित होता है। उपर्युक्त संकलन में गुलेर राज्य के राजा प्रकाश चंद्र (1760-1790 ई.) का एक चित्र कांगड़ा कलम में ही अंकित मिलता है। ऐसा लगता है कि बसोहली एवं गुलेर के चितेरे एक दूसरे राज्यों में प्रायः आया-जाया करते थे। कलाविद् गोट्ज का मत है कि अमृतपाल की अतिशय स्वतंत्रप्रियता के चलते बसोहली कलम क्रमशः बिखरने लगी थी, क्योंकि उसकी रुचि के चलते बसोहली कलम 18वीं शताब्दी के अंतिम वर्षों में मुगल कलम की ओर झुकती हुई सी दिखाई देती है। बसोहली की चित्रकला राजा मेदिनीपाल (1725) के राज्याश्रय में विशेष रूप से विकसित हुई। उसने रंगमहल की शीश का निर्माण करवाया, जो वास्तुशिल्प के साथ-साथ नायिका-भेद आदि कलात्मक चित्रण से सज्जित थे। इसकी उत्कृष्टता का उल्लेख 18वीं-19वीं शताब्दी में भारत की यात्रा पर आने वाले विदेशी यात्रियों ने भी किया है। दुर्भाग्यवश, आज इसमें से एक भी चित्र प्राप्य नहीं है। 1808 ई. में हिमालय की उपत्यका में स्थित लगभग सभी पहाड़ी रियासतें लाहौर नरेश महाराजा रणजीत

सिंह के अधीन हो गईं। बसोहली का अंतिम राजा कल्याणपाल (1834-1846 ई.) था। उसे पराजित कर महाराजा रणजीत सिंह ने बसोहली राज्य को जम्मू के राजा हीरा सिंह की रियासत में मिला दिया। ज्ञातव्य है कि कल्याणपाल के राज्य-काल में ही बसोहली के सुशिक्षित ब्राह्मणों ने अधिकांश चित्रों का संकलन किया था। 1827 ई. में कल्याणपाल की मृत्यु के उपरांत बसोहली कलम की भी लगभग इतिश्री हो गई।

उपर्युक्त पालवंशी पहाड़ी नृपतियों के संरक्षण में बसोहली कलम पर्याप्त विकसित हुई। यहां के नक्काशीदार भव्य एवं पुराने राजमहल को जिसे पश्चिमी हिमालय-क्षेत्र का सर्वोच्च आश्चर्य माना जाता था, की भित्तियों को राजा महेंद्रपाल ने बसोहली कलम के चित्रांकन से भरपूर सज्जित करवाया था।

बसोहली शैली के चित्रों के मुख्य विषय

बसोहली कलम के चित्रकारों ने 17वीं से लेकर 19वीं शताब्दी तक के समकालीन राजनीतिक, सामाजिक एवं आर्थिक जीवनधारा को रूपायित किया है। 18वीं शताब्दी इस चित्रकारी का सर्वोकृष्ट काल था। यहां के चित्रों का विषय अन्य पहाड़ी कलमों के अनुरूप ही मिलता है। धार्मिक चित्रों में वैष्णव धर्म से संबंधित चित्रों को अधिक वरीयता से अंकित किया गया है। विष्णु के दश अवतारों तथा कृष्ण की बाल एवं गोपी लीलाओं को बसोहली के कलाकारों ने बहुतायत में चित्रित किया है। इस काल में चित्रांकित रामायण की दो प्रतियां भी उपलब्ध हैं। इसमें एक प्रति विशुद्ध बसोहली कलम में चित्रांकित है तथा दूसरी प्रति पर कुल्लू कलम का प्रभाव परिलक्षित होता है। रामायण के अतिरिक्त भागवत पुराण के कथा-दृश्यों को भी बसोहिली के कलाकारों ने अपनी चित्र-रचना का प्रमुख विषय बनाया था।

धार्मिक चित्रों के अतिरिक्त बसोहली के चितेरों ने काव्य एवं रागमाला को भी अपनी सर्जना का प्रमुख विषय चुना था। चौदहवीं शताब्दी में विरचित भानुदत्त कृत *रसमंजरी* बसोहली के राजा कृपालपाल का परम प्रिय काव्य था। इसके अतिरिक्त केशवदास की 'रामचंद्रिका' के वर्ण-विषयों को भी यहां के चितेरों ने उच्चित्रित किया है। रसमंजरी में नायक-नायिका-भेद, रस एवं शृंगार आदि का बड़ा सजीव वर्णन किया गया है। परंतु इसमें कृष्ण की लीलाओं का वर्णन नहीं है। राष्ट्रीय संग्रहालय, नई दिल्ली में सुरक्षित 'रसमंजरी' के कतिपय चित्रों में कृष्ण का आदर्श प्रेमी रूप को बड़ी बारीकी से चित्रित किया गया है। ऐसा प्रतीत होता है कि राजा कृपालपाल ने अपने आश्रयी चित्रकारों के द्वारा रसमंजरी के

चित्रांकनों द्वारा कृष्ण के रूप को अंकित करवाकर उन्हें एक आदर्श प्रेमी का स्वरूप प्रदान करने की चेष्टा की थी। नायिकाओं में उल्का तथा अभिसारिका आदि का उत्कृष्ट चित्रांकन बसोहली कलम की उल्लेखनीय विशेषता मानी जा सकती है।

'रसमंजरी' के दृश्यांकनों के साथ-साथ बसोहली के चितेरों ने 12वीं शताब्दी में विरचित जयदेवकृत *गीतगोविंद* के वर्ण्य-विषयों पर अनेक सुंदर चित्रों की रचना की थी। भारत कला-भवन, बनारस हिन्दू विश्वविद्यालय, बनारस में 'रागमाला' पर आधारित कतिपय महत्वपूर्ण चित्र सुरक्षित किए गए हैं। बसोहली कलम के परवर्ती चितेरों ने 'बारहमासा' चित्रावलियों को उरेहने में भी विशेष रुचि ली थी। ध्यातव्य है कि इस कलम में चित्रित 'रागमाला' एवं 'बारहमासा' चित्रों में कृष्ण और राधा को नायक एवं नायिका के रूप में प्रदर्शित किया गया है। 'गीतगोविंद' से संबंधित बसोहली कलम के चित्र पाकिस्तान में लाहौर स्थिति सेंट्रल म्यूजियम में भी सुरक्षित किए गए हैं।[4]

बसोहली कलम के चित्रकारों ने मानवीय प्रेम के चित्रण के साथ-साथ हृदयगत एवं आध्यात्मिक भावनाओं का चित्रण भी बड़ी कुशलता के साथ किया है। कृष्ण के विरह में गोपियों की व्याकुलता के भाव को प्रदर्शित करने के पीछे कलाकार मानो मानवीय आत्मा का परमात्मा की प्राप्ति के लिए व्याप्त व्याकुल भाव को प्रदर्शित करने का भाव रखते हुए दिखाई देते हैं। ऐसा लगता है कि बसोहली के चित्रों में रहस्यात्मकता के भाव को सहज एवं मधुर संपुंजन किया गया है।

बसोहली के अधिकांश चित्रकार राज्याश्रयी थे एवं दरबारी संस्कृति से विधिवत परिचित थे। इसीलिए इस कलम में व्यक्ति-चित्रों की अधिकता मिलती है। यहां के चितेरों ने राजा, रानी, दरबार तथा समसामयिक अतिविशिष्ट कवियों, संतों तथा संगीतज्ञों आदि का भी चित्र अंकित किया है। इन विशिष्ट व्यक्तियों के चित्रों के अवलोकन से तत्कालीन पश्चिमी हिमालय की संस्कृति एवं इतिहास के अनेक महत्वपूर्ण पहलू आलोकित हो उठते हैं।

बसोहली कलम की विशेषताएं

बसोहली चित्रकला अपनी विशेषताओं के कारण तिब्बती कांगड़ा तथा राजस्थानी चित्रकला से अपनी पृथक पहचान रखती है। इसे कांगड़ा कलम की अपेक्षा अधिक प्राचीन माना जाता है। यद्यपि कांगड़ा शैली में बसोहली चित्रों की तुलना में सुकुमारता, कोमलता तथा कलागत परिमार्जन अधिक मिलता है तथापि सरलता, शक्ति, सरसता तथा चमकदार रंगों की अपूर्व संवेगात्मक गतिशीलता की दृष्टि से

बसोहली कलम अपनी अलग पहचान रखती है। इतना ही नहीं, इसमें कलाकार की स्वतंत्र अभिव्यक्ति अधिक मुखर एवं स्पष्ट है। इस कलम में रंग उजले हैं तथा गहरे लाल, पीले, नीले तथा काले रंगों की प्रधानता देखने को मिलती है। रंग शोख तथा चटकदार अवश्य हैं परंतु उनसे मानवीय भावों, यथा—करुणा, प्रेम, शोक, उल्लास अथवा व्याकुलता आदि अभिव्यक्तियों कथमपि बाधित नहीं होती है। बसोहली चित्र शैली में व्यक्तियों के हाथ एवं उंगलियों की एक खास बनाबट उसकी विशेषता मानी जा सकती है। भावांकन में उंगलियों की मुद्राएं बड़ी सहायक प्रतीत होती हैं। बसोहली कलम में हाथों एवं उंगलियों की मुद्राओं द्वारा अभिप्राय संप्रेषण के लिए एक नई भाषा तैयार की गई थी, इस बात की ओर विद्वानों का ध्यान आकृष्ट किया जा सकता है। मनोभावों की अभिव्यक्ति में हस्तमुद्राओं की अहम भूमिका को बसोहली के कलावंतों ने बड़ी गहराई से उच्चित्रित किया है। इस दृष्टि से बसोहली कला पर अजंता चित्रकला का गम्भीर प्रभाव परिलक्षित होता है।

बसोहली की चित्रकला कांगड़ा चित्रों की तुलना में अधिक सादगी तथा ग्राम्यपन लिए हुए हैं। इनमें कांगड़ा चित्रों की तरह सुकुमारता कम मिलती है। बसोहली कलम के चित्रों की भाषा सीधी-सादी है, जिसे इनकी सीधी दौड़ती रेखाओं तथा पकड़ते रंगों से सरलतया समझा जा सकता है। कांगड़ा कलम में अंकित नारी-सौंदर्य रूप, रंग, मुद्रा एवं सुकुमारता की दृष्टि से नारी सहज सौंदर्य को अधिक मुखरित करती है परंतु बसोहली चित्रकला में प्रदर्शित नारी का रूप ओजपूर्ण एवं सुकुमार तो है परंतु चित्ताकर्षक सौंदर्य की दृष्टि से किंचित न्यूनता का अहसास कराती है। बसोहली कलम में नारी का मुखमंडल कांगड़ा शैली से किंचित भिन्नता के साथ अंकित किया गया है। इस कलम में होठ अपेक्षाकृत छोटे, नाक लंबी एवं झुकी हुई, गाल भरे-पूरे, ठोड़ी किंचित गोलाकार तथा ललाट पीछे की ओर कुछ-कुछ ढलुआ सा दिखता है। परंतु आंखें बड़ी-बड़ी तथा कमल दल की भांति मनोहारी हैं। इन्हें देखकर यह पंक्ति सहजतः याद आने लगती है— "ज्यों बड़री अंखियां निरखि, अंखियन को सुख होत।" नारी-यष्टि के अंकन में भी बसोहली कलम कांगड़ा कलम से कुछ कम आकर्षक दिखाई देती है। बसोहली के चित्रों में नारी-देह, चोली, दुपट्टा, घाघरा आदि झीने वस्त्रों में झांकता हुआ परिलक्षित नहीं होता। अलंकारों एवं वस्त्रों को उनकी सूक्ष्मता में ही देखा जा सकता है। नारी के मुखमंडल पर प्रायः कपोल अथवा माथे पर लटें तथा केश राशि को वेणी या जुड़े में वृद्ध अथवा केसों को प्रायः खुला दिखाया गया है। इसी प्रकार बसोहली कलम में अंकित पुरुषों को ऊपर से किसी वस्त्र विशेष से परिवेष्ठित

अंकित किया गया है। अंगरखा का किनारा सुनहले रंग में तथा शेष भाग उजले-पीले रंगों में उरेहा गया है। बसोहली कमल में पुरुषों को प्रायः भांति-भांति के अलंकरणों से सज्जित किया गया है।

बसोहली कलम में चित्रांकनों की भूमिका में प्रायः एक ही रंग प्रयुक्त किया गया है जिसके कारण उसमें समतलता का बोध होता है। इन्हें देखकर ऐसा लगता है जैसे कलाकार ने ब्रुश की एक ही घसीट से रंग लेप कर दिया हो। इन चित्रों पर गहरा या हल्का हरा, गहरा पीला, हल्का लाल एवं सीपिया रंगों का प्रयोग किया गया है। चित्रांकनों में रंगों के प्रयोग एवं दृश्यांकनों में बसोहरी कलावंतों की शोख-दृष्टि एवं सुकुमार प्रकृति-प्रेम एवं उनके दक्षतापूर्ण कला-चित्रण का पता चलता है।

सारांशतः बसोहली चित्रकला पर जहां एक ओर अंशतः अजंता एवं न्यून ही सही किंतु मुगल चित्रकला का प्रभाव देखा जा सकता है, वहीं उस पर अन्याय पवर्ततीय तथा परंपराओं के गहरे प्रभाव को भी नजरअंदाज नहीं किया जा सकता है। बसोहली चित्रकला में लोक-प्रथाओं, मर्यादाओं, अलंकरणों एवं पहनावे के अंकन के साथ-साथ भारतीय दर्शन एवं धर्म के विविध पक्षों को भी बड़ी गहराई के साथ उच्चित्रित किया गया है। कला के साथ भारतीय दर्शन के सामंजस्य को सभी पहाड़ी चित्रकला में जितना अधिक संरक्षित किया गया है, उतना उत्तर मध्यकालीन अन्य किसी भी भारतीय कला में संरक्षण एवं चित्रण दिखाई नहीं देता है।

संदर्भ एवं टिप्पणियां

1. द्रष्टव्य, जे.सी. फैंच, *हिमालयन आर्ट,* पृ. 43
2. *द माडर्न रिव्यू,* अक्टू. 1960, पृ. 312
3. द्रष्टव्य, *द माडर्न रिव्यू,* अक्टू. 1960, पृ. 312, 'बसोहली पेंटिंग्स इन द श्री चित्रालयम् चित्रवेंद्रम 'के.पी. पद्मनाभम् टैंपी, बी.ए.
4. द्रष्टव्य, डब्ल्यू.जी. आर्चार : *इंडियन पेंटिंग इन पंजाब हिल्स,* पृ. 15 तथा द्रष्टव्य, सेंट्रल म्यूजियम, लाहौर में सुरक्षित एवं विक्टोरिया तथा अलबर्ट म्यूजियम लंदन में 1730 ई. में *गीत गोविंद* सचित्र प्रति

15. बौद्ध धर्म में अनत्त सिद्धांत : एक विवेचना

रेनु शुक्ला

बौद्ध धर्म की व्याख्या 'बुद्ध', 'धम्म', 'निब्बान', 'पटिच्च समुप्पाद', 'अर्हन', 'अनत्त' आदि शब्दों के बिना संभव नहीं है। इन्हीं शब्दों के चारों ओर बौद्ध सिद्धांतों का ताना-बना बुना गया है। प्रस्तुत शोधपत्र का उद्देश्य बौद्ध धर्म में 'अनत्त' शब्द का सही अभिप्रेत एवं अनत्त सिद्धांत पर विचार करना है। बौद्ध धर्म का यह सिद्धांत जितना महत्वपूर्ण है उतना ही विवादास्पद भी। 'अनिच्च', 'दुःख' एवं 'अनात्म' के साथ मिलकर यह बौद्ध विचारधारा को आधार प्रदान करता है। 'अनत्त' का सामान्यतः स्वीकार्य है अर्थ है—अनात्म अर्थात आत्मा जैसे किसी स्थायी, शाश्वत तत्व की सत्ता नहीं है। सभी संस्कृत पदार्थ अनित्य हैं।[1] 'जो उत्पन्न हुआ है वह नष्ट होने वाला है, यही परम ज्ञान है।'[2] अपने समय में प्रचलित आत्मवाद का अनेक प्रकार से खंडन करने वाले बुद्ध ने पंच स्कंधों, सभी भूतों एवं भौतिक पदार्थों चित्त और चैत्तसिक धर्मों में अनित्यता के लक्षण को देखा, स्वीकारा एवं संपूर्ण सांसारिक प्रपंच को अनात्मभूत कहा।[3]

ब्राह्मण सहित सभी प्रमुख धर्मों के आत्मा संबंधी सिद्धांत का बुद्ध ने 'अनत्त सिद्धांत' के द्वारा विरोध किया और पंच स्कंधों या उनमें से किसी भी एक को आत्मा के रूप में समझने से इनकार किया।[4] जब व्यक्ति यह कहता है कि "मैं हूं" तो उसका तात्पर्य यह नहीं है कि उसकी "बुद्धि", "चित्त" या "शरीर" आत्मा है। "मैं" की पहचान अविज्जा के कारण मनुष्य कभी भौतिक शरीर से करता है तो कभी मानसिक विकारों से। वह आत्मा के वास्तविक स्वरूप को भूलकर अहं को ही आत्म रूप समझने लगता है। अविज्जा को समाप्त करके ही अपने सार्वभौम स्वरूप की पहचान की जा सकती है एवं विमुक्ति को प्राप्त किया जा सकता है।[5] वस्तुतः अनत्त

सिद्धांत को लेकर दुविधा या विरोधाभास का कारण यह है कि 'अनत्त' शब्द को उसके सही अर्थ में नहीं समझा गया है। उदाहरण के लिए 'रूपं अनत्ता' का सही अनुवाद 'रूप अनात्म है' नहीं हो सकता इस अर्थ की प्राप्ति के लिए 'रूपं अनत्तं' का प्रयोग करना पड़ेगा। व्याकरण की दृष्टि से 'रूपं अनत्ता' का यही तात्पर्य हो सकता है कि 'रूप आत्मा नहीं है'। यही व्याख्या "विज्ञानं अनत्ता", "चाक्खु अनत्ता" आदि के संदर्भ में भी लागू होती है। "वेदना अनत्ता", "सञ्ञा अनत्ता", "संखारा अनत्ता", "सब्बे धम्मा अनत्ता", को वेदना, संज्ञा, संसार, सभी धर्म अनात्म हैं" कहा जा सकता परंतु इन शब्दों का यह वास्तविक अभिप्रेत नहीं है।[6] इसी प्रकार "यह अनत्ता तं न एतं मम, न एसोहम अस्मि न में सो सत्ता" का अनुवाद "वह जो आत्मा नहीं है, वह, यह मेरा नहीं है, यह मैं नहीं हूं, यह मेरा आत्मा नहीं है"—यही हो सकता है। इस तथ्य को अनदेखा करते हुए प्रायः विद्वानों ने इसकी व्याख्या बौद्ध धर्म में आत्मा के निषेध के रूप में की है।[7] विभिन्न विद्वानों ने *अनत्तलक्खण सुत्त* की भी इसी प्रकार की भ्रमात्मक व्याख्या प्रस्तुत की है।[8]

इस विषय में गहराई से विचार करने पर प्रतीत होता है कि बौद्ध धर्म में 'अत्ता' का तात्पर्य औपनिषदिक सार्वभौम आत्मा से न होकर अविद्याजन्य, संसारबद्ध अहंकारी जीव के रूप में है। बुद्ध से लेकर कमलशील तक प्रायः सब आत्मा को अहंकारी जीव ही समझते रहे और सरलतापूर्वक उसका खंडन करते रहे। हीनयान ने तो आत्मा को क्षणिक विज्ञानों के अतिरिक्त अन्य कुछ नहीं माना। नागसेन ने राजा मिलिंद से कहा कि जिस प्रकार रथ, डंडा, धुरा, पहिए आदि का समूह मात्र है और इनके अतिरिक्त और कुछ नहीं हैं उसी प्रकार आत्मा भी क्षणिक विज्ञानों का समूह मात्र है और इनके अतिरिक्त और कुछ नहीं है।[9] महापरिनिब्बान सुत्त में बुद्ध कहते हैं—"जो कुछ भी उत्पन्न हुआ है, जीवधारी के रूप में अस्तित्व में लाया गया है, स्वाभाविक रूप से स्वयं में नष्ट होने का गुण रखता है ऐसी स्थिति में ऐसा जीव मृत्यु को न प्राप्त हो यह कैसे संभव है? इस प्रकार किसी भी स्थिति का अस्तित्व नहीं हो सकता।"[10] धम्मपद में कहा गया है—'सब्बे धम्मा अनत्ता।'[11] महायान में भी आत्मा को अविद्याजन्य अहंकार, ममकार युत जीव ही माना जो न तो पंच स्कंध से भिन्न है न अभिन्न, किंतु विशुद्ध आत्मा जो विशुद्ध विज्ञान स्वरूप है बौद्ध दर्शन को सदा किसी न किसी रूप में मान्य रही थी। भगवान बुद्ध स्वयं तत्व को 'प्रज्ञा' या 'बोधि' कहते हैं। अश्वघोष उसे 'आलय विज्ञान' कहते हैं। महायानसूत्र 'प्रपंचशून्य', और 'प्रत्यात्मवेद्य' कहते हैं। यह एक महत्वपूर्ण बात है कि यद्यपि बौद्ध प्रायः विशुद्ध आत्मसत्व को आत्मा न

कहकर 'चित्त' या 'विज्ञान' कहते हैं तथापि कभी-कभी उसके लिए 'ब्रह्म' शब्द का प्रयोग किया जाता है उदाहारणार्थ *अष्टसहस्त्रिका प्रज्ञापारमिता* में कहा गया है समस्त पदार्थ न आते हैं, न जाते हैं, न शुद्ध हैं, न अशुद्ध, राग और द्वेष तथा संग और असंग से रहित हैं क्योंकि वे ब्रह्मभूत हैं। दीर्घ निकाय में ब्रह्मभूत को तथागत का बोधक कहा गया है।[12] बौद्ध दर्शन के संदर्भ में यह अत्यंत महत्वपूर्ण प्रश्न है कि क्या बुद्ध ने वास्तव में सार्वभौम आत्मा के अस्तित्व को नकार दिया अथवा केवल अनात्मभूत तत्वों में आत्मा को न देखने का उपदेश दिया।[13] इस प्रश्न पर विचार करना अत्यावश्यक है। कोई भी देश, काल अथवा परिस्थिति हो मनुष्य द्वारा स्वयं को जानने की इच्छा स्वाभाविक है।[14] विभिन्न दार्शनिकों ने अपने-अपने तरीके से इस प्रश्न का उत्तर खोजने का प्रयत्न किया और प्राप्त उत्तर की अपनी-अपनी व्याख्या की। स्पष्ट है कि मनुष्य सभी वस्तुओं की सत्ता को नकार सकता है परन्तु स्वयं की सत्ता को चुनौती नहीं दे सकता। जो आत्मा की सत्ता को नकारते हैं वे भी अपने निषेध के द्वारा उसे कहीं न कहीं स्वीकार कर लेते हैं। बौद्ध धर्म के संबंध में इस विषय को देखने से स्पष्ट है कि बुद्ध ने अनेकशः यह प्रतिपादित किया कि संपूर्ण मानसिक एवं भौतिक जगत के आधार पर पंचस्कंध 'अनत्त' (अनात्म) हैं।[15] अज्ञानी व्यक्ति शरीर एवं वेदना को आत्मा एवं आत्मा को शरीर एवं वेदना के रूप में देखता है जो सत्य नहीं है।[16] अतः बुद्ध ने जो तुम्हारा नहीं है उसे त्यागने का उपदेश दिया—"यं न तुम्हाकं तं पजहथ।"[17] उनका वास्तविक अभिप्रेत यह था कि आत्मवाद तात्विक है न अनात्मवाद। दोनों ही कोटियों के परे अनिवर्चनीय रूप से सत्य प्रतिष्ठित है।[18] आत्मा की व्याख्या विभिन्न प्रकार से की गई है परंतु आत्मा की व्याख्या का सर्वोत्तम प्रकार उसकी नकारात्मक व्याख्या है। बृहदारण्यक उपनिषद[19] में आत्मा को 'नेति नेति' कहा गया तो सांख्य दर्शन में 'नास्मि न में नाहं' और इसी प्रकार बौद्ध दर्शन में 'नेतं मम, नेसोहमस्मि ने मेसो अत्ता।'[20] जब बुद्ध ने भद्र तरुणों के एक समूह को उपदेश दिया—"अत्तानं गवेसेय्याथ"[21] तो आत्मा के लिए एकवचन प्रयुक्त किया है।[22] अर्थात आत्मा एक है और अनेक प्रतीत होता है।[23] अनेक रूपों में एक ही सत्य की व्याख्या को भिन्न नहीं बना सकती न ही सत्य इस व्याख्या से प्रभावित होता है। अविज्जा के कारण जो सार्वभौम है व्यक्तिगत प्रतीत होता है, जो अनादि और अनंत है सांसारिक प्रतीत होता है जो स्वतंत्र है अधीन प्रतीत होता है। समस्त दैहिक और चैत्तसिक पदार्थों में आत्मा का प्रतिषेध त्रिपिटक में बार-बार उपलब्ध होता है। समस्त स्कंध, धातु, और आयतन, समासतः सभी भूत और भौतिक, चित्त

और चैत्त धर्मों में अनित्यता, दुःखात्मता और परतंत्रता व्यापक है। किसी वस्तु के आत्मा होने के लिए उसे नित्य, सुखात्मक और स्वतंत्र होना चाहिए। इसके विपरीत लक्षण वाले व्यावहारिक जगत को सर्वथा अनात्मभूत मानना चाहिए।[24]

वस्तुतः 'अनत्त' शब्द को बुद्ध की शिक्षाओं के संदर्भ में भलीभांति न समझने के कारण ही यह मिथ्या धारणा उत्पन्न होती है कि बौद्ध आत्मा के विरोधी हैं। 'अनत्त' से तात्पर्य व्यक्ति के अहं भाव (मैं) का निषेध है अथवा आत्मा का, इस पर सूक्ष्म दृष्टि से विचार किए बिना प्रथम अर्थ को द्वितीय अर्थ पर आरोपित कर दिया गया। बुद्ध के द्वारा आत्मा की मिथ्या अवधारणा के निषेध को उनके द्वारा वास्तविक आत्मा के निषेध के रूप में लिया गया। 'आत्मन' शब्द सार्वभौमिक आत्मा का बोध कराता है जो सभी में सामान्य है, सत्य है। मिथ्या धारणा तब उत्पन्न होती है जब हम व्यक्तिगत आत्मा को ही आत्मा का सत्य स्वरूप मान लेते हैं। अहं भाव आत्मभाव नहीं है। अपितु इसके विपरीत यह आत्म भाव से हमारा भेद स्थापित कर हमें विशुद्ध आत्मतत्व (सार्वभौम आत्मा) से दूर ले जाने का कार्य करता है। इसे समाप्त करके ही सत्य को प्राप्त किया जा सकता है।[25] अहं भाव से परे सत्य तक पहुंचने के लिए अहं भाव का विनाश आवश्यक है। अर्हत में अहंभाव नहीं होता अतः वह सत्य स्वरूप को प्राप्त कर लेता है। अनत्त के सही अर्थ को समझने के लिए उसे अत्ता के सदर्भ में समझना होगा जैसे अंधकार को प्रकाश के संदर्भ में समझा जा सकता है। नकारात्मक स्थिति सकारात्मक की ओर संकेत करती है। जब बुद्ध पंच स्कंधों के विषय में कहते हैं—"यह मेरा नहीं है, यह मैं नहीं हूं, यह मेरा आत्मा नहीं है" तब यह प्रश्न स्वतः ही उत्पन्न होता है कि "मेरा क्या है?, मैं कौन हूं?, और मेरा आत्मा क्या है?"। मैक्स टॉप कहते हैं कि 'समस्त पदार्थ विनाशधर्मा एवं अनित्य हैं अतः आत्मा नहीं हो सकते' कथन से स्वतः ही यह निष्कर्ष निकलता है कि आत्मा नित्य और दुःख से परे है। इस प्रकार कथन की आत्मा के अस्तित्व में अविश्वास का परिचायक नहीं है।[26] 'अनिच्च', 'दुक्ख' और 'अनत्त' के विरोधी गुणों में ही वस्तुतः इनकी सत्ता समाहित है। 'अनिच्च' एवं 'दुक्ख' के विपरीतार्थी 'नित्य' और 'सुख' संस्कृत साहित्य में यथार्थ के विशेषण कहे गए हैं। पाली साहित्य में 'निच्च' के स्थान पर 'धुव' एवं 'अच्चुत' को 'निब्बान' के विशेषण के रूप में प्रयुक्त किया गया है।[27] यही नहीं शाश्वतवादियों द्वारा प्रायः (व्यक्तिगत) आत्मा के लिए प्रयुक्त नित्य शब्द एक स्थल पर निब्बान के लिए भी प्रयुक्त हुआ है।[28] निब्बान की व्याख्या सुख के रूप में की गई है।[29] बौद्ध धर्म में भी 'अनत्त' के द्वारा उसके विपरीतार्थक 'अत्ता' की सत्ता की ओर स्पष्ट संकेत है। श्रावस्ती में बुद्ध ने

उपदेश दिया—"अत्तदीपा, भिक्खवे, विहरथ अत्तसरणा अनसञ्ञसरणा।"[30] क्या बुद्ध ने उसकी शरण लेने का उपदेश दिया जो मिथ्या है। जिसकी सत्ता ही नहीं है? इसी प्रकार धम्मपद में भी यह कहा गया है कि आत्मा ही आत्मा का स्वामी है, आत्मा ही आत्मा की गति है।[31] यह सभी संदर्भ बौद्ध धर्म में आत्मा के नकार को मिथ्या सिद्ध करते हैं।

अनत्त सिद्धांत को आधार बनाकर आस्तिक ब्राह्मण एवं नास्तिक बौद्ध धर्मों में भेद दर्शाया गया परंतु अनत्त सिद्धांत की स्वीकृत व्याख्या का आधार न्यायसंगत नहीं है। वस्तुतः परम सत्य एक ही है। औपनिषदिक सत्य एवं बौद्ध धर्म का सत्य भिन्न-भिन्न नहीं हो सकते उसे देखने का दृष्टिकोण भिन्न-भिन्न हो सकता है। विभिन्न धर्मों के तुलनात्मक अध्ययन से इस सत्य को स्थापित किया गया है कि एक पारमार्थिक (सर्वोच्च) सत्य है जो ऐतिहासिक प्रक्रिया के अनुरूप विभिन्न धर्मों में वि।भेन्न प्रकार से व्यक्त किया गया है। सभी विचारक प्रारंभिक अज्ञानता की स्थिति से परे जाकर सर्वोच्च सत्य तक पहुंचे (जो एक ही है किसी नवीन सत्य की उद्घोषणा के लिए कोई आधार नहीं है) अतः यथार्थ (सत्य) संबंधी उनके विचारों में मौलिक एकता के दर्शन होते हैं जिसे विभिन्न भाषाओं में भिन्न शब्दों में व्यक्त किया गया। सत्य ब्रह्म भी है और निब्बान भी जिन्हें समान विशेषणों से शाभित किया गया है। उपनिषदों में 'अयमात्माब्रह्म'[3)] कहकर ब्रह्म और आत्मा को एक कहा गया तो भगवद्गीता[33] में ब्रह्म और निर्वाण को एक कर दिया गया।

'अनत्ता' की भ्रमात्मक व्याख्या ने बुद्ध की मौलिक विचारधारा के विपरीत उनकी शिक्षाओं को एक भिन्न रूप में स्थापित करने का प्रयास किया जो उनका सही स्वरूप प्रतीत नहीं होता। विषयों में चैतन्य, नित्य आत्मा की खोज एवं उन्हें ही आत्मस्वरूप समझ लेने का उन्होंने खंडन किया। 'विषयों में आत्मा की सत्ता नहीं है'—यह कहने का तात्पर्य आत्मा का निषेध नहीं था। संयुत्त निकाय में एक प्रश्न के उत्तर में उन्होंने 'आत्मा है अथवा नहीं है' दोनों ही विकल्पों को अस्वीकार किया[34] उनके अनुसार दृष्टियां छोड़ देने पर एवं उपशांत होने पर आत्मा एवं नैरात्म्य दोनों नहीं रह जाते। स्पष्ट है कि बुद्ध ने अनिर्वचनीय सार्वभौम आत्मा का खंडन नहीं किया अपितु तथाकथित 'अत्तभाव' जिसमें कर्तृत्व एवं भोक्तृत्व समाहित है, का खंडन किया क्योंकि इस प्रकार के कर्ता एवं भोक्ता आत्मा में नित्यता की कल्पना से अहंकार, ममकार, तृष्णा और कर्म विवृद्ध होते हैं जो निब्बान के मार्ग में बाधक हैं। इससे छुटकारा पाकर ही विराग भाव दृढ़ किया जा सकता है। इस मिथ्या आत्मभाव के विरोध को ही बौद्ध धर्म में नैरात्म्यवाद के समर्थन के रूप में गृहण किया गया।

वस्तुतः बुद्ध ने आत्मा की सत्ता का निषेध नहीं किया अपितु जो आत्मा का यथार्थ स्वरूप नहीं है उसे आत्मा समझ लेने की विचारधारा पर प्रश्नचिह्न लगाया।

संदर्भ एवं टिप्पणियां

1. 'अनिच्चा संखारा, तं कुतेत्थ लब्भा' ति। *दीघनिकाय,* II.3.23, पृ. 392, संपा. एवं अनु. स्वामी द्वारिकादास शास्त्री, वाराणसी, 1996
2. यं किञ्चि समुदयधम्मं सब्बं तं निरोधं धम्मं ति। मिलिंदपञ्ह I.1.12, पृ. 12 संपा., स्वामी द्वारिकादास शास्त्री, वाराणसी; *दि क्वेश्चन्स ऑव किंग मिलिंद,* अनु. टी.डब्ल्यू. रीज डेविड्स, प्रथम भाग, पृ. 25, (दि सेकरेड बुक ऑव दि ईस्ट, संपा. एफ. मैक्समूलर, वाल्यूम XXXV), 1996, दिल्ली
3. रूपं, भिक्खवे अनत्ता, वेदना अनत्ता, सञ्ञा अनत्ता, संखारा अनत्ता, विञ्ञाणं अनत्ता। *संयुत्त निकाय,* भाग 2, संपा. स्वामी द्वारिकादास शास्त्री, वाराणसी, 2000, III.22.14, पृ. 770
4. बौद्ध ग्रंथों में पंच स्कंधों को ही एक मात्रा सत्ता कहा गया है और आत्मा को इनमें प्रतीत एक भ्रांति। व्यक्ति का शरीर पंच स्कंधों से मिलकर बना है—रूप, वेदना, संज्ञा, संस्कार और विज्ञान। इनमें से किसी भी एक को या सभी को संयुक्त रूप से आत्मा की संज्ञा नहीं दी जा सकती क्योंकि यह सभी नष्ट हो जाने वाले हैं और मनुष्य इन पंच स्कंधों के अतिरिक्त और कुछ है भी नहीं। अतः सभी कुछ अस्थायी है, क्षणिक है। यह वह ज्ञान है जो व्यक्ति में दीक्षित होकर प्राप्त करता है और इसी प्रज्ञा से वह मोह मुक्त होकर निर्वाण की ओर बढ़ता है। ऐसी स्थिति में आत्मा की सत्ता की संभावना नहीं है। *मिलिंदपञ्ह,* II.1.12., पृ. 21, *दि क्वेश्चन्स ऑव किंग मिलिंद,* प्रथम भाग, पृ. 45
5. रूपं, भिक्खवे, अनत्ता, वेदना अनत्ता, सञ्ञा अनत्ता, संखारा अनत्ता, विञ्ञाणं अनत्ता। एवं परस्स, भिक्खवे सुतवा अरियसावको रूपस्मि पि निब्बिदन्ति, वेदनाय पि निब्बिदन्ति, संञ्ञाय पि निब्बिदन्ति संखारेसु पि निब्बिदन्ति, विञ्ञाणस्मिं पि निब्बिदन्ति। निब्बिन्दं विरज्जति; विरागा विमुच्चति। विमुत्तस्मिं विमुत्तमिति ञाणं होति। *संयुत्त निकाय,* भाग 2, III.2.12, पृ. 170
6. चौधरी, आर. पी., 'इंटरप्रेटेशन ऑव दि अनत्त डाक्टरिन ऑफ बुद्धिज्मः ए न्यू अप्रोच', देखें *इंडियन हिस्टारिकल क्वार्टरली,* वाल्यूम XXXI., पृ. 52-53, 1955
7. कुमारस्वामी ने अनत्त की व्याख्या करते हुए लिखा, "किसी वस्तु में किसी अपरिवर्तनीय तत्व की सत्ता नहीं है न ही किसी व्यक्ति में कोई शाश्वत आत्मा है।" द्रष्टव्य कुमारस्वामी, ए.के., *बुद्धा एंड दि गॉस्पेल ऑफ बुद्धिज्म,* पृ. 198, नई दिल्ली, 2003
8. चौधरी, आर. पी., पूर्वोद्धृत, पृ. 53
9. मिलिंदपञ्ह II.1.1, पृ. 21, 'परमत्थतो पनेत्थ पुग्गलो नूपब्मति। *दि क्वेश्चन्स ऑव किंग मिलिंद,* प्रथम भाग, पृ. 44-45

10. सेकरेड बुक ऑव द ईस्ट, XI, 63, पृ. 69
11. धम्मपाद, 279, संपा. एवं अनु. स्वामी द्वारिकादास शास्त्री, वाराणसी 2001; *दि सेकरेड बुक ऑव दि ईस्ट,* संपा. एवं अनु. एफ. मैक्समूलर, वाल्यूम, X, 2006, दिल्ली, पृ. 69
12. *दीघनिकाय,* III.4.2 पृ. 655
13. रीजडेविड्स का यह विचार *शाक्य, 'बुद्धिज्म', 'व्हाट वाज दि ओरीजनल गॉस्पेल* इत्यादि में विभिन्न स्थलों पर देखा जा सकता है।
14. मंदिरों में "Know thyself" उक्ति का प्राप्त होना मनुष्य की इसी इच्छा की अभिव्यक्ति है।
15. जनक ने घोषित किया—"मिथिलयं दह्यमानाय न में किञ्चि अदह्यत", *जातक,* VI, 54
16. शरीर विनाश धर्मा होने के कारण आत्मा नहीं हो सकता और वेदनाएं विविध और अनित्य होने से आत्मा नहीं हो सकतीं। इससे भी महत्वपूर्ण तथ्य है कि यदि आत्मा वेदनधर्मा है तो वेदनाओं का निरोध होने पर आत्मा का भी निरोध हो जाएगा। द्रष्टव्य पांडे, गोविंद चंद्र, *बौद्ध धर्म के विकास का इतिहास,* पृ. 83, लखनऊ, 2006
17. *संयुत्त निकाय,* भाग 3, IV.35.5, पृ. 1217
18. *मूलमाध्यमकाकारिज दे नागार्जुन एवेक ले प्रसन्नपद,* संपा. ला वाली पूसिनद्ध, 18.6
19. *बृहदारण्यक उपनिषद,* IV.4,23
20. *संयुत्त निकाय,* भाग 2, II.18.21, पृ. 698
21. *विनय पिटक, महावग्ग,* पृ. 25, नालंदा
22. व्याकारणीय प्रतिबद्धताओं को छोड़कर प्रायः आत्मा के लिए एकवचन का ही प्रयोग किया गया है।
23. एकं सत् विप्रा बहुधा वदन्ति, द्रष्टव्य ऋग्वेद, I.164,4
24. द्रष्टव्य, पांडे, जी.सी., पूर्वोद्धृत, पृ. 82
25. विभिन्न समय और परिस्थितियों में उत्पन्न विभिन्न विचारकों ने भिन्न-भिन्न प्रकार से इस परम सत्य का ज्ञान दिया। ईसा ने विरोधी वक्तव्यों द्वारा इसे व्यक्त करते हुए कहा—"जो अपने जीवन की रक्षा करना चाहता है उसे खो देता है; और जो अपने जीवन को खो देता है वह उसे बचा लेता है।" द्रष्टव्य, सेंट ल्यूक, 17.33
26. उपाध्याय, काशीनाथ, *अर्ली बुद्धिज्म एंड भगवद्गीता,* पृ. 303, दिल्ली, 1998
27. "इदं सच्चं इदं धुवं इदं सासतं इदं केवलयं इदं अचवनधम्मं"
28. *पटिसंभिदामग्ग,* I, 238
29. निब्बानं परमं सुखं
30. भिक्षुओ! तुम अपना आधार स्वयं बनो, अपना शरण-स्थल स्वयं बनो, किसी दूसरे की शरण में जाने का प्रयास मत करो....। *संयुत्त निकाय,* III, 5.43, च. 797
31. धम्मपाद, 160, 380; एवं अनु. *दि सेकरेड बुक ऑफ दि ईस्ट,* संपा. एवं अनु. एफ. मैक्समूलर, वाल्यूम X., पृ. 45, 89
32. *मॉण्डूक्य उपनिषद,* 2
33. ब्रह्मनिर्वाणम्, श्रीमद्भगवद्गीता, II, 72
34. *संयुत्त निकाय,* भाग 3, IV. 44.10, पृ. 1605; *संयुत्त निकाय, महावग्ग,* 56,1,8, पृ. 2153

16. बौद्ध दर्शन में अनात्मवाद

दुर्गेश कुमार त्रिपाठी

बौद्ध दर्शन के आविर्भाव की पृष्ठभूमि में एक महान दार्शनिक परंपरा निहित है, जिसमें स्वयं संहिताएं भी सम्मिलित हैं। दर्शन एक ऐसा आध्यात्मिक ज्ञान है जो आत्मारूपी इंद्रिय के समक्ष संपूर्ण रूप से प्रकट होता है। आध्यात्म और नैतिकता का समन्वय बौद्ध दर्शन की महत्वपूर्ण देन हैं। भारतीय संस्कृति अनेक प्रकार के विचारों का विकसित रूप है। ये विचार प्राचीनकाल से अनेक धाराओं में बहते चले आ रहे हैं। इन्हें मुख्य रूप से दो भागों में विभक्त किया जा सकता है—एक वैदिक परंपरा, दूसरी श्रमण परंपरा। श्रमण परंपरा की अनेक शाखाएं रही हैं, किंतु वर्तमान समय में केवल दो शाखाएं ही देखने को मिलती हैं—जैन परंपरा एवं बौद्ध परंपरा। ये दो परंपराएं ही अन्य परंपराओं की भांति धर्म एवं दर्शन के संरक्षण में पुष्पित-पल्लवित और विकसित हुईं।

एक विचार के अनुसार भारतवर्ष में जितने दर्शन हैं, उनका लक्ष्य मोक्ष की प्राप्ति है। इस अर्थ में सब दर्शन मोक्षशास्त्र हैं।[1] अनात्म में आत्म-ग्रह-मिथ्या-ज्ञान है। 'मैं हूं' इस प्रकार का मोह, अहंकार अर्थात् अनात्मा को (देह आदि) आत्मा के रूप में देखना, यह दृष्टि अहंकार है। शरीर, इंद्रिय, मन, वेदना, बुद्धि यह पदार्थ-समूह (अर्थ-जात) है, जिसके विषय में अहंकार होता है। जीव आदि पदार्थ-समूह को 'मैं हूं' यह निश्चित कर शरीर आदि के उच्छेद को आत्मोच्छेद मानता है। वह शरीर आदि की चिर-स्थिति के लिए व्याकुल होता है और बार-बार उसका ग्रहरण कर जन्म-मरण के निमित्त यत्नशील होता है।[2] बौद्ध दर्शन चार हैं। सर्वास्तिवाद-वैभाषिक मत का अत्यधिक प्रचार कनिष्क के समय में हुआ। चीनी यात्रियों में फाहियान (399-414 ई.) एवं इत्सिंग (671-692 ई.) इसके मर्मज्ञ थे।[3] सौत्रांत्रिक मत के संस्थापक

कुमारलात थे। इस कथन की पुष्टि ह्वेनसांग द्वारा होती है। अन्य अनुयायी शिष्य श्रीलाभ, धर्मत्रात, बुद्धदेव, यशोमित्र के नाम मिलते हैं।[4] विज्ञानवाद-योगाचार मत बौद्ध दर्शन के विकास का एक महत्पूर्ण अंग समझा जाता है। मैत्रेय, असंग और वसुबंधु ने इस दिशा में उल्लेखनीय कार्य किये।[5] माध्यमिक-शून्यवाद के प्रवर्तक आचार्य नागार्जुन थे, जो आंध्र राजा गौतमी पुत्र यज्ञश्री (166-196 ई.) के समकालीन बतलाए जाते हैं। इनके शिष्यों में आर्यदेव (200 ई. - 224 ई.), स्थविर बुद्धपालित, भावविवेक, चंद्रकीर्ति, शांतरक्षित के नाम महत्वपूर्ण हैं।[6]

मन अपनी ऊर्ध्वतम अवस्था में भी केवल एक पुद्गल है, एक स्कंध है, विविध तत्वों का एक पुंजमात्र है। अतः पुद्गल का स्कंधों से वही संबंध है, जो अग्नि का ईंधन से है, ऐसे में तुमको स्वीकार करना पड़ेगा कि वह क्षणिक परिवर्तनशील और विनांशशील है। बौद्ध दर्शन क्षण-क्षण परिवर्तित मन से परे किसी भी नित्य जीवात्मा को नहीं मानता। बौद्ध दर्शन को समझने के लिए दुःखवाद, अनित्यतता और अनात्मवाद तीन मूलभूत सिद्धांत हैं। चूंकि कोई वस्तु शाश्वत नहीं है, प्रत्येक वस्तु नश्वर है, इससे स्वतः यह स्पष्ट होता है कि आत्मा का स्वयमेव कोई अस्तित्व नहीं है।[7] पंचवर्गीय भिक्षुओं के उपसंपदा के तुरंत बाद भगवान बुद्ध ने उनको अन्नत (अनात्म) के बारे में शिक्षा दी और जोर देकर कहा कि रूप, रस, वेदना, संस्कार एवं विज्ञान, ये अनात्म हैं।[8] "भिक्षुओ! रूप (भौतिक पदार्थ) अन्-आत्मा है। यदि रूप (पुरुष) की आत्मा होती तो यह पीड़ादायक न बनती, और रूप में—मेरा रूप ऐसा होता, मेरा रूप ऐसा न होता, यह पाया जाता, चूंकि रूप अनात्म है, इसलिए रूप पीड़ादायक होता है।"[9] सुत्तनिपात में वर्णित है कि अनात्मा में आत्मदर्शी देवताओं के लोक को देखो। नामरूप में निर्दिष्ट वह समझता है, यही सत्य है, किंतु उसका वह विनश्वर और गत्वर सत्व मोषधर्म है। निर्वाण अमोषधर्म है।[10] यदि आत्मा और स्कंध एक ही आत्मा है तो आत्मा, अनित्य और नाशवान हुई, और यदि वह स्कंधों से अलग है तो उसी प्रकार हुई जैसे गायों के साथ गोपाल। इसलिएः न यही कहा जा सकता है कि आत्मा और स्कंध एक है और न यही कि दोनों अलग हैं।[11] अतः भिक्षुओ! वर्तमान चक्षु अनित्य है, जो अनित्य है वह दुःख है; जो दुःख है वह अनात्म है; जो अनात्म है वह न मेरा है, न मैं हूं और न मेरी आत्मा है; इसे भलीभांति प्रज्ञापूर्वक समझ लेना चाहिए।[12] संपूर्ण संसार को अनित्य, अनात्म एवं दुःखरूप मानने वाले व्यक्ति को ही ज्ञान, प्रीति, की प्राप्ति होती है। अनात्म चिंतन से ही मनुष्य यथाभूत परमार्थ सत्व का दिग्दर्शन करता है।[13]

"दीप स्वयं प्रकाशित होता है"— यह चित्त में जानकर कहा जाता है। "चित्त

प्रकाशित होता है।" यह किससे जानकर कहा जाता है? "चित्त स्वयं प्रकाशवान है या नहीं" यह बात किसी द्रष्टा के अभाव में चाहे जितनी कही जाए वह बंध्या-पुत्री के विलास की भांति मिथ्या है।[14] बुद्ध आत्मा को नहीं मानते, उसकी जगह वे चित्त मन और विज्ञान को मानते हैं, मन शरीर नहीं है, किंतु साथ ही मन काया आश्रित है।[15] हम यह जानते हैं कि इंद्रियों के बिना बुद्धि (मन, ज्ञान) नहीं होती, साथ ही इंद्रियां भी बुद्धि के बिना नहीं होतीं। अतः इंद्रियां और बुद्धि एक दूसरे पर आश्रित हैं। जब बुद्धि के सामने भाव और अभाव दोनों ही नहीं रहते, तब उसके सामने और कोई गति नहीं होती कि वह स्वयं ठहर सके। इसलिए अंत में आलंबन न होने के कारण वह भी शांत हो जाती है।[16] अपना स्वरूप मन, बुद्धि, शरीर आदि के साथ दिखता है, पर वास्तव में इनके साथ है नहीं। सामान्य रूप से प्रत्येक व्यक्ति यह अनुभव कर सकता है कि बचपन से लेकर अब तक शरीर, इंद्रियां, मन, बुद्धि आदि सबके सब बदल गए, पर मैं वही हूं। अतः मैं बदलने वाला नहीं हूं।[17] एक नित्य आत्मा और नित्य असंचारी मन, विशिष्ट संयोग का होना, जो विशिष्ट चित्त के लिए आवश्यक है, इसे कैसे सिद्ध कर सकते हैं? क्या आप यह कहेंगे कि यह विशिष्टता बुद्धि-विशेष के कारण होती है, जो आत्मा का गुण है? लेकिन बुद्धि में भी वही समस्या है, जो मन में है। जब आत्मा विशिष्ट है, तो बुद्धि कैसे विशिष्ट होगी? क्या आप कहेंगे कि संस्कार विशेष आत्मा और मन का संयोग-विषेष होता है, और इस विशेष से बुद्धि-विशेष होता है? इस कथन से आत्मा निष्प्रयोजनीय हो जाती है।

पुराणों में वर्णित है कि आत्मा स्वच्छंद विचरण कर सकती है। इसके संबंध में विभिन्न विद्वानों के वैचारिक मत हैं। जब तक मन चंचल है, तब तक मन के हर कार्य पर गहरी दृष्टि रखना अत्यावश्यक है, क्योंकि मन ही जीवात्मा का मित्र और मन ही जीवात्मा का शत्रु है। इंद्रियों में अनित्य, दुःख, अनात्म से विमुक्ति का वर्णन मिलता है।[18] जिस जीवात्मा द्वारा मन और इंद्रियों सहित शरीर जीता हुआ है, उस जीवात्मा का तो वह आप ही मित्र है, और जिसके मन तथा इंद्रियों सहित शरीर नहीं जीता गया, उसके लिए वह आप में शत्रु सदृश्य करता है।[19]

कुछ मर्मज्ञों का मानना है कि गौतम बुद्ध आत्मा के किसी रूप विशेष में आस्था नहीं रखते थे। उनका धर्म पूर्णतया अनात्मवादी था।[20] रीज डेविड्स के मतानुसार बुद्ध के समय में उत्तर-भारत में बहु-ईश्वरवाद, द्वैतवाद, अद्वैतवाद एवं जगदीश्वरवाद की विचारधाराएं प्रचलित थीं। आत्मा का विश्वास इन सभी विचारधाराओं में मूल रूप से मौजूद था। बुद्ध इसे नकारा ही नहीं, अपितु यहां तक माना कि ये

विचारधाराएं, आध्यात्मिक उत्कर्ष में बाधक हैं।[21] पालि साहित्य से भी अनात्मवाद का समर्थन मिलता है,[22] लेकिन कुछ स्थलों पर आत्मवाद का समर्थन मिलता है।[23] श्रीमती रीज डेविड्स ने अपनी पूर्व कृतियों में बौद्ध धर्म के अनात्म संबंधी सिद्धांत को नकारा है।[24]

एक विचार के अनुसार आत्मा कर्म-कर्ता नहीं, परंतु उनके फलों की भोक्ता है। वह निपुण, निष्क्रिय है, वह अपरिवर्तनशील या अविकारी सत्ता का परिवर्तनशील सत्ता के साथ संयोग किसी भी दशा में नहीं हो सकती, न अपरिवर्तनशील आत्मा परिवर्तनशील प्रकृति की भोक्ता हो ही सकती है। जो नित्य और अपरिवर्तनशील है, उसे सदा वैसा ही बने रहना चाहिए और परिवर्तनशील वस्तु के साथ उसका कभी संयोग नहीं होना चाहिए।[25] सांख्य लोगों का मानना है कि आत्मा प्रकृति से भिन्न है और मारना, मरवाना आदि बातों का परिणाम उस पर नहीं होता।[26] इस कथन की पुष्टि 'भगवद्‌गीता' से भी होती है।[27] वहीं श्रीमती रीज डेविड्स ने इस विचारधारा पर जोर दिया है कि बुद्ध ने अनात्मा के सिद्धांत को प्रतिपादित ही नहीं किया बल्कि ये बाद में ब्राह्मण धर्म के मूल सर्वमान सिद्धांत (आत्मा के अस्तित्व) के विरोध में विकसित हुआ।[28] संयुत्त के एक पद्य की तुलना उन्होंने भद्रनायक के एक कथनांक से करते हुए कहा कि मेरे विश्वास से यह बहुत कुछ संभव है कि मूलपद्य के कथाकार ने अत्त शब्द का प्रयोग उसी भाव में किया है, जिस भाव में आत्मा शब्द उपनिषदों में प्रयुक्त हुआ है।[29] इस विचारधारा पर कुमारस्वामी[30] और राधाकृष्णन[31] ने यथा अपेक्षित परिवर्तनों सहित पुनर्बल दिया है। एक स्थान पर राधाकृष्णन ने स्पष्ट रूप से कहा है कि गौतम बुद्ध के मतानुसार आत्मा का कोई अस्तित्व नहीं है, यह कहना गलत होगा।[32] गीता में वर्णित है कि अनादिकाल से जीवात्मा जीवन की विविध योनियों में और विभिन्न लोकों में लगभग निरंतर, यात्रा करती रहती है। यद्यपि वह किसी निश्चित वस्तु के रूप में नहीं होती, तथापि वह प्रत्येक योनि का आधार होती है। यह गौतम बुद्ध का भी विचार है, लेकिन वे इसे निश्चित रूप से नहीं कहते हैं।[33] कहने का आशय यह है कि जैसे पृथ्वी से दूर जल है, जल से दूर तेज, तेज से दूर वायु, वायु से दूर आकाश, आकाश से दूर महतत्व, महतत्व से दूर प्रकृति और प्रकृति से दूर जीवात्मा है। अतः दूर से दूर होते हुए भी वह जीवात्मा व्यापक रूप से सब में है, क्योंकि जीवात्मा सबका कारण है और सब कार्यों में रहता है।

बौद्ध धर्म में आत्मा के अस्तित्व को स्वीकार किए जाने का यह भी प्रमाण है कि बौद्ध धर्म ध्यान पर बल देता है। बिना आध्यात्मिक सिद्धान्त को स्वीकार किए

हुए उच कर्तव्य ज्ञान को सत्यापित करना असंभव है।[34] भगवान बुद्ध ने कहा है कि श्रेष्ठतर चित्त की साधना में लगे हुए भिक्षु को समय-समय पर समाधि, निमित्त, प्रग्रह निमित्त तथा उपेक्षा निमित्त को मन में स्थान देना चाहिए।[35] जब कोई ध्यानी अपनी प्रज्ञा द्वारा 'सभी धर्म अनात्म हैं' ऐसा साक्षात कर लेता है तब वह दुःखों के प्रति वैराग्यवान हो जाता है। यही चित्त विशुद्धि का सर्वोत्तम मार्ग है।[36] नारद ने भी ध्यान का महत्व बताते हुए कहा है कि ध्यान से पाप नष्ट होते हैं, ध्यान से मोक्ष मिलता है, ध्यान से भगवान प्रसन्न होते हैं। ध्यान से समस्त साधनों में सिद्धि मिलती है।[37] मनुष्य की मृत्यु के पश्चात् उसका चित्त या विनाना (उपनिषदों में वर्णित आत्मा के समान) ही शेष बचता है, यह सिद्धांत निश्चित रूप से बुद्ध से पूर्व का है। बुद्ध इसे सुधारते हुए न कि नकारते हुए प्रतीत हुए हैं।[38] अनेक विद्वानों ने यह कहा है कि भगवान बुद्ध ने अपने समय में प्रचलित आत्मवाद का खंडन किया और संसारी को संसरण प्रवाह में निमग्न कर दिया।[39] इसके विपरीत कुछ मर्मज्ञों ने यह कहा है कि इस प्रकार का नैरात्म्यवाद परवर्ती भिक्षुओं और आचार्यों की बुद्धि की उपज है। तथागत ने केवल अनात्मभूत तत्वों में आत्मा को न देखने का उपदेश दिया था। आत्मा का सर्वथा तिरस्कार नहीं।[40] जब बुद्ध से सीधे आत्मा के अस्तित्व के बारे में प्रश्न पूछा गया, तो उन्होंने आत्मा के अस्तित्व के विषय में स्वीकारात्मक या नकारात्मक उत्तर देने से मना कर दिया। कीथ[41] का मानना है कि यह उनके अनीश्वरवाद का परिणाम है। अतः बुद्ध ने आत्मा की स्वतंत्र सत्ता का तो निषेध कर दिया, लेकिन वे मन और मानसिक वृत्तियों की सत्ता सदैव स्वीकार करते हैं। इन वृत्तियों में तृष्णा, वेदना, दुःख, राग, द्वेष आदि वर्णित हैं।[42] अविद्या, संस्कार पूर्व जन्म से संबंधित है; विज्ञान, स्कंध, नामरूप, षडायतन, स्पर्ष, वेदना, तृष्णा, उपादान, वर्तमान जीवन से संबंधित हैं; वहीं भव, जाति जरामरण, भविष्य से संबंधित हैं।[43] इस प्रकार तथागत ने आत्मवाद और अनात्मवाद दोनों का उपदेश दिया, किंतु उनका वास्तविक अभिप्राय यह था कि न आत्मवाद तात्विक है, न अनात्मवाद। दोनों ही कोटियों के परे अनिर्वचनीय रूप से सत्य प्रतिष्ठित हैं।[44]

उपर्युक्त विवरण से संकेत मिलता है कि जीवात्मा क्या है? उसका क्या स्वरूप है? इस संबंध में बौद्ध दर्शन, ब्राह्मण धर्म एवं उपनिषदों में वर्णित तथ्यों के दृष्टिगत सभी मर्मज्ञ/धर्मावलंबी में वैचारिक मतभेद कायम हैं। लेकिन जीवात्मा के अस्तित्व को प्रत्यक्ष ब्राह्मण ग्रंथ/उपनिषद तथा अप्रत्यक्ष रूप से बौद्ध दर्शन भी स्वीकार करता है। भगवान बुद्ध ने अपने उपदेशों में स्वयं को स्वयं द्वारा विभिन्न लोकों में भ्रमण

किया जाना कहा है। जातक कथाओं में भी उनके पूर्वजन्मों का उल्लेख मिलता है। बुद्ध ने स्वयं स्वर्ग और नरक योग्य कर्मों के अनुसार जीवात्मा का विभिन्न योनियों में जन्म लेने तथा निर्वाण, जिसे उपनिषदों में मोक्ष कहा गया है, का उपदेश दिया है। इससे विदित होता है कि चित्त प्रवाह में कोई स्थिर जीवात्मा अवश्य है, यदि नहीं, तो कर्म-फल का भोग कौन करता है, निर्वाण सुख का भोग कौन करता, स्वर्ग-नरक किसको प्राप्त होता है? या तो ये सब परिकल्पनाएं भ्रम हैं या जीवात्मा का चित्त-प्रवाह में अस्तित्व अवश्य है। चूंकि आत्मा शरीर के अन्य अंगों की तरह मूर्तरूप में नहीं होती, अतः इसका अनुभव ज्ञान के द्वारा ही किया जा सकता है। समस्त धर्मों में जीवात्मा के अस्तित्व को प्रत्यक्ष या परोक्ष रूप से स्वीकार किया गया है। बौद्ध दर्शन में अनात्मक के सम्यक अध्ययन से यही सिद्ध होता है कि बौद्ध दर्शन भी इस विचारधारा से अछूता नहीं है।

संदर्भ एवं टिप्पणियां

1. नरेंद्रदेव, आचार्य, *बौद्ध धर्म-दर्शन,* (मोतीलाल बनारसीदास पब्लिशर्स प्राइवेट लिमिटेड, दिल्ली, पुनर्मुद्रण, 1994), पृ. 221
2. वही, पृ. 222
3. उपाध्याय, बलदेव, *बौद्ध दर्शन-मीमांसा,* (प्रकाशक, चौखंबा विद्याभवन, वाराणसी, पंचम संस्करण, 1999 ई.), पृ. 147-148
4. वही, पृ. 184-187
5. पांडे, गोविंद्र चंद्र, *बौद्ध धर्म के विकास का इतिहास,* (उत्तर प्रदेश हिंदी संस्थान, लखनऊ, चतुर्थ संस्करण, 2006), पृ. 320
6. उपाध्याय, बलदेव, पूर्वोद्धृत, पृ. 236-237, 239-240, 242
7. महाबोधि, LXXIV, नं. 9-10, पृ. 194-196; श्रीराम गोयल, *ए रिलिजियस हिस्ट्री ऑव एंशियंट इंडिया अप टू सी. 1200 ए.डी.,* (कुसुमांजति प्रकाशन, मेरठ, 1984), पृ. 236
8. *संयुत्तनिकायपालि, राधसंयुत्तं,* (बौद्धभारती, वाराणसी, 2000 ई.) द्वितीय भाग, संपादक एवं अनुवादक स्वामी द्वारिकादास शास्त्री, 17, अनत्तासुख, पृ. 994 : रूपं, अनत्ता, वेदना अनत्ता, सञ्ञा अनत्ता, सङ्खारा अनत्ता, विञ्ञाणं अनत्ता।; सुत्त-पिटके संयुत्त-निकाय, अनुवादक, भिक्षु जगदीश कश्यप एवं त्रिपिटकाचार्य भिक्षु धर्मरक्षित, (प्रकाशक, महाबोधि सभा, सारनाथ, बनारस, 1954), भाग-द्वितीय, उदासीयुत्त, 34.4.3.7, पृ. 519
9. महावग्गपालि, विनयपिटक, (नव-नालंदा, महाविहार, 1980 ई.) प्रधान संशोधक, भिक्षु जगदीसकस्सपो, 8. अनत्तपरियायो, पृ. 16 : अथ खो भगवा पञ्चवग्गिये भिक्खू

आमन्तेसि रूपं, भिक्खवे, अनत्ता। रूपं च हिदं, भिक्खवे, अत्ता अभविस्स, नायिदं रूपं आबाध्य संवत्तेय, लब्मेथ च रूपे–एवं में रूपं होतु, एवं में रूपं मा अहोती।

10. सुत्तनिपात, द्वयतानुपस्सनासुत्त, (मोतीलाल बनारसीदास, वाराणसी, द्वितीय संस्करण, 1983), पृ. 200-202, सुत्त 33-35 : "अनत्तनि अत्तमानिं, पस्स लोकं सदेवकं। निनिट्ठं नामरूपस्मिं, इदं सच्चाति मञ्ञति।। तं हिं तस्स मुसा होति, मोसधम्मं हि इत्तरं।। अमोसधम्मं निब्बाणं, तदरिया सच्चतो विदू। ते वे सच्चाभिसमया, निच्छाता परिनिब्बुता।।"
11. *मज्झिमनिकाय,* (बांबे, 1937, प्रथम भाग), एन.के. भागवत, पृ. 95-96 : तं जीवं तं सरीरं इति पि, अञ्ञं जीवं अञ्ञं सरीरं।
12. सुत्त-पिटके संयुत्त-निकाय, सट्ठि पेय्याल, यदनिच्च सुत्त, 34.4.2.39, पृ.514
13. पांडे, ब्रजमोहन, *बौद्ध साधना और दर्शन,* (अमन प्रकाशन, नई दिल्ली), पृ. 171
14. बोधिचर्यावतार, (बुद्ध विहार, लखनऊ, 2527 बुद्धाब्द : 1983), आचार्य शांतिदेव, अनुवादक, शांतिभिक्षु शास्त्री, पृ. 101, श्लोक 22-23 : द्वीपः प्रकाशित इति ज्ञावा ज्ञावेन कथ्यते। बुद्धि प्रकाशत इति ज्ञात्वेदं केन कथ्यते।। प्रकाशा वाप्रकाशा वा यदा दृष्टा न केन चित्त्। वन्ध्यादुहितृलीलेव कथ्यमानापि सा मुधा।।
15. सांकृत्यायन, राहुल, *बौद्ध दर्शन* (प्रकाशक, किताब महल, 2005), पृ. 146
16. बोधिचर्यावतार, पूर्वोद्धृत, पृ. 104 : यदा न भावो नाभावो मतेः संतिष्ठते पुरः। तदान्यगत्यभावेन निरालंबा प्रशाम्यति।।
17. *श्रीमद्भगवतगीता,* स्वामी रामसुखदास, (गीताप्रेस, गोरखपुर, 86वां संस्करण, सं. 2060), पृ. 798, अध्याय 12, श्लोक 8 : मय्येव् मन आध्त्स्व मयि बुद्धिं निवेशय। निवसिष्यसि मय्येत अत ऊर्ध्वं न संशयः।।; संयुत्तनिकाय, अंग्रेजी अनुवाद रीज डेविड्स एवं एफ.एल. वुडवर्ड, (लंदन, 1917, 1930), 4.54
18. *सुत्त-पिटके संयुत्त-निकाय,* पूर्वोद्धृत, भाग-1, 17-राहुल संयुत्त, 1-चक्खुसुत्त, 17.1.1, पृ. 297 से आगे।
19. *श्रीमद्भगवतगीता,* पूर्वोद्धृत, पृ. 399, अध्याय 6, श्लोक 6 : बंधुरात्मात्मनस्तस्य येनात्मैवात्मना जितः। अनात्मनस्तु शत्रुत्वे वर्तेतात्मैव शत्रुवत्।।
20. सांकृत्यायन, राहुल, *बौद्ध दर्शन* (इलाहाबाद, 1692), पृ. 22-23; महाबोधि, LXXIV नं. 5-6, पृ. 63-69
21. डेविड्स, टी.डब्ल्यू. रीज, *हिस्ट्री ऑफ इंडियन बुद्धिज्म,* (लन्दन, 1877), पृ. 95-99
22. सुत्त-पिटके संयुत्त-निकाय, पूर्वोद्धृत, भाग-2, राध सुत्त, 34.2.3., पृ. 472
23. वाले पुंसा, दि आत्मन् इन दि पालि केनन, *इंडियन कल्चर,* भाग-2, 1935-36, पृ. 821-824
24. डेविड्स, सी.ए.एफ. रीज, *बुद्धिज्म, एक स्टडी, ऑफ दि बुद्धिस्ट नॉर्म,* (लंदन, 1912); जर्नल ऑफ दि रॉयल एशियाटिक सोशायटी, बांबे ब्रांच, बांबे, 1903
25. बाजपेयी, कृष्णदत्त एवं नलिनाक्ष दत्त, *उत्तर प्रदेश में बौद्ध धर्म का इतिहास,* (प्रकाशन ब्यूरो, उत्तर प्रदेश सरकार, लखनऊ, प्रथम संस्करण, 1956), पृ. 156
26. कोसंबी, धर्मानंद, *भगवान बुद्ध : जीवन और दर्शन* (लोक भारती प्रकाशन, इलाहाबाद,

1987), पृ. 166

27. *भगवद्गीता,* पूर्वोद्धृत, अध्याय 2, श्लोक 19, पृ. 70 : य एनं वेत्ति हन्तारं यश्चैनं मन्यते हतम्। उभौ तौ न विजानीतो नायं हन्ति न हन्यते।।
28. डेविड्स, सी.ए.एफ. रीज, *शाक्याज ऑर बुद्धिस्ट ओरिजिंस* (लंदन, 1931)।
29. *संयुत्तनिकायपालि,* 38-अरूपीअत्तासुत्तं, संपादक एवं अनुवादक स्वामी द्वारिकादास शास्त्री, (बौद्ध भारती, वाराणसी, 2000 ई.), भाग 2, पृ. 1027; विश्वनाथ प्रसाद वर्मा, *अर्ली बुद्धिज्म एंड इट्स ओजिरजिंस,* (नई दिल्ली, 1973), पृ. 156
30. कुमारस्वामी, ए.के., एंड हर्न, *लिविंग थॉट्स ऑफ गौतम दि बुद्ध,* (लंदन, 1948); हरी सिंह गौर, *दि स्पिरिट ऑफ बुद्धिज्म,* (कलकत्ता), पृ. 285
31. राधाकृष्णन, सर्वपल्ली, *इंडियन फिलॉसफी,* (लंदन, 1923), भाग-1, पृ. 386-389
32. वही
33. वही, पृ. 388; *बुलेटिन ऑफ रामकृष्ण मिशन इंस्टीटयूट ऑफ कल्चर,* भाग-14, कलकत्ता, पृ. 9-15
34. डेविड्स, सी.ए.एफ. रीजि, *ध्यान इन अर्ली बुद्धिज्म, इंडियन हिस्टोरिकल क्वाअर्ली,* भाग-3, कलकत्ता, 1927, पृ. 689-715.
35. *अंगुत्तर-निकाय,* प्रथम भाग, अनुवादक, भदंत आनंद कौसल्यायन, (प्रकाशक, महाबोधि सभा, कलकत्ता) पृ. 265
36. धम्मपद, बुद्धोपदेशसंग्रह, संपादक एवं अनुवादक, स्वामी द्वारिका दास शास्त्री, (प्रकाशक, चौखंबा संस्कृत सीरीज, वाराणसी, 2005), पृ. 20, मग्ग वग्गो वीसतिमो गाथा 279 : सब्बे धम्मा अनत्ता ति, यदा पञ्ञाय पस्सति अर्थ निब्बिन्दति दुक्खे, एस मग्गो विसुद्धिया।।
37. *बृहन्नारदीयपुराणम्,* पूर्व भाग, हिंदी अनुवाद सहित, अनुवादक तारिणीशस झा, (हिंदी साहित्य सम्मेलन, प्रयाग, 1989), अध्याय 33, श्लोक 139, पृ. 218 : ध्यानात्पापानि नश्यन्ति ध्यानान्मोक्षं च विंदति। ध्यानात्प्रसीदति हरिद्धर्यापात्सर्वार्थसाधनम्।।
38. *जर्नल ऑफ दि अमेरिकन ओरियंटल सोसायटी,* न्यू हेवल, भाग-84, सं. 3, पृ. 254-259
39. डेविड्स, उदा. टी.डब्ल्यू. रीज, *अमेरिकन लेक्चर्स,* पृ. 36-41; जी.पी. श्चेरबात्स्की, *दि यूनिक डॉक्ट्राइन ऑफ बुद्धिज्म,* (लंदन, 1922), पृ. 73
40. डेविड्स, सी.ए.एफ. रीज, *शाक्याज ऑर बुद्धिस्ट ओरिजिंस,* (लंदन, 1931)।
41. कीथ, ए.बी., *बुद्धिस्ट फिलॉसफी,* भाग-1, (कैंब्रिज, 1925), पृ. 39-46
42. *सुत्त-पिटके संयुत्त-निकाय,* पूर्वोद्धृत, भाग-1, मज्झिम पण्णासक, 7-पञ्चवग्गियसुत्त, 21.2.1.7, पृ. 351-352
43. *संयुत्तनिकायपालि,* पूर्वोद्धृत, 2-निदानवग्गो, पृ. 391-394
44. पांडे, गोविंद चंद्र, पूर्वोद्धृत, पृ. 80

17. प्राचीन भारत में तंतुवायों की सामाजिक स्थिति

एक अध्ययन

सुषमा श्रीवास्तव

आधुनिक काल में भारतीय इतिहास लेखन के मार्क्सवादी दृष्टिकोण के तहत बीसवीं शती के पांचवें-छठे दशक में सामाजार्थिक अध्ययन को प्रधानता मिली। इस संदर्भ में अनेक शिल्पी वर्ग की सामाजार्थिक स्थिति पर महत्वपूर्ण अध्ययन हुआ है, जिसमें तंतुवायों की सामाजिक स्थिति पर भी शोध पत्र प्रकाशित हुआ है[1]। किंतु इस संदर्भ में कतिपय महत्वपूर्ण साहित्यिक स्रोतों एवं अभिलेखों का अध्ययन अपेक्षित है। अतः प्रस्तुत शोध-पत्र में कतिपय साहित्यिक एवं पुरातात्विक स्रोतों की पुनर्व्याख्या की गई है तथा तंतुवायों की आर्थिक स्थिति ने उनकी सामाजिक स्थिति को कहां तक प्रभावित किया है उस पर भी प्रकाश डाला गया है।

उल्लेखनीय है कि भारत में कृषि कर्म के बाद सबसे महत्वपूर्ण व्यवसाय वस्त्र उद्योग था जिसके प्रमाण सैंधव सभ्यता से प्राप्त होने लगते हैं। सैंधवकालीन पुरास्थल आलमगीरपुर के उत्खनन से वस्त्र का एक टुकड़ा प्राप्त हुआ है। मोहनजोदड़ो से तांबे की वस्तुएं सूत के कपड़े में लपेटी हुई प्राप्त हुई हैं।[2] अतः यह स्पष्ट है कि सैंधव काल में बुनकर वर्ग अस्तित्व में आ गया था। ऐतिहासिक कालक्रम में सबसे प्राचीनतम साहित्य ऋग्वेद में वस्त्र के लिए *'वासस'* शब्द का प्रयोग मिलता है।[3] *ऋग्वेद* में मरुत देव को स्वर्ण के तारों से कढ़ा वस्त्र पहने हुए वर्णित किया गया है।[4] इसी ग्रंथ में पूषन देवता (सूर्य) को *वासोवाय* अर्थात वस्त्र का निर्माता कहा जाता है।[5] *ऋग्वेद* में वस्त्र निर्माण के संबंध में एक दार्शनिक व्याख्या भी मिलती है। इसमें वर्णित है कि दिन एवं रात के युग्म से काल यानी समय का वस्त्र बुना जाता है।[6] *ऋग्वेद* में बुनने के संबंध में उक्त धार्मिक एवं

दार्शनिक विवरण प्राप्त होते हैं। साथ ही, तंतुवाय (बुनकर) हेतु 'वाय' एवं 'सिरी' दो शब्दों का उल्लेख मिलता है।[7] *ऋग्वेद* में तंतुवायों के उल्लेख के साथ-साथ उनके द्वारा प्रयुक्त उपकरणों का भी उल्लेख है जैसे तसर (ढरकी)[8] तथा मयूख (खूंटी)[9] का भी उल्लेख है, अतः स्पष्ट है कि ऋग्वैदिक काल में वस्त्र का व्यवसाय महत्वपूर्ण रहा होगा।

उत्तरवैदिक काल (ई. पू. 1000-600 ई. पू.) में व्यवसायगत कौशल में अभिवृद्धि हुई। अतः तंतुवाय भी व्यवसायगत जाति के रूप में अस्तित्व में आए। उत्तर वैदिक काल के साहित्य में बुनाई की प्रक्रिया में *ओतु* (तंतु, बाना woof), ताना (warp, length wise thread) शब्दों का उल्लेख है।[10] उल्लेखनीय है कि उत्तर वैदिक काल में 'वयित्री' संज्ञा का प्रयोग स्त्री बुनकरों के लिए हुआ है।[11] ब्राह्मण ग्रंथों में उल्लेख है कि स्त्रियां भी इस उद्योग में संलग्न थीं।[12] अतः स्पष्ट रूप से कहा जा सकता है कि वैदिक काल में तंतुवाय एक व्यावसायिक वर्ग के रूप में अस्तित्व में आ गए थे। उल्लेखनीय है कि वैदिक काल में तंतुवायों को वैश्य वर्ग के अन्तर्गत परिगणित किया जाता था।[13] वैदिक काल में व्यवसायगत श्रेष्ठता एवं हीनता की अवधारणा नहीं थी।[14] अतः न तो तंतुवायों का व्यवसाय हीन था एवं न ही उनकी सामाजिक स्थिति निम्न थी।

ई. पू. 600 शती में नागरिक प्रवृत्ति के विकास के साथ-साथ वस्त्रों एवं परिधान के विविध स्वरूप मिलने लगते हैं। पाणिनि की *अष्टाध्यायी* (लगभग 500 ई. पू.) में तंतुवायों का उल्लेख मिलता है।[15] साथ ही, बुनकरों के तकनीकी उपकरणों का भी विस्तार से उल्लेख है। वस्त्रोद्योग के विकास का अनुमान इस शिल्प में प्रयुक्त विशिष्ट शब्दावलियों से लगाया जा सकता है जैसे, जहां वस्त्र बुना जाता था उस स्थान को आवाय,[16] करघे को तंत्र,[17] ढरकी को प्रवाणी[18] तथा जो वस्त्र उसे करघे से बुनकर उतारा गया हो उसे *तंत्रक*[19] *नवक या निष्प्रवाणि* कहा जाता है। अष्टाध्यायी में स्पष्ट वर्णित है कि इस काल में विभिन्न व्यवसायों में शूद्र संलग्न थे। शूद्रों की दो कोटियां थीं जो क्रमशः निर्वासित तथा अनिर्वासित शूद्र थे। उल्लेखनीय है कि तंतुवायों की गणना अनिर्वासित शूद्रों में थी[20] क्योंकि वह उच्च्व सामाजिक वर्ग के समीप आवासित होते थे। कालक्रम में तंतुवायों के संबंध में महाकाव्यों से भी विस्तृत जानकारी मिलती है। इस उद्योग एवं तंतुवायों के महत्व का अनुमान *रामायण* (400 ई. पू.-200 ई.) के एक प्रसंग से लगाया जा सकता है। इसमें वर्णित है कि राम के वनवास काल में जब भरत राम से मिलने के लिए अयोध्या से शृंग्वेरपुर जाते हैं तो वे अपने साथ विभिन्न व्यवसायियों एवं शिल्पकारों को ले जाते हैं। उल्लेखनीय है कि

लगभग 24 व्यवसायियों की सूची में *सूत्रकर्म विशेषज्ञों* अर्थात तंतुवायों का उल्लेख तृतीय स्थान पर है।[21] अतः यह कहा जा सकता है कि राज्य की दृष्टि में बुनकरों का महत्व था एवं इस शिल्प एवं जाति को हीन नहीं माना जाता रहा होगा। *महाभारत* (400 ई. पू.-200 ई.पू.) में भी रेशमी, सूती, मलमल, ऊनी सभी प्रकार के वस्त्रों का उल्लेख मिलता है। इसमें संदर्भित है कि भारत के विभिन्न भागों से आए हुए वस्त्र युधिष्ठिर को भेंट किए गए थे।[22] स्पष्ट है कि उस काल में विभिन्न प्रकार के वस्त्रों का निर्माण हो रहा था।

भारतीय विकसित वस्त्रोद्योग का अनुमान इस तथ्य से भी लगाया जा सकता है कि ईसा पूर्व की अंतिम एवं ईसवी की प्रारंभिक शताब्दियों में सूती वस्त्र, मलमल एवं रेशम का निर्यात किया जाता था। *पेरिप्लस ऑफ द इरीथ्रियन सी* नामक ग्रंथ से ज्ञात होता है कि भारतीय मलमल एवं रेशम की विदेशों में अत्यधिक मांग थी।[23] भारतीय मलमल की गुणवत्ता एवं श्रेष्ठता के संबंध में विदेशी लेखक टेवेरनियर के विवरण से ज्ञात होता है कि आस्ट्रिच के अंडे के बराबर के नारियल में 60 क्यूबिट नाप का अर्थात लगभग 30 मीटर की पगड़ी हेतु वस्त्र रखा जा सकता था[24]। प्राचीन एवं मध्यकालीन विदेशी यात्रियों ने भारतीय सूत्री वस्त्र की गुणवत्ता के संबंध में लिखा है कि उत्तम कोटि का 20 गज लंबा एक गज चौड़ा वस्त्र ऊंगूठी के मध्य भाग से निकल सकता था।[25] अतः स्पष्ट है कि ईसा पूर्व की अंतिम शताब्दियों में भारत का वस्त्रोद्योग अत्यंत विकसित था जिसके संबंध में पालि बौद्ध ग्रंथों से भी पर्याप्त साक्ष्य मिलते हैं। बौद्ध जातक ग्रंथ में (ई.पू. 300-200 ई.पू.) बुनकरों का श्रेणी में संगठित होने का उल्लेख मिलता है।[26] एक जातक में तंतुवायों के कार्य करने के स्थान को *तन्तवित्थानम* कहा गया है।[27] बौद्ध ग्रंथ *विनयपिटक* (300 ई. पू.) में कपड़े बुनने के उपकरण को तंतभण्ड[28] कहा जाता था। इस काल में विभिन्न व्यवसायियों की वीथिकाओं का उल्लेख मिलता है जैसे—दंतकार वीथि, रंगरेज वीथि तथा तंतुवायों की भी वीथियां थीं।[29] उल्लेखनीय है कि विभिन्न शिल्पों एवं व्यवसाय को निश्चित क्षेत्र या स्थान में आवासित करने का एक कारण यह भी हो सकता है कि शिल्पगत व्यवसायों में अपेक्षाकृत वृद्धि के कारण शिल्पियों के वर्गों हेतु विभिन्न स्थानों को निर्धारित कर दिया गया होगा।

पालि बौद्ध ग्रंथों में इस व्यवसाय के साथ तंतुवायों की सामाजिक स्थिति के संबंध में भी पर्याप्त जानकारी प्राप्त होती है। *विनयपिटक* (300 ई. पू.) में उल्लेख मिलता है कि बुद्ध भिक्षुओं को निर्देश देते हैं कि वे भिक्षुओं की पूर्व जाति, सिप्प एवं कम्म का हवाला देकर उन्हें अपमानित न करें व संघ में भेद पैदा न करें।[30] अतः

यह निष्कर्ष निकाला जा सकता है कि इस काल में शिल्पगत एवं जातिगत श्रेष्ठता एवं हीनता की अवधारणा विकसित हो चुकी थी। *विनयपिटक* में नलकार, कुंभकार, पेसकार (बुनकर), चम्मकार (चर्मकार), नहापित (नाई) के व्यवसाय को हीन कोटि का कहा गया है[31] जबकि दीघनिकाय[32] (300 ई. पू.) में बुनकर के शिल्प को सामान्य कोटि में रखा गया है। उल्लेखनीय है कि पालि ग्रंथों में वर्णित हीन जातियों में तंतुवायों को परिगणित नहीं किया गया है।[33] *दीघनिकाय* (ईसा पूर्व 300 शती) में जन्म से निम्न जाति एवं निम्न व्यवसाय करने वालों में भेद किया गया है जिन्हें क्रमशः *हीन जातियों* तथा *हीन-सिप्पानि* कहा गया है। उल्लेखनीय है कि तंतुवायों की गणना जन्म से हीन जाति वर्ग में नहीं की गयी है।[34] *भीमसेन जातक* का एक संदर्भ तंतुवायों के संदर्भ में अत्यंत महत्वपूर्ण है। इसमें यद्यपि तंतुवाय को हीन कहा गया है किंतु एक धनुर्धारी ब्राह्मण द्वारा इस व्यवसाय को अपनाने का उल्लेख है।[35] *लामक कम्म जातक* में भी तंतुवाय के व्यवसाय को हीन बताया गया है[36]। पालि बौद्ध ग्रंथों में तंतुवायों के व्यवसाय के संबंध में भिन्न-भिन्न मत मिलते हैं किंतु सामान्यतः यह कहा जा सकता है कि तंतुवाय जाति के रूप में हीन नहीं थे किंतु उनका शिल्प हीन कोटि में परिगणित होने लगा था।

कौटिल्य के *अर्थशास्त्र* से भी तंतुवायों के संबंध में विशिष्ट जानकारी मिलती है। इस ग्रंथ से ज्ञात होता है कि राज्य के अधीन बुनकर विभाग था एवं उनका प्रधान *सूत्राध्याय* होता था।[37] जिनके अधीन बुनकर कार्य करते थे। *अर्थशास्त्र* में यह भी उल्लेख है कि स्त्रियां भी इस कार्य में संलग्न थीं।[38] इसमें यह भी संदर्भित है कि राज्य के कोष संवर्धन के लिए बुनकरों से कर लिया जाता था। 'सूत्र' नामक कर सूत (वस्त्र) पर लिया जाता था।[39] *अर्थशास्त्र* के अनुसार आपत्ति काल में कोष वृद्धि हेतु सूत एवं कपड़े के व्यवसायी को अपनी लागत का चालीसवां हिस्सा राज्य को कर के रूप में देने का प्रावधान था।[40]

अर्थशास्त्र के संदर्भों से दो तथ्य स्पष्ट है कि राज्य के अधीन बुनकर विभाग था अतः स्पष्ट है कि राज्य के अधीन श्रमिक बुनकर कार्य करते थे जिनमें स्त्रियां भी संलग्न थीं। प्राक्-मार्य काल में बुनकर गहपति या श्रेणी प्रमुख के अधीन कार्य करते थे किंतु अब मौर्यकाल में राज्य उन्हें बड़ी संख्या में नियोजित करने लगा था। यह भी उल्लेखनीय है कि उनके आवास की व्यवस्था राजधानी एवं महत्वपूर्ण नगरों तक सीमित थी। *अर्थशास्त्र* में यह निर्देशित है कि जो शिल्पी ऊनी और सूत्री वस्त्र आदि बनाते हैं उन्हें राजभवन के पश्चिम की ओर स्थान दिया जाना चाहिए।[41] *अर्थशास्त्र* में यह भी उल्लेख है कि नगर के छोर पर खाली स्थान पर जुलाहों... को

बसाया जाना चाहिए।[42] इन तथ्यों से यह निष्कर्ष निकाला जा सकता है कि वस्त्र उद्योग तो विकसित था एवं बुनकरों के व्यवसाय से राज्य को अत्यधिक लाभांश प्राप्त होता था किंतु यह कहा जा सकता है कि मौर्यकाल में अधिकांश बुनकर स्वतंत्र रूप से कार्य नहीं करते थे। अतः उन्हें संभवतः अपेक्षाकृत लाभ प्राप्त होता रहा होगा।

ऐतिहासिक कालक्रम में लगभग 100 ई. पू. से 300 ई. तक विभिन्न धार्मिक ग्रंथों एवं अभिलेखों से भी इस व्यवसाय के संबंध में जानकारी मिलती है। इस काल में तंतुवायों के लिए विभिन्न अभिधानों का प्रयोग मिलता है। महावस्तु[43] (लगभग 100 ई.) में बुनकरों के कौशल विशिष्ट्य के आधार पर 4 प्रकार के अभिधानों का उल्लेख है जैसे, *तंत्रवाय* (सूती वस्त्र बुनकर), *उर्णवायक* (ऊनी वस्त्रों के बुनकर), *वरूथतंत्रवायक* (कवच बुनकर) तथा *तूलवाय* (सूत कातने में कुशल)। *दिव्यावदान* (200 ई. पू.) में बुनकर के लिए *कुविंद*[44] तथा *तंत्रवाय*[45] शब्दों का उल्लेख मिलता है। बौद्ध ग्रंथ *मिलिंदपञ्ह* (ई.पू. 100-200 ई.पू.) में बुनकर को *तंतीवाप* (पेसकार) कहा गया है।[46] *मिलिंदपञ्ह* से ज्ञात होता है कि बुद्ध की विमाता गौतमी वस्त्र निर्माण की पांच प्रक्रिया जानती थीं।[47] बौद्ध ग्रंथ से यह भी ज्ञात होता है कि दासों से भी शिल्प का कार्य लिया जाता था। जो दास वस्त्र बुनने का कार्य करते थे उन्हें पेसकारदास कहा जाता था।[48]

जैन ग्रंथों से भी तंतुवायों तथा वस्त्र के व्यवसाय के संबंध में महत्वपूर्ण जानकारी मिलती है। इसमें वस्त्र के व्यापारी को *दोसिय*, बुनकर को *सोत्तिय* तथा सूत के व्यापारी को *कप्पासिय* कहा गया है।[49] *आवश्यक निरुक्ति* में तंतुवाय का एक अभिधान *णनतिक्क* है।[50] जैन ग्रंथ *पण्णवणा*[51] से भी ज्ञात होता है कि ईसा की प्रारंभिक शताब्दियों में वस्त्र निर्माण एवं विशेषकर रेशम बुनकरों के व्यवसाय में वृद्धि हुई थी। रेशम बुनकर को *पट्टकार* कहा गया है[52]। अतः स्पष्ट है कि ईसा की प्रारंभिक शताब्दियों में रेशम के भी वस्त्र निर्माण के कौशल में वृद्धि हो रही थी[53]।

अब प्रश्न उठता है कि ईसा की प्रारंभिक शताब्दियों में तंतुवायों की सामाजिक स्थिति कैसी थी? लगभग 100 ई. से 300 ई. कुषाण काल तथा प्राक् गुप्तकाल में तंतुवायों की सामाजिक एवं आर्थिक स्थिति के संबंध में साहित्यिक एवं आभिलेखिक साक्ष्यों के समवेत अध्ययन से कई महत्वपूर्ण पक्षों पर प्रकाश पड़ता है।

ईसा की प्रारंभिक शती में वस्त्र भारतीय निर्यात का प्रमुख उत्पाद था। इस व्यवसाय से लाभ भी अधिक होता था। अतः तंतुवायों की आर्थिक स्थिति अन्य शिल्पी वर्ग की अपेक्षा अच्छी थी किंतु अधीनस्थ श्रमिक तंतुवायों की आर्थिक स्थिति स्वतंत्र रूप से कार्य कर रहे शिल्पियों की अपेक्षा हीन थी। अतः कहा जा सकता

है कि समस्त बुनकरों की सामाजिक एवं आर्थिक स्थिति समान नहीं थी। इस संदर्भ में पुरातात्विक साक्ष्यों से भी कतिपय प्रकाश डाला जा सकता है। ईसा की प्रथम शती में सातवाहन राज्य में विभिन्न श्रेणियों के पास ब्याज की प्रत्याशा से धन जमा करने के प्रमाण मिलते हैं जिनमें बुनकर श्रेणी का उल्लेख मिलता है।[54] इसके अतिरिक्त नासिक के गुहालेख (120 ई.) से ज्ञात होता है कि शक शासक उषवदत्त ने गोवर्धन में निवास करने वाली बुनकर श्रेणी के पास 2000 कार्षापण निवेशित किए तथा एक अन्य बुनकर श्रेणी के पास 1000 कार्षापण जमा किए जिनमें प्राप्त ब्याज से नासिक गुफा में निवास करने वाले भिक्षु संघ के वस्त्र एवं कुषण (अर्थ स्पष्ट नहीं है) के लिए प्रयोग किया जाता था।[55] उपरोक्त साक्ष्यों से यह द्योतित होता है। तंतुवायों की संगठित श्रेणियां लाभ की स्थिति में रही होंगी फलस्वरूप वह अक्षयनीवियों पर ब्याज दे सकती थीं। तंतुवायों द्वारा व्यक्तिगत दान के भी उल्लेख मिलते हैं।[56]

गुप्तोत्तर काल में लगभग चौथी-पांचवीं शती में तंतुवायों की आर्थिक स्थिति में ह्रास दिखाई देता है जिसके संबंध में पुरातात्विक एवं साहित्यिक साक्ष्य समवेत रूप से प्रकाश डालते हैं। गुप्तकालीन ग्रन्थ *अमरकोश*[57] में जुलाहे के केवल दो नामों का उल्लेख है—*तंतुवाय एवं कुविंद*। इस काल के अभिलेखों में बुनकरों के लिए कोलिक संज्ञा का भी प्रयोग किया गया है[58]। उल्लेखनीय है कि इस काल में बुनकरों के लिए प्रयुक्त होने वाले अभिधान पूर्व काल की अपेक्षा कम हैं। अतः यह अनुमान लगाया जाता है कि इस काल में विभिन्न प्रकार के वस्त्रों के निर्माण में कमी आई थी।

ईसा की चौथी शताब्दी में पश्चिमी विश्व के साथ होने वाली व्यापारिक गतिविधियों में ह्रास हुआ जिसकी पुष्टि पुरातात्विक एवं साहित्यिक साक्ष्यों से भी होती है। मंदसौर (दसपुर) अभिलेख से जानकारी प्राप्त होती है कि लाट के बुनकर दशपुर में जाकर बस गए एवं उन्होंने अन्य पेशों को अपना लिया।[59] आभिलेखिक साक्ष्यों से ज्ञात होता है कि मंदसौर (दसपुर) में रेशम बुनकरों ने शिल्प द्वारा उपार्जित धन से 436 ई. (मालव संवत 493) में एक सूर्य मंदिर बनवाया और 472 ई. (मालव संवत 472 ई.) में उसका जीर्णोद्धार करवाया।[60] यद्यपि यह साक्ष्य भी तंतुवायों द्वारा धार्मिक कार्य के निर्माण हेतु दान दिए जाने का उल्लेख कता है किंतु इससे यह निष्कर्ष नहीं निकाला जा सकता है कि इस काल में बुनकर श्रेणियों की आर्थिक स्थिति अच्छी रही होगी। उल्लेखनीय है कि मंदसौर में बुनकर श्रेणियों द्वारा बनवाया गया मंदिर मात्र 36 वर्ष में जीर्ण हो गया था। इस संबंध में ओम प्रकाश श्रीवास्तव का मत है कि वह सूर्य मंदिर सामान्य एवं छोटा रहा होगा। उनके अनुसार विशाल

मंदिर के इतनी अल्प अवधि में गिरने की संभावना कम होती है। अतः मंदिर निर्माण से बुनकरों की आर्थिक स्थिति के सुदृढ़ होने की पुष्टि नहीं होती है।[61] तंतुवायों की आर्थिक स्थिति में ह्रास की पुष्टि साहित्यिक साक्ष्यों से भी होती है। गुजरात के कांठियावाड़ क्षेत्र में लगभग चौथी-पांचवीं शताब्दी ईसवी में विष्णु शर्मा कृत *पंचतत्र*[62] से भी रेशम बुनकर की सामाजार्थिक स्थिति पर महत्वपूर्ण प्रकाश पड़ता है। इस ग्रंथ में वर्णित है कि 'महाभाग्य सोमलिक' बुनकर जो रेशम वस्त्रों का निर्माण करता था किन्तु वह मुश्किल से अपनी जीविकोपार्जन कर पाता है। अतः वह अपनी पत्नी से गुजरात के लाट नामक स्थान को छोड़कर वर्धमान नामक स्थान पर बसने के लिए कहता है।[63] सोमलिक नामक बुनकर कहता है कि जो तन्तुवाय सामान्य कोटि के वस्त्र बुन रहे हैं वह अपेक्षाकृत अधिक समृद्ध हो रहे हैं।[64] अतः उक्त उद्धरणों से स्पष्ट है कि रेशम वस्त्र निर्यात में ह्रास हुआ किंतु वस्त्र निर्माण एक आवश्यक उद्योग की श्रेणी में आता है। अतः इस उद्योग में तंतुवायों की संलग्नता बनी रही एवं आजीविका हेतु धन मिलता रहा।

पंचतंत्र के अन्य उद्धरण से भी तंतुवायों की आर्थिक स्थिति की जानकारी मिलती है, जिसमें एक जुलाहे द्वारा प्रतिदिन बीस गज कपड़ा बनाने का उल्लेख है।[65] एक जुलाहे द्वारा एक दिन में बीस गज कपड़ा बुना जाना यह संकेत देता है कि वह बुनकर सामान्य प्रकार का वस्त्र (सूती या ऊनी) बुनता होगा क्योंकि उच्च कोटि का रेशम एवं मलमल का 20 गज वस्त्र एक व्यक्ति द्वारा बुना जाना असंभव नहीं तो कठिन अवश्य है। अतः यह भी निष्कर्ष निकाला जा सकता है कि उच्चकोटि के वस्त्र का निर्यात न होने के कारण बुनकर द्वारा स्थानीय या देशी खपत के लिए ही वस्त्र बुने जाते थे। इस काल (चौथी-पांचवीं शती) में पश्चिमी विश्व में रोम के साथ होने वाला रेशम व्यापार समाप्त प्राय हो गया था। फलस्वरूप उनकी आर्थिक स्थिति में ह्रास हुआ था, जिसके कारण उनका सामाजिक स्तर भी प्रभावित हुआ।

भातीय इतिहास का पूर्व मध्यकाल 600 ई.-1200 ई. राजनीतिक, सामाजिक एवं आर्थिक दृष्टि से परिवर्तनशील काल था। इस काल में शौच-अशौच की प्रवृत्ति विकसित हो रही थी। पूर्व काल में कई व्यावसायिक जातियां जो शूद्र थीं एवं उनके शिल्प भी हीन थे। किंतु वह अंत्यजों की श्रेणी में नहीं परिगणित थीं किंतु पूर्व मध्यकाल में अनेक शिल्पी वर्ग अंत्यजों के वर्ग में रखे गए। पूर्व मध्यकाल में विभिन्न ग्रंथों एवं क्षेत्रों में तंतुवायों के सामाजिक स्तरीकरण के संबंध में विभिन्न उल्लेख मिलते हैं। जैन साहित्यिक साक्ष्यों से भी तंतुवायों की सामाजिक स्थिति पर प्रकाश पड़ता है। जैन ग्रंथ में आर्य वर्ग में परिगणित शिल्पियों की सूची में सोत्तिय

(तंतुवायों) एवं पट्टगार (रेशम बुनकर) को रखा गया है।[66] लेकिन यहां यह उल्लेख करना आवश्यक है कि कतिपय जैन ग्रंथों में *कोसेज्ज* (रेशम वस्त्र) व्यवसाय को *सिप्प जुंगित* (हीन शिल्प) की कोटि में वर्णित किया गया है।[67] ऐसा प्रतीत होता है कि जैन धर्म में अहिंसा का अत्यधिक महत्व था। रेशम के वस्त्र बनाने के लिए रेशम के कीड़ों को मारा जाता था। अतः अहिंसक सिद्धांत के समर्थकों ने रेशम व्यवसाय को निम्न कोटि का माना। जैन ग्रंथ में *जम्बूद्वीप प्रज्ञप्ति* (800 ई.) से 18 श्रेणियों के संबंध में जानकारी प्राप्त होती है। इस ग्रंथ में पटैल्ला (तंतुवाय) को नारुआ (स्पृश्यों) की कोटि में रखा गया है।[68] जैन ग्रंथों में सामान्यतः शिल्पकारों को अहम (अधम) कोटि में रखा गया है किंतु कुछ शिल्पकारों के शिल्प को हीन नहीं माना गया है। *त्रिषष्टिशलाकापुरुष चरित* (12वीं शती) में बुनकर, दर्जी, कुंभकार, नापित आदि के कार्य को हीन या निम्न कोटि में नहीं रखा गया है।[69] जैन साक्ष्यों के अनुसार न तो तंतुवाय का व्यवसाय हीन था न ही वे अस्पृश्यों की कोटि में रखे गए थे। यह भी उल्लेखनीय है कि जैन भिक्षुक निम्न जाति के लोगों से जिनमें बुनकर भी शामिल थे, से अन्न ग्रहण करते थे।[70] जैन साहित्यिक साक्ष्यों से स्पष्ट ज्ञात होता है कि तंतुवायों को हीन शिल्पियों में वर्गीकृत नहीं किया गया है। संभवतः इसका कारण यह भी हो सकता है कि जैन धर्म में कृषि की अपेक्षा व्यवसाय एवं व्यापार को प्रधानता दी गई थी, अतः व्यवसाय में संलग्न शिल्पी अधिकांशतः ग्रंथों में हीन नहीं कहे गए हैं किंतु रेशम व्यवसाय को हीन शिल्प के अंतर्गत रखा गया है।

पूर्व मध्यकाल के धर्मशास्त्रीय ग्रंथ एवं ऐतिहासिक ग्रंथों से भी बुनकरों के सामाजिक स्तर के संबंध में भी विस्तृत जानकारी मिलती है। उल्लेखनीय है कि प्राचीन काल की धर्मशास्त्रीय सूची[71] में सात हीन जातियों का उल्लेख है किंतु उसमें तंतुवायों का उल्लेख नहीं है। *याज्ञवल्क्य स्मृति*[72] के टीकाकार मिताक्षरा (12वीं शती) ने भी अंत्यजों की सूची में भी तंतुवायों का उल्लेख नहीं किया गया है। हेमाद्रि ने चतुवर्ग चिंतामणि[73] (लगभग 13वीं शती) में अंत्यजों की पूर्व उल्लिखित सूची में 9 अन्य अंत्यजों की गणना की है किंतु हेमाद्रि ने भी तंतुवायों का उल्लेख अंत्यजों की सूची में नहीं किया है।

ब्रह्मवैवर्त पुराण[74] (13वीं शती) में कुबिंदक (तंतुवाय) उत्तम शिल्प की श्रेणी में रखा गया है। *बृहद्धर्म पुराण* में शिल्पियों को क्रमशः उत्तम, मध्यम एवं निम्न श्रेणी में वर्गीकृत किया गया है किंतु उल्लेखनीय है कि तंतुवायों की गणना उत्तम कोटि के शिल्पियों में की गयी है।[75] धर्मशास्त्रीय सूची, स्मृति ग्रंथ तथा पौराणिक साक्ष्यों में भी तंतुवाय अंत्यजों एवं अस्पृश्यों की श्रेणी में नहीं रखे गए हैं। किंतु अरब यात्री

अलबरूनी (11वीं शती) तंतुवायों की गणना अंत्यजों में करता है[76] किंतु पूर्व मध्यकालीन कतिपय ग्रंथ भी बुनकरों को हीन ही नहीं वरन अंत्यजों की कोटि में रखते हैं। लक्ष्मीधर के *कृत्यकपतरू*[77] (12वीं शती) में भी उल्लेख है कि ब्राह्मण? को बढ़ई, लोहकार, तंतुवाय, मालाकार तथा चित्रकार के हाथ से स्पर्श किया भोजन नहीं ग्रहण करना चाहिए। उल्लेखनीय है कि इस काल में उशना[78] ने आयोगवों के लिए तंतुवायों के शिल्प को अपनाने का विधान दिया। आयोगव अंत्यजों की श्रेणी में थे, अतः एक कारण यह भी था कि तंतुवाय अंत्यज कहे जाने लगे। *प्रबंध चिंतामणि* से ज्ञात होता है कि राजा भोज ने विद्वानों को आवासित करने के लिये अपने क्षेत्र से बुनकरों को विस्थापित कर दिया था। संभवतः इसका एक कारण यह भी हो सकता है कि बुनकरों का व्यवसाय राज्य के लिये पूर्व काल की अपेक्षा कम लाभप्रद हो गया था।[79]

पूर्व मध्यकाल में जो तंतुवाय राज्य के संरक्षण में थे व राज परिवार के लिए कार्य करते थे उनकी सामाजार्थिक स्थिति अपेक्षाकृत श्रेष्ठ थी, जैसे चोल वंशी राजेंद्र चोल (10-11वीं शती) के अभिलेख से जानकारी प्राप्त होती है। कांची के बुनकर, जो राजपरिवार के वस्त्र निर्माण में संलग्न थे उनकी स्थिति अपेक्षाकृत अच्छी थी, यद्यपि वह निम्न वर्ण के थे किंतु उन्हें अपनी जाति से अधिक सम्मान दिया जाता था, वह कई प्रकार के कर से भी मुक्त थे।[80]

बंगाल के सेन शासन काल में धोयी नामक तंतुवाय के संबंध में महत्वपूर्ण साक्ष्य प्राप्त होता है। यह ज्ञात होता है कि धोयी को लक्ष्मण सेन के दरबार में उच्च कोटि के कवि का दर्जा प्राप्त हुआ था[81]। इस संबंध में कहा जा सकता है कि धोयी अपने ज्ञान के कारण उच्च पद पाने में समर्थ हुआ। यह संदर्भ भारतीय सामाजिक वर्ण व्यवस्था के नियम को काटती प्रतीत होती है। पूर्व मध्यकालीन ग्रंथ बुनकरों को अंत्यजों की श्रेणी में रखते हैं, दूसरी ओर कतिपय संदर्भ उनकी उच्च सामाजार्थिक स्थिति की भी जानकारी देती है।

अब प्रश्न यह उठता है कि विभिन्न ऐतिहासिक कालक्रम में तंतुवायों का सामाजिक स्तर कैसा था? वैदिक काल में तंतुवायों की सामाजिक स्थिति अच्छी थी। ई. पू. 600 से 600 ई. के मध्य तंतुवायों की सामाजार्थिक स्थिति अपेक्षाकृत अच्छी थी किंतु इस काल में तंतुवाय शूद्र वर्ग में परिगणित किये जाने लगे थे। सामान्यतः बौद्ध एवं जैन साहित्य ने न तो उनके व्यवसाय को ही माना है और न ही उनकी जाति हीन कोटि में रखा गया है। किंतु बौद्ध साहित्य में कहीं-कहीं उनके व्यवसाय को हीन कहा गया हैं। कतिपय जैन साहित्य में रेशम वस्त्र के

व्यवसाय को हीन शिल्प के अंतर्गत रखा गया है। पूर्व मध्यकाल सामाजिक परिवर्तन का काल था। इस काल में धर्मशास्त्रीय ग्रंथों की सूची, पुराणों एवं विभिन्न टीकाकारों ने इनकी गणना अंत्यजों में नहीं की। किंतु कालांतर में अलबरूनी ने इनकी गणना अंत्यजों में की। अतः निष्कर्ष रूप में कह सकते हैं कि तंतुवायों की सामाजिक स्थिति क्रमशः अवनत हुई। दक्षिण भारत में वस्त्र विकसित अवस्था में था किन्तु उनकी प्रतिबद्धता मंदिरों के साथ भी निर्धारित कर दी गई थी। अतः उनसे भी उनकी आर्थिक स्थिति प्रभावित हुई। पूर्व मध्यकाल में वैदेशिक व्यापारिक ह्रास भी उनकी सामजिक स्थिति को प्रभावित करने का प्रमुख कारक था।

संदर्भ एवं टिप्पणियां

1. ए.पी. ओझा, 'प्राचीन एवं मध्यकालीन भारत में तंतुवायों की सामाजिक स्थिति : एक ऐतिहासिक विश्लेषण', *जर्नल ऑफ द गंगानाथ झा केंद्रीय संस्कृत विद्यापीठ,* जिल्द XXXV, जनवरी-जून 1979, भाग 1-2, पृ. 202-212
2. के.के. थपल्याल एवं एस.पी. शुक्ला, *सिंधु सभ्यता,* तृतीस संस्करण, लखनऊ 1992, पृ. 1199
3. *ऋग्वेद,* 1.34.1; 115.4; 162.16; VIII.3.2.4; X.26.6; 102.2
4. *वही,* V.55.6, *हिरण्ययाम अतकाम, हिरण्ययान प्रत्यत्कां*
5. *वही,* X.26.6
6. *वही,* V.47.6
7. *वही,* X.26.6, *वासोवायोऽवीनाम;* X.71.9, *सिरीस्तंत्रं तन्वते;* ए.बी. कीथ तथा ए.ए., मेक्डॉनल, *वैदिक इडैक्स ऑफ नेम्स एवं सब्जेक्ट्स,* जिल्द II, दिल्ली, 1987, पृ. 123
8. *वही,* X.130.2
9. *वही,* VII.99.3
10. दृष्टव्य, *वैदिक इडैक्स,* भाग I, पृ. 123, *अथर्ववेद,* XIV.2 51, X.3.6
11. *पंचविश ब्राह्मण,* 1.8.9
12. *ऐतरेय ब्राह्मण,* 6.30.1
13. दृष्टव्य, बी.एन.एस. यादव, *सोसाइटी एंड कल्चर इन नार्दन इंडिया,* इन द ट्वैल्थ सेंचुरी, ए.डी., इलाहाबाद, 1973, पृ. 97, पादटिप्पणी 467
14. आर. एस. शर्मा, *शूद्रों का प्राचीन इतिहास,* दिल्ली, 1997, पृ. 53
15. पाणिनि कृत *अष्टाध्यायी,* VI. 2.76
16. *वही,* III.3.12, *आवयन्ति अस्मिन*
17. *वही,* V.2.70

18. *वही,* V.6-160
19. *वही,* V.2.70, *तंत्रादचिरापहृते*
20. *वही,* II.IV.10
21. *रामायण,* II.83.12
22. *महाभारत,* सभा पर्व; 47.11
23. डब्ल्यू.एच. शॉफ, *पेरिप्लस ऑफ द इरीथ्रियन सी,* 1912, द्वितीय संस्करण, 1974, नई दिल्ली, पृष्ठ 258: *दीघनिकाय* I.283, उदधृत रिज डेविड्स *बुद्धिस्ट इंडिया,* दिल्ली, पुनर्मुद्रित, 2005 पृ. 90
24. *पेरिप्लस,* पृ. 256-257, टिप्पणी यदि 60 क्यूबिट को मीटर में मापे तो उसका लगभग 30 मीटर एवं 48 से.मी. का होगा। 1 क्यूबिट=1 हाथ, 1 हाथ=20 इंच अतः 60 क्यूबिट × 20 इंच=1200 इंच होगा। 1200 इंच=30 मीटर के लगभग होगा।
25. *वही,* पृ. 256
26. *द जातकाज* (संपा.), कावेल, ई.बी., सं. 538, जि. VI पृ. 14
27. *वही,* 1.424
28. *विनयपिटक,* II, पृ. 135, द्रष्टव्य एम.एम. सिंह, *बुद्धकालीन समाज एवं धर्म,* पटना, 1972, पृ. 75
29. *दिव्यावदान,* (संपा), पी.एल. वैदय, दरभंगा, 1959, पृ. 184
30. विनयपिटक, IV, 4.11
31. वही, IV.6
32. *दीघनिकाय,* I.15
33. *मज्झिम निकाय* (विनयपिटक का भाग) III, 169-78, II.152, 183-4, *सुत्तविभंग पाचित्तिय,* II.2.1
34. टी.डब्ल्यू रिज डेविड्स, *पूर्वोक्त,* पृ. 57
35. ई. बी. कावेल, सम्पादक, द *जातकाज,* भाग I, सं. 80, दिल्ली, पुनर्मुद्रित 1994
36. *जातक* (संपा) वी. फासबाल, जिल्द I, सं. 356, जिल्द 1-7, लंदन 1877-97
37. *अर्थशास्त्र,* II.23
38. *वही*
39. *वही,* II.6.23
40. *वही,* V.2
41. *वही,* II.40
42. *वही,* II.4
43. आर.जी. बसाक, *जे.एन. बनर्जी, वाल्यूम,* कलकत्ता, 1960, पृ. 40
44. कावेल, ई.बी. एवं आर.ए. (संपा), द *दिव्यावदान पेट्रोग्रेड,* 1902, पृ. 184
45. *वही,* पृ. 171
46. उद्धृत, रेनु शुक्ला, *मिलिंदपञ्ह : एक अध्ययन,* 2004, पृ. 184, *मिलिंदपञ्ह* V.4.1 पृ. 234-35

47. *मिलिंदपञ्ह,* अनुवादक, रिज डेविड्स, लंदन, 1928, पृ. 240
48. *सामंतपासादिक,* 1.215 (संपादक), तकाकुसु एवं नागाई, खंड-1 से 6, 1925-47, सियामी लिपिका संस्करण खंड, 1-2 बेंकाक, 1918;
49. जगदीशचंद्र जैन, *लाइफ इन ऐश्येंट इंडिया एज डिपिक्टिट इन द जैन कैनन एंड कमेंट्रीज (सिक्स सेंचुरी बीसी टू सेविंटींथ सेंचुरी ए-डी,* दिल्ली, द्वितीस संस्करण), पृ. 127 एवं 186
50. *आवश्यक निरुक्ति,* 207, दृष्टव्य, जगदीश चंद्र जैन, *पूर्वोक्त,* पृ. 127
51. *पण्णवणा,* 1.61
52. वही, I.50
53. विस्तार के लिए देखिए श्रीवास्तव, 'भारत में रेशम उत्पादन की प्राचीनता; *फेसेट्स ऑफ इंडियन हिस्ट्री,* दिल्ली, 2006, पृ. 390-395
54. ल्यूडर्स लिस्ट सं. 1133
55. *एपिग्रेफिया इंडिका,* VII, पृ. 82; सं. 12, पृ. 82, X.X.1133, पृ. 126
56. आर.एन. मिश्र, *ऐंश्येंट आर्टिस्ट एंड आर्ट ऐक्टीविटी,* शिमला, 1975, पृ. 3
57. *अमरकोश,* II.10.06
58. *सलेक्ट इंस्क्रिप्शंनम,* I, जि. III, संख्या 37, पंक्ति 25, उद्धृत आर.एस. शर्मा, *शूद्रों का प्राचीन इतिहास,* पृ. 290
59. *कार्पस इंस्क्रिपशनम इंडिकेरम,* जिल्द III, सं. 18
60. जे.एफ. फ्लीट (संपादक), *कार्पस इंस्क्रिपशनम इंडिकेरम,* जिल्द III, लंदन 1888, पृ. 68 एवं 79
61. ओम प्रकाश, री अप्रेजल ऑफ मंदसौर-इंस्क्रिप्शन ऑफ कुमारगुप्त I; *रीजनल इंडियन हिस्ट्री,* नई दिल्ली, 2008, पृ. 86 से आगे
62. पंचतंत्र का चीनी भाषा में 416 ईसवी में अनुवाद किया गया, दृष्टव्य एम. विंटरनिट्ज, *हिस्ट्री ऑफ इंडियन लिटरेचर,* भाग III, दिल्ली, 1977, द्वितीय संस्करण, पृ. 374 एवं 364
63. विष्णु शर्मा कृत *द पंचतंत्र,* मित्र संप्राप्ति, संख्या 5 पृ. 303 से आगे
64. *वही,* पृ. 303
65. *पंचतंत्र कथा* संख्या-8
66. दृष्टव्य, जगदीश चंद्र जैन, *पूर्वोक्त,* पृ. 186-187
67. *निशीथ भाष्य,* II.3.708, *व्यवहार भाष्य,* 3.94
68. *जम्बूद्वीप प्रज्ञप्ति* पर शांति चंद्र वाचक ने प्रमेय मंजूषा टीका लिखी है। दृष्टव्य बी. एन. एस. यादव, *पूर्वोक्त,* पृ. 96, सन्दर्भ सं. 465
69. *त्रिषष्टिशलाकापुरुष चरित,* जि. II. पृ. 118
70. आर.एस. शर्मा, *पूर्वोक्त,* पृ. 124
71. अत्रि 199; यम 3, दृष्टव्य यादव, *पूर्वोक्त,* पृ. 98, पाद टिप्पणी 512
72. *याज्ञवल्क्य स्मृति,* III. 260

73. *चतुवर्ग चिंतामणि*, प्रायश्चित खंड, पृ. 298; द्रष्टव्य बी.एन.एस. यादव, *पूर्वोक्त*, पृ. 46
74. *ब्रह्मवैवर्त पुराण*, ब्रह्मखंड, अध्याय 10
75. *बृहद्धर्म पुराण*, III,13
76. सचाऊ, *अलबीरूनीज इंडिया*, भाग I. पृ. 101-2; दृष्टव्य बी.एस.एन. यादव, *पूर्वोक्त*, पृ. 46
77. कृत्यकल्पतरू नित्यकाल खंड, Vol. III, गायकवाड़, ओरिएंटल सिरीज, बड़ौदा, सं. XI, 1950, पृ. 262-63
78. उशना, 13
79. मेरुतुंग की *प्रबंध चिंतामणि*, संपादक, जिनविजय मुनि, शांति निकेतन, 1933, अनुवादक, सी.एच. टावने, कलकत्ता, 1901, पृ. 29, (1.17)
80. रोमिका थापर, *पूर्वकालीन भारत* (प्रारंभ से 1300 ई. तक, दिल्ली, 2008, पृ. 467)
81. *ऐपिग्रेफिया इंडिका*, XIX, पृ. 277 से आगेः XXIII.141

18. जैन दर्शन के आधारभूत तत्वों का समीक्षात्मक अध्ययन
(जिनसेनकृत हरिवंश पुराण के विशेष संदर्भ में)

एस.के. जायसवाल

भारतीय क्षितिज पर अवतरित जैन धर्म ने ब्राह्मण और बौद्ध धर्म के बीच आध्यात्मशास्त्र अथवा आध्यात्मज्ञान के साधनों का प्रतिनिधित्व करते हुए दोनों धर्मों में प्रतिपादित आचार संबंधी सिद्धांतों को व्यावहारिक रूप प्रदान करके उन्हें पुनर्जागृत करने का सफल प्रयास किया है।[1] आदि काल से ही यह धर्म भारतीय संस्कृति को सुसंस्कृत, सुपल्लवित एवं सुपुष्पित करता हुआ आत्मा और प्रकृति के सही स्वरूप को स्पष्ट करता आया है। धर्म, अर्थ एवं काम की प्रवृत्ति तथा मोक्ष की निवृत्ति को आधार रूप में स्वीकारते हुए इसने सम्यक दर्शन, सम्यक ज्ञान एवं सम्यक चरित्र के रूप में[2] आचार एवं विचार का समन्वय स्थापित करते हुए आत्मज्ञान के सही स्वरूप को स्पष्ट करने का प्रयास किया है। विविध प्रकार के भौतिक दुःखों से पीडित व्यक्ति उनसे छुटकारा पाने के ध्येय से आत्मसाक्षात्कार के माध्यम से और रागद्वेषादि द्वंदों से परे होकर सुख शांति का मार्ग तलाशने में तल्लीन हो जाता है। अतएव आत्मजिज्ञासा और जीवन संघर्ष को विवेचित करने हेतु जैन धर्म आत्म-तत्व, पुनर्जन्म एवं साधनात्मक प्रक्रिया का विश्लेषण प्रस्तुत करता है। यह धर्म बाह्य शुद्धि और कर्मकांड को निरर्थक बताकर विशुद्ध आचरण पर बल देता है।[3] इसके अनुसार जो सदाचार से युक्त है, जो श्रेष्ठ संयम का पालन करते हुए समस्त अपराधों पर नियंत्रण कर लेता है और जो विपुल, उत्तम और ध्रुवगामी है, मोक्ष को प्राप्त करने में सफल होता है।[4] यदि जीव के साथ साबद्ध अजीव तत्व के संपर्क की धारा रोक दी जाए एवं उत्पन्न हुए बंधनों को जर्जरित कर दिया जाए तो जीव तत्व अपने शुद्ध एवं मुक्तावस्था को प्राप्त हो जाता है।[5]

जड़ को चैतन्य रूप आत्मा अथवा जीव से अलग कर उसे अपने सही रूप में वास कराना ही जैन दर्शन का मुख्य लक्षण है।

आचार्य जिनसेन[6] ने अपनी प्रसिद्ध कृति *हरिवंश पुराण* में वर्गचतुष्ट्य के साथ आचार, दर्शन एवं धर्मभावना के तत्वों पर प्रकाश डालते हुए यह स्पष्ट किया है कि आत्मा अत्यंत सूक्ष्मता को प्राप्त है। उनके अनुसार यह जीव *(आत्मा)* अनादिनिधन है।[7] आचार्य जिनसेन का मत है कि आत्मा शरीर के अवयवों से पृथक द्रव्य है।[8] जिस तरह बालू आदि से तेल की उत्पत्ति और अभिव्यक्ति नहीं हो सकती, उसी प्रकार पृथ्वी आदि चार तत्वों से चैतन्य की उत्पत्ति और अभिव्यक्ति नहीं हो सकती।[9] *आत्मा* कर्म के अधीन होकर एक-दूसरे से गति प्राप्त करती रहती है।[10]

जैन दर्शन में जीव का दार्शनिक अर्थ आत्मचेतना से लगाया जाता है। जीव में अनुभव की शक्ति के परिणामस्वरूप दर्शन तथा बाह्य पदार्थों को समझने की शक्ति रहती है। जहाँ भी इन दो गुणों की उपयोग शक्ति है वहीं यह जीव अर्थात् आत्मा जैसा तत्व विद्यमान है।[11] जैन दर्शन के अनुसार इस विश्व में मूल रूप से जीव एवं अजीव नामक दो प्रमुख तत्व हैं जिनके संयोग से यह जीव नाना प्रकार की आवश्यकताओं का अनुभव करता है। जैन परंपरा में *जीव, पुदगल,*[12] *धर्म, अधर्म, आकाश* और *काल* नामक द्रव्य विश्व के समस्त सत्तात्मक पदार्थों का निर्माण करते हैं। जैन धर्म का मानना है कि बंधन का दुःख जीव को भोगना पडता है। स्वभाव से पूर्ण अनंत एवं चैतन्य जीव जब शरीर धारण कर लेता है तो उसके सामने अनेक बंध आ जाते हैं। जब ये बंधनजनित बाधाएं दूर हो जाती हैं तो अनंत ज्ञान, अनंत दर्शन एवं अनंत आनंद की प्राप्ति होती है। बंधन जीव के स्वाभाविक गुणों को ढक लेता है, उस पर पर्दा डाल देता है। जैन दर्शन में मनुष्य के जीवन से निर्वाण तक सात तत्वों को अभिव्यक्त किया है—जीव (soul), अजीव (non-soul), आश्रव (contract अर्थात आत्मा एवं पुद्गल परमाणुओं का सम्पर्क), बंध, समवर (आश्रव और बंध को रोकने वाला तत्व), निर्जरा (पूर्व संचित कर्म पुद्गलों को क्षय करने की साधना) एवं निर्वाण[13] जीववाद में जीवात्मा की अवधारणा है।[14]

हरिवंश पुराण के विविध उल्लेखों में जैन धर्म को जिनधर्म,[15] सिद्धमार्ग,[16] एवं संयत धर्म[17] की संज्ञा से विभूषित करते हुए ज्ञान के साधन में प्रमाण, नय, निक्षेप, सप्तभंगी स्याद्वाद, हेतुवाद, जीवस्थान, मार्गणास्थान, गुणस्थान, एवं अनुयोग का बहुत सुंदर उल्लेख मिलता है। प्रस्तुत पुराण में प्रमाण शब्द के एकमात्र उल्लेख से उसे संसारी जीव के निश्चयीकरण में सहकारी बताया गया है।[18] प्रमाण समग्र वस्तु अखंडरूप में ग्रहण करता है। *हरिवंश पुराण* में वस्तु के अनेक स्वरूपों में

से किसी एक निश्चित स्वरूप को ग्रहण करने वाले ज्ञान को नय कहा गया है।[19] प्रमाण और नय दोनों का घनिष्ठ संबंध होता है। पहला समस्त पदार्थों के धर्मों का व्याख्यान करता है, तो दूसरा केवल प्रसंग प्राप्त का ही निर्णय करता है। उसे उस समय अन्य पर्यायों से कोई प्रयोजन नहीं होता।[20]

द्रव्य का स्वरूप नाना प्रकार का है और उसको समझने समझाने के लिए हम जिन पद्धतियों का उपयोग करते हैं, वे 'निक्षेप' कहलाती हैं। हरिवंश पुराण में नाम, स्थापना, द्रव्य एवं भाव नामक चार निक्षेपों की सूचना मिलती है।[21] जैन धर्म में निश्चय पर पहुंचने के लिए सात प्रकार के विचारों की कल्पना की गयी है। यही सप्तभंगीनय है। हरिवंश पुराण में यह सात प्रकार के विचार इस प्रकार बताए गए हैं—सत्, असत, उभय, अवक्तव्य, सद्अवक्तव्य, असद अवक्तव्य एवं उभय अवक्तव्य।[22] जैन दर्शन में सत न केवल कूटस्थ तथा क्षणिक ही है अथवा न केवल नित्य एवं अनित्य ही है तथा चेतन एवं अचेतन ही है, वरन वह सब कुछ है।[23]

जैन दर्शन के सिद्धांतों के अंतर्गत स्याद्वाद एक ऐसा सिद्धांत है, जो वस्तु के यथार्थ रूप को अपेक्षाकृत वर्णन कर सभी को एक साथ संतुष्ट कर सकता है। इसके समर्थक तर्क-बल पर विश्वास करते हैं।[24] हेतुवाद के समर्थक भी ऐसा मानते हैं। 'स्यात' पूर्वक जो 'वाद' अर्थात वचन अथवा कथन है वही स्याद्वाद है। कहीं-कहीं स्याद्वाद को अनेकांतवाद भी कहा जाता है। अनेकांतवाद वास्तविक सत्य का साक्षात्कार करने में सहायक होता है और इस अनेकांत का प्रतिपादकवाद स्याद्वाद कहलाता है।[25] स्याद्वाद के अभाव में किसी भी विषय का ठीक-ठीक प्रतिपादन करना कठिन है। जीवन के दैनिक व्यवहार से लेकर मोक्षपर्यंत सभी विषयों में स्याद्वाद का उपयोग होता है।[26]

जीव स्थान द्वारा जीव द्रव्य के कथन की बात हरिवंश पुराण में कही गयी है और बताया गया है कि यह संख्या चौदह हैं,[27] परंतु इनका विस्तृत उल्लेख नहीं किया गया है। प्रस्तुत ग्रंथ में मार्गणास्थान के अंतर्गत चौदह मार्गणाओं का वर्णन मिलता है— गति, इंद्रिय, छहकाय, योग, वेद, कषाय, ज्ञान, संयम, सम्यकत्व, लेश्या, दर्शन, संज्ञित्व, भव्यत्व एवं आहार। इनमें जीव द्रव्य का कथन किया जाता है।[28] मोह और योग के निमित्त से होने वाले आत्मा के क्रमिक विकास को गुण स्थान कहा गया है। जहां तक अनुयोग का प्रश्न है, प्रस्तुत पुराण में द्वादश अनुयोगों (श्रेत्रानुयोग, काल अनुयोग, गति अनुयोग, लिंग अनुयोग, तीर्थ अनुयोग, चरित्र अनुयोग, बुद्ध एवं बोधिसत्व अनुयोग, ज्ञान अनुयोग, अंतर अनुयोग, अन्य अनुयोग एवं संस्था

अनुयोग) की चर्चा मिलती है।[29] पुराण में वर्णित द्वादश अनुयोगों का विवरण तत्वार्थसूत्र के अनुरूप प्रतीत होता है।

हरिवंश पुराण में कर्म द्वारा संचालित पुनर्जन्म का बड़ा सरल चित्र उपस्थित किया गया है। लोग अपने कर्मानुसार मनुष्य से देव और देव से पुनः मनुष्य हो जाते हैं।[30] कर्म का सीधा संबंध आत्मा और शरीर से है।[31] पुराण में कर्म के आठ भेद इस प्रकार गिनाए गए हैं[32]–

(i) **ज्ञानावरणीय**–आत्मा के ज्ञान को ढकने वाला,
(ii) **दर्शनावरणीय**–आत्मा की सम्यक दर्शक शक्ति को रोकने वाला,
(iii) **वेदनीय**–दुःख-सुख के सम्यक को रोकने वाला,
(iv) **मोहनीय**–जीव को मोह में डालने वाला,
(v) **आयु**–आयु को निर्धारित करने वाला कर्म,
(vi) **नाम**–मनुष्य की गति, शरीर, परिस्थिति आदि को निर्धारित करने वाला कर्म,
(vii) **गोत्र**–मनुष्य के गोत्र, ऊंच-नीच स्तर को निर्धारित करने वाला एवं
(viii) **अन्तराय**–सत्कर्मों में बाधा डालने वाला कर्म

आचार्य जिनसेन ने दोनों वादों–भाग्यवाद अर्थात दैववाद[33] एवं पुरुषार्थवाद अर्थात कर्मवाद[34] की चर्चा अवश्य की है, परंतु अपना विशेष पक्ष पुरुषार्थवाद पर ही केंद्रित किया है। जैन दर्शन का पुनर्जन्मवाद का सिद्धांत कर्मवाद पर ही आधारित है। इस दर्शन में वर्णित उपरोक्त अष्ट कर्मों में से चार कर्म–ज्ञानावरण, दर्शनावरण, मोहनीय एवं अंतराय को घातिकर्म तथा शेष को अघाति कर्म कहा जाता है।[35]

जैन दर्शन में ज्ञान के सिद्धांत पर विशेष प्रकाश डालते हुए स्पष्ट किया गया है कि जीव की आत्मा में पूर्ण ज्ञान रहता है। इस दर्शन में ज्ञान के पांच प्रकार बताए गए हैं जिनकी सूचना *हरिवंश पुराण* में भी दी गई है।[36] यह पांच ज्ञान हैं–**श्रुति** अर्थात सुनकर प्राप्त करने वाला ज्ञान, मति अर्थात इंद्रियों से प्राप्त होने वाला ज्ञान, अवधि अर्थात दिव्य ज्ञान जो किसी भी काल और किसी भी स्थान की किसी भी वस्तु के बारे में ज्ञान प्राप्त किया जा सकता है, मनःपर्याय अर्थात दूसरे के मन मस्तिष्क की बात जान लेने वाला ज्ञान एवं कैवल्य पूर्ण ज्ञान जो जितेंद्रियों को प्राप्त होता है। हरिवंश पुराण में भगवान नेमिनाथ को कैवल्यज्ञान प्राप्त होने का विशद वर्णन प्राप्त होता है।[37]

इस प्रकार आचार्य जिनसेन ने जिनभक्ति का वैशिष्ट्य उल्लेख करते हुए इसके

विविध आयामों को स्पष्ट करने का पूरा प्रयास किया है। विभिन्न दार्शनिक पक्षों पर यथेष्ट प्रकाश डालते हुए उसके विविध रूपों का जो चित्र हमारे समक्ष उपस्थित किया है, वह अपने आप में अद्वितीय है और मानव को उसकी गतिविधियों का बोध कराता है। उन्होंने स्पष्ट करने का पूरा प्रयास किया है कि समस्त सांसारिक सुख अनित्य हैं और आत्मा के सिवाय कोई स्थिर नहीं है। जीव अकेला ही उत्पन्न होता है और अकेला ही मृत्यु को प्राप्त होता है, एक धर्म को छोड़कर दूसरा उसका कोई सहायक नहीं होता। धर्म ही सर्वोपरितत्व है जिसमें जीव शोभन जाति को प्राप्त कर सकता है। चित्त की चंचलता को दूर करने के लिए अंर्तध्यान, रौद्रध्यान, धर्म्यध्यान एवं शुक्लध्यान का जो मार्मिक चित्रण आचार्य जिनसेन ने प्रस्तुत किया है, वह जैन धर्म की विशिष्टता को स्पष्ट करने में न केवल सहायक है, बल्कि मानव को सम्यक पथ की ओर अग्रसर करने का सही संदेश देता है। अणुव्रत, गुणव्रत और शिक्षाव्रत को आधार बनाकर एक श्रावक परम गति को प्राप्त कर सकता है, ऐसा आचार्य का मानना है। निश्चित रूप से आचार्य जिनसेन ने अपने पुराण में वैज्ञानिक तथ्यों के आधार पर जो दार्शनिक सिद्धांत प्रस्तुत किए हैं वे किसी भी धर्म के आधारभूत तत्व स्वीकार किए जा सकते हैं और मानव जीवन के उत्थान में उनका महत्वपूर्ण स्थान निर्देशित किया जा सकता है। जैन दर्शन के समस्त आधारभूत तत्वों को स्पष्ट करने का जो प्रयास प्रस्तुत पुराण में किया गया है, उसका अध्ययन लोक-कल्याण की दृष्टि से काफी महत्वपूर्ण है और जैन सिद्धांतों को सही अर्थों में समझने के लिए सर्वहितकारी है।

संदर्भ एवं टिप्पणियां

1. दृष्टव्य, ई. वासवर्न हापकिंग्स, *दि रिलिजन्स ऑफ इंडिया,* बोस्तोन, 1895, पृ. 283, दृष्टव्य बाल कृष्ण गोविंद गोखले, *अर्ली बुद्धिज्म एंड दि ब्राह्मणस,* स्टडीज इन हिस्ट्री ऑफ बुद्धिज्म (सम्पा. ए.के. नारायण), दिल्ली, 2010, पृ. 67-77
2. *सूत्रकृतांग,* 1.12.11, *स्थानांग सूत्र,* 2.62
3. *उत्तराध्ययनसूत्र* 12. 38-39
4. वही, 20.52
5. दृष्टव्य, हीरा लाल, जैन, *भारतीय संस्कृति में जैन धर्म का योगदान,* भोपाल, 1962, पृ. 215
6. आचार्य जिनसेन ने अपनी प्रस्तुति कृति का समय स्वयं निर्देशित किया है, इसलिए इसकी रचना काल के संदर्भ में कोई मतभेद की गुंजाइश नहीं रह जाती। इस पुराण

की रचना शक संवत् 705 (सन् 783 ई.) में हुई थी। इस पुराण की रचना दो स्थानों पर हुई बताई जाती है। प्रथम स्थान वर्धमानपुर तथा दूसरा दोस्तटिका का शांतिनाथ जिनालय था। वर्धमानपुर सौराष्ट्र का प्रसिद्ध नगर वधवाण है। वधवाण से गिरिनगर जाते समय मार्ग दोत्तडि नामक स्थान की ही पहचान दोस्तटिका से की जाती है। पुराण में जिनसेन ने जैन धर्म से संबंधित अनेक दार्शनिक विषयों का प्रतिपादन बड़ी सुंदरता से प्रस्तुत किया है।

7. हरिवंश पुराण, वाराणसी संस्करण, 58.30-33

   द्रव्यभतः स्वयं जीवो ज्ञातः दृष्टिस्ति कारकः।
   भोक्ता मोक्ताव्ययोत्पाद ध्रौव्यवान् गुणवान् सदा ॥
   असंख्यात प्रदेशात्मा संसहार विसर्पणः,
   स्वशरीरप्रमाणस्तु मुक्तवर्णादिविंशतिः ॥
   श्यामाकणमात्रो न न चाकाशाणुमात्रकः,
   नांगुष्ठर्वभागो य न पत्रवृशतयोजनः ॥
   देहे-देह सवृत्तित्वे प्रदेशैः सकलैः सह,
   न स्वार्थ प्रतिपद्येत स्पर्शनं चक्षुरादिवत्॥

8. वही, 58.25
9. वही, 58.16
10. वही, 58.27
11. दृष्टव्य, हीरालाल जैन, *पूर्वनिर्दिष्ट,* पृ. 217
12. जैन दर्शन में स्पर्श, रस, गंध, वर्ण नामक चार द्रव्यों से युक्त पदार्थ पुद्गल अजीव द्रव्य है। तत्वार्थ सूत्र, 5.4 मोट तौर पर हम जो कुछ देखते हैं, छूते, सूंघते हैं, खाते हैं और सुनते हैं, वह सब पुद्गल द्रव्य है। कैलाश चंद्र शास्त्री जैनधर्म, काशी, 1955, पृ. 86
13. द्रष्टव्य, वी.सी. पांडेय, अनूप पांडेय, *ए नींव हिस्ट्री ऑफ् एंशियंट इंडिया,* जालंधर, 1998, पृ. 128
14. दृष्टव्य, एस.एल. दोषी, पी.सी. जैन, *सामाजिक विचारक,* जयपुर, 1997, पृ. 288
15. *हरिवंश पुराण,* 10.36, 21.151, 60.45, 552, 66.51
16. वही, 9.67, 81.127
17. वही, 65.6
18. वही, 58.38
19. वही, 58.38-40
20. दृष्टव्य, विश्राम तिवारी, *आचार्य जिनसेनकृत हरिवंश पुराण : एक अध्ययन,* वाराणसी, 2007, पृ. 227
21. हरिवंश पुराण, 2.108, 58.38
22. वही, 10.54-58
23. दृष्टव्य, उमेश मिश्र, *भारतीय दर्शन,* लखनऊ, 1964, पृ. 125-30
24. हरिवंश पुराण, 12.77

25. दृष्टव्य, देवेंद्र मुनि शास्त्री, धर्म और दर्शन, आगरा, 1967, पृ. 104. अहिंसावाद की तरह ही अनेकावाद जैन संस्कृति का अभिन्न अंग माना जाता है। दृष्टव्य पी.सी. जैन, *हरिवंश पुराण का सांस्कृतिक अध्ययन,* जयपुर, 1983, पृ. 51
26. दृष्टव्य, कामता प्रसाद जैन, महावीर एंड बुद्ध, *बुद्धिस्टिक स्टडीज* (संपा. बिमल चरण ला) दिल्ली, 2004, पृ. 73-174.
27. हरिवंश पुराण, 2.107, 16, 34.100
28. वही, 2.107, 58.36-37
29. वही, 68.87-105
30. वही, 34.33-35, 64.142
31. दृष्टव्य, मोहनलाल मेहता, *जैन धर्म दर्शन,* वाराणसी, 1974, पृ. 445
32. *हरिवंश पुराण,* 3. 95-99, 58. 205-209, 215, 218
33. वही, 43. 68, 61.77, 62.44, 62.46
34. वही, 62.51
35. कैलाश चंद्र शास्त्री, *पूर्वनिर्दिष्ट,* 1955, पृ. 140
36. *हरिवंश पुराण,* 2.106, 64.14
37. वही, 56. 111-114

19. प्रारंभिक वैदिक समाज में जल-पूजा–एक अध्ययन

सुनील कुमार

मनुष्य के जीवन में जल का स्थान अत्यंत महत्वपूर्ण है। जल तथा वायु मानव जीवन के मूलाधार हैं। प्रकृति के इन अभिव्यक्तियों के प्रति आदिमानव में श्रद्धा उत्पन्न होना स्वाभाविक था और इनके प्रति उसने कई प्रकार की कल्पनाएं कर अनेक प्रकार की मान्यताओं तथा आस्थाओं का समाज में विकास किया। जल के प्रति पूजा का भाव विभिन्न मानव समुदायों में उनकी अनुभूतियों तथा सामाजिक परिवेश के अनुसार कई रूपों में विकसित हुआ।

वैदिक काल में जल-पूजा कई रूपों में की जाती थी। तत्कालीन समाज में जल का पूजन भिन्न-भिन्न साधनों के रूप में तथा विभिन्न देवताओं के रूप में संपन्न होता था। भारत सहित विश्व के अनेक प्राचीन देशों तथा उनकी प्राचीन संस्कृतियों में जल से संबंधित बातों की व्यापक-चर्चा की गई है। जल का मानव जीवन में कितना अधिक महत्व है और उनके धार्मिक जीवन को किस हद तक प्रभावित करता है, इनसे जल संबंधी भौतिक तथा यातुधानीय परिकल्पना में जल का नाग, चंद्रमा, मगर आदि से विशिष्ट संबंध, जल की धार्मिक मान्यता तथा जल पर नियंत्रण आदि के संबंध में जानकारी प्राप्त होती है। जल के संबंध में यह बताया गया है कि जल प्रजनन शक्ति से सुसंपन्न होता है तथा उसके प्रयोग मात्र से व्यक्ति न केवल पवित्र होता है बल्कि रोग-मुक्त भी होता है, अर्थात जल में रोगों की उन्मूलनशीलता का गुण प्रमुख रूप से विद्यमान होता है। जल-पूजा का स्वरूप धीरे-धीरे विकसित होता गया तथा आद्यऐतिहासिक एवं ऐतिहासिक कालों में यह समाज के सामने कई रूपों तथा मान्यताओं में दृष्टिगत होता है। पूर्व वैदिक साहित्य तथा उत्तर वैदिक साहित्य में जल-पूजा की जानकारी मिलती है। *ऋग्वेद* के प्रथम नव मंडलों

को पूर्व वैदिक काल तथा ऋग्वेद के दसवें मंडल, यजुर्वेद, सामवेद एवं अथर्ववेद तथा ब्राह्मणों, आरण्यकों, उपनिषदों को उत्तर काल का साहित्य माना जाता है। अनेक साहित्यों में जल-पूजा की परंपरा, उसकी धार्मिक मान्यताएं, मानव जीवन के साथ उसका संबंध आदि की विस्तृत व्याख्या की गई है। जल-पूजा के क्रमिक विकास की एक लंबी प्रामाणिक ऐतिहासिक परंपरा है। यहां तक कि हड़प्पा काल में जो संकेत लिपियां प्रयुक्त हो रही थीं उनमें से एक जल नागों से भी संबंधित है। हड़प्पा के लेखों में कुछ जगहों पर इस संकेतलिपि (इडियोग्राम) का प्रयोग किया गया है।

वैदिक साहित्य में जल-पूजा कई रूपों में दृष्टिगत होती है। तत्कालीन समाज में विभिन्न जल देवताओं को आपः देवता कहा जाता था। इस संबंध में सूयकांत[1] का कहना है कि वह शब्द अवेस्ता के आपो शब्द के समकक्ष है। इस संबंध में यह विचार व्यक्त किया गया है कि आपः एक हिंद-ईरानी देवता है। इतना ही नहीं ऋग्वेद के एक सूक्त में पवित्रताकारिणी माता (अम्बयो) तथा देवी (अपो देवी रूप) के रूप में आपः देवताओं का वर्णन मिलता है।[2] इन्हें स्वर्गीय तथा धाराओं से प्रभावित होने वाला[3] तथा इंद्र, वरुण, मित्र, अग्नि, औषधि, वन तथा मरुतों के साथ कल्याण प्रदान करने वाला बताया गया है।[4] इनकी स्तुति कुछ देवताओं के साथ प्रसन्नता की प्राप्ति के लिए की गई है जैसे—सूर्य, दिशाओं, पर्वतों, तथा नदी आदि।[5]

जल देवी-देवता :—पूर्व वैदिक काल में हिंद-ईरानी देवता वरुण का स्थान तत्कालीन समाज में अत्यंत महत्वपूर्ण था यह असंदिग्ध है। सर्वशक्तिमान, ऋत के स्वामी, आकाश—देव वरुण वस्तुतः आदि वैदिक देव-कुल के प्रमुख देवता थे जो उत्तर काल में मात्र जल देवता रह गए। इनका स्थान कालांतर में इंद्र ने ले लिया। इंद्र भी वृष्टि देवता होने के कारण जल से ही संबंधित है। इस प्रकार वरुण तथा इंद्र दोनों का जल से घनिष्ठ संबंध होना यह प्रमाणित करता है कि वैदिक काल के समाज में जल का महत्व अत्यधिक था। इन प्रमुख देवताओं के साथ अनेक लघु जल-देवों की परिकल्पना तत्कालीन समाज में की गई।

जल के संबंध में ऋग्वेद का निम्नलिखित श्लोक महत्वपूर्ण है—

> शतपवित्राः स्वधाया मदन्ती देवोदेवानामपि यन्ति पाथः।
> ता इंद्रस्य न मिनन्ति व्रतानि सिंधुभ्योहव्यं धृत वज्जुहोत।।[6]

आप देवता को अन्न-प्रदायक बताते हुए इसे केवल जल-देवता के रूप में नहीं बल्कि कृषि-देवता के रूप में भी जोड़ कर देखा गया है। ऋग्वेद में ही इसे संरक्षक के रूप

में देखा गया है। इस संबंध में कहा गया है कि आपः देवता (स्वयं जल देवता) उन जलों से संरक्षण प्रदान करें जिनके अधिपति वरुण हैं तथा जिनमें सोम एवं अग्नि का निवास है।[7] इनसे प्रतीत होता है कि जल देवता विभिन्न प्रकार के दैवीकृत रूपों में पूजे जाते थे।

ऋग्वेद के एक सूक्त में विभिन्न प्रकार के जलों, यथा—आकाशीय, धरातलीय, खनिज, स्वतः उद्भूत तथा समुद्र की ओर गतिशील पवित्र एवं दैवी जलों (आपः) से संरक्षण की याचना की गई है।[8] जल के महत्व को बताते हुए कहा गया है कि आपः देवता अमृत तथा औषधियों से युक्त हैं, इसलिए पुरोहितों को इनकी स्तुति के लिए तत्पर रहना चाहिए।[9]

इनकी स्तुति से ही मानव के रोग एवं पाप से मुक्त होने की बात कही गई है।[10] एक तरफ जल को सूर्य से संबद्ध करते हुए यज्ञ के कल्याणार्थ स्तुति करने की बातें कही गई हैं, जबकि वहीं पर दूसरी ओर एक स्थल पर दैवी जलों को आहुति प्रदान करने का उल्लेख किया गया है।[11] इस प्रकार ऋग्वेद में जल संबंधित सूक्तों के अध्ययन से इस बात की प्रामाणिक जानकारी मिलती है कि ऋग्वैदिक काल में आपः देवता का बड़ा महत्व था तथा लोग अपने विभिन्न उद्देश्यों की पूर्ति के लिए इनकी स्तुति किया करते थे और अधिक प्रसन्न करने के लिए जल की आहुति देने की बात कही गई है, जिससे ऐसा लगता है कि अन्य महत्वपूर्ण देवताओं की तरह आपः देवता भी ऋग्वैदिक काल में महत्वपूर्ण देवता थे तथा इनकी स्तुति भी अन्य देवताओं की स्तुति की तरह की जाती थी।

आपः देवता की तरह पूर्व-वैदिक काल में अन्य जल-देवता की परिकल्पना अपांनपात के रूप में की गई। यद्यपि इस जल-देवता का विकास कई रूपों में परिस्थिति विशेष में हुआ है लेकिन मूल रूप से इसका स्वरूप दुष्टात्मा का है। ऋग्वेद में इसकी चर्चा वृष्णी भूमस्य गर्भः अर्थात भूमि से उत्पन्न शक्तिशाली जीव के गर्भ के रूप में हुई है।[12] इस संबंध में डांगे का कहना है कि यह विशेषण अहिर्बुधन्य हेतु प्रयुक्त हुआ है।[13] ऋग्वेद में अजएकपाद, अहिबुर्धन्य, समुद्र आदि के साथ इसकी स्तुति की गयी है।[14] इसका अहिर्बुधन्य के साथ प्रार्थित होना यह संकेत करता है कि दोनों में आंतरिक संबंध रहे होंगे। इसी संबंध को दृष्टि में रखते हुए डांगे ने कहा कि अपांनपात अपने मूल रूप में अन्धकार का सर्प तथा अहिर्बुधन्य का एक पक्ष था। सर्वविदित है कि प्रागैतिहासिक काल से ही सर्प जल की चेतन-शक्ति के रूप में मान्य था। यह देवता वैदिक युग से ही चेतन-शक्ति के रूप में परिकल्पित है। इसे विद्युत-युक्त[15] (विद्युतं वसानः) लोगों के कल्याणार्थ पहुंचा

हुआ,[16] विविध रूपों को धारण करने वाला[17] स्वर्णिम आभा से युक्त बताया गया है।[18]

अपांनपात के संबंध में वर्णित है कि यह उस जल में निवास करता है जो मनुष्य की पहुंच के सीमा-क्षेत्र में आता है। इस संबंध में एक विशेषण नाट्य[19] प्रयुक्त हुआ है जो आकाशीय और धरातलीय दोनों जलों का बोधक है। इस संबंध में ऋग्वेद में प्रामाणिक तौर पर यह कहा गया है—*उपेमसृक्षि वाजयुर्वचस्यां चनो दधीत नाथो गिरो में।*[20] इस धरातलीय जल अर्थात नदियों के जल में अपांनपात की उपस्थिति के आधार पर डांग ने इसे एक चारागाहीय देवता माना है।[21] डांगे द्वारा इस देवता का चारागहीय स्वरूप इस तथ्य से भी सिद्ध होता है कि उसे अपने निवास में गाय (धेनु) रखने वाला गया है। डांगे ने इस विषय पर विचार करते हुए कहा है कि अपांनपात की धेनु नदी की स्त्री आत्मा के अतिरिक्त कुछ भी नहीं है। इन्होंने अपने मत को प्रमाणित करने के लिए सरस्वती नदी की आत्मा सरस्वान की अवधारणा का आश्रय लिया है। इनका कहना है कि अपांनपात तथा सारस्वान की अवधारणाओं में अद्भुत साम्य है। दोनों को ही जल का शिशु तथा वृषभ संबोधित किया गया है। दो प्रकार की चेतन-शक्ति को यहां पर दिखलाने का प्रयास किया गया है। एक, अपांनपात जो जल की नर चेतना-शक्ति है और दूसरा नदी-रूप में स्त्री-चेतन-शक्ति अपांनपात का एक ही साथ जल का शिशु तथा वृषभ (पति) दोनों ही रूप इस विश्वास पर न्यायोचित ठहराया गया कि विश्व के कतिपय भागों में यह धारणा व्यक्त है कि नर एक साथ पृथ्वी माता का पुत्र तथा पति दोनों हैं।[22] यहां तक कि कृषि विशेषज्ञों में भी यह धारणा प्रचलित है। ऋग्वेद के अध्ययन से अपांनपात का चारागहीय रूप इस बात से भी प्रमाणित होता है कि इस साहित्य से अपांनपांत को मधुमय लहरों (मधुमतऊर्मि) का नियंत्रक कहा गया है।[23] इस विशेषण का संबंध अपांनपात तथा सारस्वान देवताओं के अतिरिक्त केवल क्षेत्रपति नामक कृषि देवता से जोड़ा गया है।[24] स्पष्ट है कि क्षेत्रपति देवता तथा अपांनपात के गुणों में काफी हद तक समानता है, इस कारण अपांनपात एक चारागाहीय देवता के रूप में माने जा सकते हैं।

अपांनपात को और कई तत्वों से संबंधित किए जाने के साक्ष्य मिलते हैं। अश्व से संपृक्त कर इसे आशुहेमा[25] कहा गया है। अपांनपात से संबंधित ऋग्वेद के एक मंत्र में कहा गया है कि यहां अश्व और सूर्य दोनों का जन्म हुआ है।[26] अग्नि के लिए आशुहेमा विशेषण का प्रयोग हुआ है। इसमें अग्नि की स्तुति अश्वप्राप्ति के लिए की गई है।[27] इन साक्ष्यों से यह प्रमाणित होता है कि अपांनपात जल में स्थित सूर्य है। अपांनपात देवता के इस द्विपक्षीय समीकरण में एक तो सूर्य का वह पक्ष है जो पृथ्वी की जलधाराओं में रहता है तथा दूसरा वह पक्ष है जो चारागाहीय रूप

में कृषि देवता क्षेत्रपति से संबंधित है। अन्न,[28] संतति,[29] कल्याण[30] तथा सरंक्षण प्राप्ति हेतु[31] इसकी स्तुति तथा धन प्राप्ति हेतु[32] इसे हवि प्रदान करने के उल्लेख किए गए हैं।

अपांनपात अवेस्ता में भी प्रतिष्ठित हैं जिससे स्पष्ट है कि वह हिंद-इरानी देवता है। अपांनपात का वर्णन वहां भी चारागाहीय देवता के रूप में किया गया है। इसका संबंध नक्षत्र-अश्व तिस्त्र से दिखलाया गया है। इस संबंध में यह मान्यता प्रचलित है कि अश्व समुद्र में उसे उबालने हेतु प्रवेश करता है। समुद्र के बारे में लोगों में यह धारणा व्याप्त थी कि समुद्र जब उबलेगा तभी वर्षा होगी। वर्षा को तिस्त्र अश्व का बीज कहा गया है। इस संबंध में यह भी कहा गया है कि तिस्त्र में जलों को बीज-युक्त करने का गुण अपांनपात से आता है।[33] ऋग्वेद में इस प्रकार का वर्णन आया है कि अपांनपात जल से अपनी उपस्थिति से उसे गर्भयुक्त कर देता है।[34] इस प्रकार स्पष्ट है कि वेदों के अपांनपात होम्या अवेस्ता के दोनों के गुणों में काफी समानता है।

पर्जन्य—पूर्व वैदिक काल में आपः तथा अपांनपात जल देवताओं के अतिरिक्त पर्जन्य नामक जल देवता के विषय में विवरण मिलता है। पर्जन्य की परिकल्पना वर्षा के देवता के रूप में की गई है। ऋग्वेद में पर्जन्य द्वारा वर्षा कराने की बात कही गई है। ऐसा विवरण मिलता है कि मेंढक ब्राह्मणी की तरह व्रतपालक होते हैं। वे वर्ष भर तपस्या करते हैं और पर्जन्य देवता की अराधना करते हैं।[35] कहा गया है कि वर्षा होने पर मेंढक ठीक उसी प्रकार आवाज करते हैं जैसे गाय अपने बछड़ों के साथ।[36] ऋग्वेद में वर्णन है कि पर्जन्य देवता वर्षा ऋतु में जब मेंढक पर जल-वृष्टि करते हैं तो मेंढक एक बार पुनः पर्जन्य देवता के प्रति धन्यवाद ज्ञापित करते हैं।[37] वर्षा के उद्देश्य से मेंढकों द्वारा पर्जन्य देवता की स्तुति करने की बात से वे पुरोहित वर्ग में सम्मिलित माने जायेंगे। मनुष्य समाज में पुरोहित वर्ग वर्षा कराने के उद्देश्य से पर्जन्य देवता की स्तुति करते हैं, अतः दोनों का गुण समान होने से यह कहा जा सकता है कि मेंढक जल में जीवों के बीच ब्राह्मणों की तरह है। वर्षा के अतिरिक्त भी दूसरे उद्देश्यों की पूर्ति हेतु पर्जन्य देवता की प्रार्थना की गई है, जैसे एक स्थान पर इस देवता की स्तुति सविता, उषा तथा सरस्वती के साथ प्रसन्नता प्राप्ति हेतु की गई है—[38]

> शं नो देवः सविता त्रायमाणः शं नो भवन्तूषसोविभातोः।
> शं नः पर्जन्यो भवतु प्रजाम्भ्यः शं नः सरस्वती सहधीमिरस्तु।।

पूर्व वैदिक काल में जल-पूजा की प्रथा का व्यापक रूप में प्रचलन था। विभिन्न जलाधानों, नदियों एवं समुद्रों की पूजा करना इसका प्रमाण है। ऋग्वेद में नदियों का मातृवत[39] तथा देवी[40] के रूप में वर्णन किया गया है जिसके फलस्वरूप इनका धार्मिक महत्व बढ़ता गया और यही कारण है कि आज भी जल धर्म का अभिन्न अंग है।

ऋग्वेद के नदी-सूक्त से तत्कालीन समाज में नदियों का महत्व स्पष्ट होता है। ऋग्वैदिक आर्यों के जीवन में नदियों का महत्व निर्विवाद है क्योंकि प्रकृति-प्रेमी आर्यों ने वनों तथा नदियों के सान्निध्य में सभ्यता का विकास किया। नदी तट पर निर्मित कुटियों में बैठे जल-प्रवाह के कलकल निनाद, भ्रमर के मधुर गुंजन तथा पक्षियों के कूजन के रूप में प्रकृति द्वारा प्रस्तुत संगीत की पृष्ठभूमि में उन्होंने वैदिक ऋचाओं की रचना की। जिस नदी के जल का वे जीवन रक्षा हेतु पान करते थे और जिसमें स्नान कर स्फूर्ति का अनुभव करते थे उसमें उन्होंने देवत्व की कल्पना की थी। क्योंकि प्रकृति के वैभव को उन्होंने विश्व पुरुष का ही रूप माना था। उस समय की प्रमुख नदियों को श्रद्धास्पद माना गया और जलपूजा की परंपरा के कारण उन्हें धार्मिक महत्व प्रदान किया गया।

सिंधु नदी—ऋग्वेद मे सिंधु के प्रवाह को समस्त नदियों की जलधाराओं के वेग से श्रेष्ठतर कहा गया है।[41] कहा गया है कि सिंधु नदी की धारा के मार्ग का निर्माण वरुण द्वारा किया गया।[42] सिंधु नदी को अति सौंदर्यमयी के विशेषण से विभूषित कर अन्न-प्राप्ति हेतु उसकी स्तुति की गई है।[43] सिंधु नदी के साथ उसकी सहायक नदियों को भी महत्व प्रदान किया गया था। इन नदियों के विषय में कहा गया है कि वे सिंधु नदी में विलीन होने के लिए उसी प्रकार दौड़ती हैं जिस प्रकार बालक अपनी माता की ओर।[44] सिंधु की समस्त सहायक नदियों को मिलाकर सप्त-सिंधु नाम दिया गया था। सप्त-सिंधु की स्तुति अन्न-प्राप्ति हेतु की गई है।[45] जिससे स्पष्ट है कि सिंधु एवं उसकी सहायक नदियों का कृषि के लिए उनकी उपयोगिता की दृष्टि से विशेष महत्व था।

सरस्वती—ऋग्वेदकालीन भारत में कई नदियों को महत्व दिया गया, परंतु सरस्वती नदी की प्रतिष्ठा सर्वोपरि थी। इसे माता रूप में, नदी रूप में तथा देवी रूप में सर्वश्रेष्ठ घोषित किया गया है। इसकी कतिपय जगहों पर स्तुति भी की गई है।[46] कई स्थानों पर इसे पवित्रतम।[47] सर्वशक्तिशालिनी[48] तथा सौंदर्य-युक्त[49] नदी के रूप में वर्णित किया गया है। कृपा, आश्रय, सौभाग्य, अन्न, धन तथा संरक्षण-प्राप्ति हेतु छवि प्रदान कर इसकी पूजा की गई है।[50]

ऋग्वेद में वर्णित है कि किस प्रकार भिन्न-भिन्न व्यक्तियों ने इस नदी की पूजा-अर्चना करके मनोवांछित फल प्राप्त किए। इसका उल्लेख है कि सुनहोत्रों द्वारा प्रजा-प्राप्ति हेतु सरस्वती नदी की स्तुति की गई।[51] इस बात की भी चर्चा है कि 'नहुष' के द्वारा स्तुति किए जाने पर सरस्वती नदी ने उन्हें जल और घृत प्रदान किया था।[52] वशिष्ठ ने सरस्वती नदी की पूजा अन्न-प्राप्ति के लिए की थी।[53] इसी क्रम में कहा गया है कि वशिष्ठ ने शक्तिशाली मंत्रों द्वारा प्रार्थिव एवं आकाशीय सरस्वती की पूजा की थी।[54] वशिष्ठ से भी पूर्ण जगदग्नि ने सरस्वती नदी की पूजा की थी इस बात का भी उल्लेख किया गया है।[55]

सरस्वती नदी के संबंध में एक अलग मान्यता थी कि इसमें सरस्वान नामक देवता निवास करते हैं। इस देवता को सरस्वती नदी का शिशु तथा वृषभ दोनों कहा गया है।[56] सरस्वती नदी गाय के रूप में भी वर्णित हैं।[57] अपांनपात जल देवता की तरह सरस्वान भी सरस्वती नदी की नर आत्मा है। डांगे ने इस विषय पर भी अपना विचार तर्कपूर्ण ढंग से व्यक्त किया है और कहा है कि सरस्वती तथा सरस्वान के इस स्वरूप पर चारागाहीय प्रभाव परिलक्षित होता है।[58] यही कारण है कि सरस्वान की पूजा शक्तिशाली पुत्र, स्त्री, धन तथा संरक्षण-प्राप्ति हेतु की जाती थी।

धार्मिक महत्व से जुड़ जाने के कारण सरस्वती नदी सर्वत्र विश्वस्तर पर अत्यधिक रूप में परिकल्पित होने लगी तथा एक जगह पर तो यहां तक वर्णन किया गया है कि इस नदी में संपूर्ण सृष्टि सन्निहित है।[59] सरस्वती नदी को विश्वस्तर पर परिकल्पना के साथ इसके पार्थिव तथा आकाशीय दो रूपों की भी कल्पना की गई।[60] यद्यपि ये दोनों ही रूप, पृथक धार्मिक अवस्थाओं के बोधक हैं, परंतु इनके मूल में सरस्वती नदी के देवत्व की भावना निहित है।

विपाशा तथा शुतुद्री—प्रारंभिक वैदिक काल में विपाशा और शुतुद्री नदी को भी देवत्व प्रदान किया गया था। ऋषि विश्वामित्र के साथ इन दोनों नदियों का संभाषण हुआ था, इसकी चर्चा ऋग्वेद के एक सूक्त में की गई है।[61] भरतों सहित विश्वामित्र ने इनकी स्तुति की थी। इन दोनों नदियों के संबंध में बतलाया गया है कि ये श्वेत गौ माता (गावेव) शुभ्र मातरा है। गति में परस्पर स्पर्धा करते हुए अश्वों के समान हैं।[62] इसके साथ ही इनका प्रवाह-मार्ग पर्वत से लेकर समुद्रपर्यंत कहा गया है।[63] यह भी कहा गया है कि ये दोनों ही नदियां अन्न, धन तथा सौभाग्य प्रदान करने वाली हैं।[64]

इस काल में यह विशेषता देखने को मिलती है कि विभिन्न उद्देश्यों की पूर्ति हेतु नदियों की सामूहिक रूप से भी पूजा की जाती थी। एक स्थान पर चर्चा है कि

मातृवत नदियां स्तुतिकर्ता का भक्षण न करें।[65] इस प्रार्थना का आशय यही रहा होगा कि नदियां लोगों को डुबाएं नहीं। रत्न-प्रदाता नदियों की स्तुति ऋभुओं, आदित्यों, पर्वतों तथा सविता के साथ कृपा प्राप्ति के लिए की गई है।[66] नदियों की स्तुति सूर्य, दिशाओं, पर्वत तथा आप देवताओं के साथ प्रसन्नता प्राप्ति हेतु भी की गई है।[67] नदियों का आदर बड़े व्यापक पैमाने पर किया गया है। इसके जल को दैवी, पवित्रकारी तथा अन्नप्रदायक आदि गुणों से संपन्न कहा गया तथा निर्देश दिया गया कि लोग नदियों को धृताहुति प्रदान करें।[68]

आज की तरह पूर्व वैदिक काल में नदी-स्नान को धार्मिक महत्व प्रदान किया गया था। इस संबंध में ऋग्वेद में उपलब्ध विवरणों से तत्कालीन समाज में नदी-स्नान की धार्मिक मान्यता का संकेत मिलता है—

> "आपो अद्यान्वचारिष रसेन समगस्महि।
> पयस्वानग्न आगहि तंमा संसृस वर्चसा।।"[69]

इस प्रकार विभिन्न साक्ष्यों से ज्ञात होता है कि पूर्व वैदिक काल से ही जल की महत्ता, पवित्रता तथा शुद्धता के विषय में यथेष्ट जानकारी प्राप्त होती है जो इस तथ्य की तरफ संकेतित करता है कि जल का धार्मिक महत्व होने के साथ ही साथ उसकी अपनी वैशिष्ट्यता है।

संदर्भ एवं टिप्पणियां

1. सूर्यकांत, *वैदिक कोश*, पृ. 37
2. *ऋग्वेद*, 1/23/16-18
3. *ऋग्वेद*, 7/47/3
4. *ऋग्वेद*, 7/34/25/7/56/25
5. *ऋग्वेद*, 7/35/8
6. *ऋग्वेद*, 7/47/3
7. *ऋग्वेद*, 7/48/3/4
8. *ऋग्वेद*, 7/49/1-2
9. *ऋग्वेद*, 1/23/19-20
10. *ऋग्वेद*, 1/23/21-22
11. *ऋग्वेद*, 1/23/17-18
12. *ऋग्वेद*, 5/41/10
13. डांगे, सदाशिव अंबदास, *पैस्टोरल सिंबोलिज्म फ्रॉम द ऋग्वेद*, पृ. 42

14. *ऋग्वेद,* 7/35/13
15. *ऋग्वेद,* 2/35/9
16. डांगे, सदाशिव अंबदास, *पेस्टोरल सिंबोलिम्म फ्रोम ऋग्वेद,* पृ. 40
17. *ऋग्वेद,* 2/35/15
18. *ऋग्वेद,* 2/35/13, 2/35/10
19. *ऋग्वेद,* 2/35/1
20. वही
21. डांगे, सदाशिव अंबदास, *पेस्टोरल सिंबोलिज्म फ्रोम द ऋग्वेद,* पृ. 38
22. मैकेंजी, डी., *मिथ्स ऑफ बेबिलोनिया एंड असीरिया,* पृ. 38
23. *ऋग्वेद,* 7/47/2
24. *ऋग्वेद,* 4/57/2
25. *ऋग्वेद,* 2/31/6, 35/1/7, 47/2
26. *ऋग्वेद,* 2/35/6
27. *ऋग्वेद,* 2/1/5
28. *ऋग्वेद,* 2/35/1
29. *ऋग्वेद,* 7/35/15
30. *ऋग्वेद,* 7/34/15
31. *ऋग्वेद,* 5/41/10
32. *ऋग्वेद,* 2/35/7
33. डांगे, सदाशिव अंबदास, *पैस्टोरल सिंबोलिज्म फ्रोम द ऋग्वेद,* पृ. 42
34. *ऋग्वेद,* 2/35/13
35. *ऋग्वेद,* 7/103/2
36. *ऋग्वेद,* 7/103/2
37. *ऋग्वेद,* 7/103/3
38. *ऋग्वेद,* 7/35/10
39. *ऋग्वेद,* 1/158/5, 3/33/3
40. वही, 2/441216—7
41. *ऋग्वेद,* 10/75/1
42. *ऋग्वेद,* 10/75/2
43. *ऋग्वेद,* 10/75/7-9
44. *ऋग्वेद,* 10/75/4
45. *ऋग्वेद,* 10/43/3
46. *ऋग्वेद,* 2/41/16-17
47. *ऋग्वेद,* 7/95/2
48. *ऋग्वेद,* 7/96/1
49. *ऋग्वेद,* 7/96/2

50. ऋग्वेद, 7/95/4-5, 7/96/2-3
51. ऋग्वेद, 2/41/17
52. ऋग्वेद, 7/95/2
53. ऋग्वेद, 7/95/6
54. ऋग्वेद, 7/96/1
55. ऋग्वेद, 7/96/3
56. ऋग्वेद, 7/95/3
57. ऋग्वेद, 7/194/49, 7/95/2
58. डांगे, सदाशिव अंबदास, *पैस्टोरल सिंबोलिज्म फ्रोम द ऋग्वेद*, पृ. 38
59. ऋग्वेद, 2/41/17
60. ऋग्वेद, 7/96/1
61. ऋग्वेद, 3/33/1-13
62. ऋग्वेद, 3/33/3
63. ऋग्वेद, 3/33/1-2
64. ऋग्वेद, 3/33/12-13
65. ऋग्वेद, 1/158/5
66. ऋग्वेद, 4/34/8
67. ऋग्वेद, 4/35/8
68. ऋग्वेद, 7/47/3
69. ऋग्वेद, 1/23/23